Cultural Critique takes an interdisciplinary approach to cultural criticism, covering literary, philosophical, anthropological, and sociological studies and using Marxist, feminist, psychoanalytic, and poststructural methods. International in scope, it draws on a large group of corresponding editors to gather articles that examine intellectual controversies, trends, and movements throughout the world.

Cultural
Critique

41

WINTER 1999

Horace Pippin and the African American Vernacular

John W. Roberts

By most informed estimations, Horace Pippin is one of the most important African American visual artists of the twentieth century. During his relatively brief career as an artist, Pippin produced some one hundred paintings and a number of burnt wood panels on themes as varied as war, family and community life, religion, and nature. In their mammoth study, *A History of African American Artists*, Romare Bearden and Harry Henderson attribute Pippin's success to the fact that "his need to organize and express the reality of life visually cut through all impediments so directly and profoundly that he arrived at concepts in painting that were extremely modern" (356). Whether it was his ability to produce modernist images or his exotic style, as others claim, Pippin's work was immediately embraced by art historians and connoisseurs from the moment that it was brought to public attention. Since the late 1930s, when his work was first shown, Pippin has been one of the most often exhibited African American visual artists. In addition, his works are still avidly sought out by private collectors and museums. Today, his works hang in the homes of many prominent Americans and are part of the permanent collections of major museums across the country including the Metropolitan Museum of Art, Whitney Museum of American Art, Hirshhorn Museum, Phillips Collection, Philadelphia Museum of Art, Pennsylvania Academy of Fine Arts, and others (Bearden and Henderson 356; S. Wilson 3).

From these obvious signs of extraordinary accomplishment in the visual arts as evidenced in his embrace by representatives of the elite art world, one might be inclined to conclude that Horace Pippin enjoys a secure place alongside other masters of American visual art. When one reviews the considerable amount of commentary on his career, however, mainly in the form of biographical sketches and exhibition reviews, one is struck by the adjectives used to describe his work. "Naive," "primitive," "folk," and "self-taught" are descriptors frequently employed to characterize the products of his verdant creative imagination.[1] In assigning the work of Pippin to these categories, art historians and other commentators are undoubtedly seeking to align his creative endeavors with those of others whose process of creativity he seems to share. In their efforts to establish a relationship between Pippin and these other artists with whom they associate him, however, scholars tend to offer little or no analysis, comparative or otherwise, to justify his inclusion in these ill-defined categories of creative cultural production. Rather, they most often rehearse Pippin's biography in order to demonstrate similarities in his life history to those of other artists with whom he is most often compared.

The tendency of scholars to resort to the biographical in discussions of Pippin's art represents a common approach in examination of the work of most artists whose created products do not fit into an identifiable Western academic tradition.[2] Often in these biographical discussions, the early impoverished childhood of the artist is invoked as well as early signs of a sensibility or talent for aesthetic construction. This discussion is usually followed by a listing of the succession of jobs or other (pre)occupations that the artist accepted and that, by implication, prevented him or her from pursuing an artistic career or otherwise finding fulfillment in artistic endeavor early on in life. Although the individual is frequently portrayed as having worked haphazardly in producing artistic pieces as a sideline throughout his or her life, more often than not, the individual, usually following some personal trauma or tragic event or even retirement, is portrayed as turning to art as a way of restoring equilibrium or finding meaning for his or her existence. Even though his or her art is envisioned as part of a self-prescribed therapeutic program or even as a hobby, the artist is eventually "discovered" by an art collector or other representative of the academic and/or elite art world and his or her individual genius is finally brought to the attention of a wider public art community.

In the case of Horace Pippin—and, I would venture to say, most artists whose works do not seem to fall into an identifiable Western tradition of artistic production—the emphasis on biography represents an attempt to account for the seeming emergence of individual artistic genius in a sociocultural milieu and in an artistic medium in which such genius is presumed to be nonexistent. Whether Pippin's career as an artist is addressed in elaborate detail or causally invoked in brief discussions, his life story is almost invariably the focus and follows the usual formulaic pattern just outlined.[3] For most of Pippin's biographers, his identity as an African American male who produced works of visual art that rivaled those of his academically trained contemporaries in symbolic complexity would seem to provide sufficient justification to initiate a search for the source of his artistic talent. Although his biographers often point out that he showed early signs of artistic ability during his years as a public school student, won an art competition as a youngster, and continued to work to perfect his artistic skills by sketching during his years in the army, they do not place much emphasis on these early productions as those of an artist honing and nurturing his skills. Nor do they envision Pippin's early creative efforts as artistic endeavors revelatory of budding genius. Instead, his biographers repeatedly point to his early childhood in a small African American community in Goshen, New York, his having been raised in an impoverished single-parent household, his limited formal education, and his unpretentious career in a succession of menial jobs to establish his unlikely candidacy for artistic accomplishment worthy of attention by representatives of the elite art world.

To explain Pippin's extraordinary accomplishments in art under such unlikely circumstances, his biographers most often suggest that, despite his rather commonplace existence as an African American in the early decades of the twentieth century, his ability to produce art of uncommon quality stems from his unique circumstances as an African American—circumstances that set him apart from and within his own community. Invariably they point to his loss of the use of his right arm in World War I and the pension he received as a result as the most important event in his life and the defining moment in his becoming an artist. Pippin's disability and the government check on which he was forced to live, though insufficient to provide for the needs of his family, it is claimed, not only set him apart in the small town of West Chester, Pennsylvania, where he moved after he was discharged from the army, but also afforded him an unusual opportunity as an African American for contemplation and the ability to indulge his imagination. To emphasize his isolation from his community, the solitary scenes of his working laboriously to burn images into pieces of wood with a fireplace poker by balancing the wood with his maimed arm and his painting with illumination from a single lightbulb in his modest home in West Chester are rehearsed endlessly in the telling of his life story. His achievements in overcoming the limitations imposed on him by his disability are represented as not only a solitary endeavor, but most often a heroic one. Although the biographical narratives disagree on exactly how and by whom Pippin's artistic genius was discovered, this culminating chapter in his life story most often unfolds in a grand way in that it is claimed that he was discovered by some of the giants of modern art during his day. Generally, his biographers contend that his talent was accidentally discovered by N. C. Wyeth, the father of artist Andrew Wyeth, and Christian Brinton, famed art historian (Rodman; Lewis; Stein 1993).[4]

Although the biographical information that accompanies discussions of Pippin's art may be useful in situating him and his art in a particular sociocultural milieu at a particular moment in history, it hardly serves as a substitute for critical discussion. In most respects, the inordinate emphasis on the biographical emerges from a view that the art produced by Pippin cannot be understood or appreciated within a traditional Western academic perspective. The same can be said for labeling his work as "naive," "primitive," "folk," or "self-taught." In recent scholarship, all of these modifiers as applied to artistic traditions and producers of aesthetic forms have been critiqued and found wanting in one way or another.[5] Commonly, scholars point out that these labels more accurately describe a relationship of power and privilege and share more of a concern with mentality than tradition; that is, the scholarly discourses in which products of the creative imagination are labeled as "naive," "primitive," "folk," or "self-taught" are based on a pronounced evolutionary perspective that inscribes an ethnocentric and binary we/they division. Within this evolutionary perspective, an allachronic discourse is produced that assigns those so labeled as living and creating in the past of more enlightened and modern others (Fabian 1983, 25–35).

Of equal importance, the use of labels such as "naive," "primitive," "folk," and "self-taught" to describe Pippin's work effectively places it in categories of creative cultural production in which artists and artistic products unrelated not only temporally but also culturally are judged and evaluated in similar terms; that is, these terms do not describe any particular cultural tradition of creativity. Rather, they affiliate products of disparate creative cultural traditions into a seemingly homogeneous category without regard for the cultural tradition of origin, the aesthetics of specific creating communities, or the criteria of evaluation within these communities. Moreover, these terms have historically allowed for the development of discourses that (re)produce otherness as a pathological condition (Roberts 1993, 162–63). In many ways, the inordinate emphasis placed on the biographical—or, rather, the particular aspects of the artist's life story that get emphasized—reflects the art historian's view of the art placed in these categories as the expressive embodiment of pathology; that is, in the production of these biographies, art historians endlessly rehearse those conditions and situations such as poverty, lack of formal education, and even nontraditional family structures that have historically acted as signs of social and cultural pathology in discussions of culturally different others.

In her introduction to the catalog for an exhibition of African American art titled *Another Face of the Diamond,* Judith McWillie suggests another vantage from which to examine the issues involved in the classification process as it relates to the art of Horace Pippin. She argues that the tendency of art historians to assign African American visual artists and art to problematic categories stems from a scholarly tradition that commenced in the 1930s—the historical moment that scholars first took serious note of artists such as Pippin. She asserts that the "fine arts intelligentsia of the 1930's" chose to ignore the most obvious creative process used in the production of African American art—syncretism—because otherwise it would have had to acknowledge that this art "so closely parallel[s], in some instances, works of the early modernists who, only a generation before, had experimented with their own versions of Afro/European syncretism" (7). Rather than embrace obvious parallels between the processes employed by African American vernacular artists and those of European modernists, art collectors and dealers created new categories of artistic classification. This move, according to McWillie, was designed to protect the cultural and economic value of European art as well as the emerging folk art market. She continues:

> In this climate, a host of diversionary labels became attached to Afro Atlantic traditional art, including "folk art," "primitivism," and "outsider art," each representing the intellectual and economic investments of those who appropriate the work. Rather than admit that the splendid accomplishments of individuals might reflect on the brilliance and resourcefulness of African American culture as a whole, most dealers and collectors continued to ignore the international continuity of Afro Atlantic art, in an intransigence that served to mask what was fast becoming obvious: that even before Derain, Matisse,

and Picasso began to unfix the classical boundaries of Western imagination and form, blacks in the Americas were synthesizing African,
European, and Native American idioms to create non-objective assem-
blages and narrative improvisations that prefigured the aesthetic revo-
lutions to come; and that African consciousness, in spite of history's
most profound shocks and disassociations, is able to sustain itself
independently, flavoring and transforming, without exception, every
culture that comes in contact with it. (7)

McWillie's critique of this important moment in the history of American
art reveals that the desire to avoid associations and comparisons between
European and African American art that would devalue both led representatives of the fine arts world to remove "Afro Atlantic traditional art
from its social context and suspended it in an atmosphere of irony and
exoticism" (ibid.). As a result, African American art became suspended in
a kind of categorical limbo. Cornel West, in an essay that examines the
dilemma in art criticism posed by the work of Horace Pippin, suggests
that the problematic classifications of African American art and artists
that arose during the 1930s must also be seen as one result of the Harlem
Renaissance's emphasis on the folk, which accorded well with a Euro-
American fascination with primitivism. He argues that the class issues
among Renaissance intelligentsia that led them to seek their other in the
African American primitive folk were translated into racial terms by fine
arts enthusiasts.[6] In so doing, the art fine art world created a dilemma in
which "Pippin's burden of being a black artist in America required that
he do battle with either primitivist designations or claims of the inferiority
of his art" (West 48).

   Also, in the case of artists such as Pippin, the situation that influences efforts to classify them as artists has been further complicated by
what Gerald Davis has called "the nettlesome business of discovery" (296).
As Davis notes, the process of discovery that brings the work of many
African American artists to public attention structures a discourse on
these artists' work that situates it most often not only in problematic eval-
uative categories, but also in inappropriate cultural contexts, by denying
the existence of a "previous validating recognition" (296). Davis goes on
to assert that the "artist's aesthetic community is rarely given credibility by
collectors or discoverers" (297). The implications of Davis's assessment of
the situation that complicates and problematizes the art historian's efforts
to assess the work of "discovered" African American artists is both pro-

found and useful. By failing to recognize and give credibility to possible already existing criteria and standards of artistic judgment, art historians and others in most instances devote little energy to investigating either the esoteric processes for mastering techniques of aesthetic construction or the standards by which diverse communities are able to recognize and accept seemingly nontraditional artists and art forms as acceptable expressions of culture-specific ideals.

Although various factors have undoubtedly conspired over time to complicate and problematize the classification of African American art and artists, the removal of labels that place Pippin and his art in some other category does not bring automatic or easy understanding of his unique accomplishments as an artist any more than would dismissal of discussions that evaluate his work in relationship to or, as has most often been done in the past, in contrast to the work of his academically trained contemporaries. In reality, analyses of his work that evaluate it in terms of unmarked categories, as well as those that place it in a relationship with his academically trained contemporaries, are equally problematic in illuminating his creative process and the products of his imagination. In attempting to find a more appropriate focus for a discussion of the art of Pippin, what is needed is a way to place it within a conceptual framework that envisions it as part of a tradition of creative cultural production. In this regard, perhaps we should take seriously the position of Bearden and Henderson, who conclude that "He is wholly an African-American artist. His life as an African-American is the basis of everything he painted" (374). In offering this assessment of Pippin as an artist, Bearden and Henderson seek to reclaim him from what they see as the limiting and even demeaning category of "folk artist"—a categorization that they claim has been detrimental to a full appreciation of his artistic accomplishments and vision. They suggest that, as an African American artist, Pippin's art can and should be evaluated from an African American cultural and historical perspective and within traditions of creative cultural production associated with people of African descent.

Within the African American tradition of creative cultural production, products of the creative imagination that have historically been labeled "naive," "primitive," "folk," or "self-taught" may be thought of as the result of a process of vernacular creativity or folklore. However, our understanding of African American folklore has been complicated by an insidious discourse of folkness. A discourse of folkness, which may be described as a mode of ideation that perceives an ontological and

epistemological distinction between "folk" and "nonfolk," has traditional-
ly served as the basis of folkloristic theorizing. Moreover, it is deeply
inscribed in the history of folklore study (Roberts 1993, 158). This discursive tradition has problematized not only discussions of African American
vernacular creativity, but also our understanding of the complexity and
diversity of creative cultural production in African American communities. The problematic for African American creative cultural study arising
from a discourse of folkness began in the late nineteenth century when
American folklorists attempted to inaugurate a folkloristics in the United
States that maintained continuity with European folkloristics, a scholarly
tradition in which the term *folk* referred exclusively to European peasants.
This conception of the folk in the European context of the late nineteenth century was made possible by a hierarchical and evolutionary view
of society (Dundes 2–4). Moreover, in this conception of folkness, scholars envisioned a cultural and historical continuity between the folk and
the nonfolk as evidenced by a tendency to view folklore as survivals of traditions created by the nonfolk in relatively culturally homogeneous
European societies in earlier times.

In the United States in the late nineteenth century, folklorists set
about to institutionalize the study of folklore in the culturally pluralistic
American society in ways that maintained continuity with the European
tradition.[7] In the absence of a culturally homogeneous population,
American folklorists embraced an affiliative process of creating a "folk" in
which groups characterized by cultural difference and social marginality
became the focus of folklore study in the United States (Newell 3).[8]
Despite vast cultural, historical, and social differences among and within
the groups originally identified, folkloristic theorizing in America sought,
and in many ways continues, to constitute these diverse groups as a homogeneous category of cultural producers called the American "folk." As a
result, folkness in the American context has come to be defined more
often by a non-European and/or socially marginal identity than by a
process of creativity.

The tendency to equate folkness with cultural and social difference
continues to exist in the popular imagination despite the acceptance and
definition of folklore as a process of creativity by contemporary folklorists.
Of the groups originally identified as folk early on in the American context, African Americans, as a perennial folk, continue to figure prominently in the imagination of scholars and the study of creative cultural
production in African American culture continues to be influenced by a

discourse of folkness. The influence of a Eurocentric discourse of folkness on African American creative cultural production necessitates envisioning African American art as either vernacular or occupying a pathological space within the creative universe, or both. This view derives from the fact that, within the United States, European creative traditions and forms continue to be viewed as the original and all others as either vernacular or imitations. Therefore, many African American artists have been forced to accept designations that consign their work to an unmarked category called the "vernacular" or have their created work denigrated as a mere imitation of European forms. Inasmuch as the vernacular apprehended by such terms as *naive, primitive, folk,* and *self-taught* does not represent an aesthetic tradition but rather an affiliative category, scholars most often spend more time trying to establish the "folkness" of African American artists through biographical analysis than in evaluating their created work as a unique artistic accomplishment.

The point is that, over time, a discourse of folkness has complicated the study of African American creative cultural production by obscuring African American artistic diversity through a problematic comparative process. This is not to deny that a tradition of African American vernacular creativity does exist as an important mode of creative cultural production in African American communities in the United States. However, it represents only one of the creative processes by which African Americans express an aesthetic sensibility. Although it is difficult to define, Ralph Ellison offers a useful discussion of the concept of vernacularity in his *Going to the Territory:*

> I see the vernacular as a dynamic process in which the most refined styles from the past are continually merged with the play-it-by-eye-and-play-by-ear improvisations which we invent in our efforts to control our environment and entertain ourselves. And this not only in language and literature, but in tools and technology. In it the styles and techniques of the past are adjusted to the needs of the present, and in its integrative action the high styles of the past are democratized. (139)

As Ellison suggests, the vernacular, though most commonly associated with a level of language use within a specific cultural community, can be thought of in more processual terms. Contemporary folklorists, for example, use the term *vernacular* to characterize a process of creativity through which certain kinds of aesthetic performances and products are created in cultural communities. The vernacular, then, is a term that can be used to confound the problematic associations and meanings inscribed in the term *folk*. Unlike *folk*, *vernacular* makes the basis of classification the process of creativity rather than the identity of the creators of aesthetic products. Most folklorists would agree with Henry Louis Gates Jr. (xxii), who has argued that the vernacular exists as "a parallel discursive universe" with other modes of creative cultural production within an African American cultural context; that is, African American vernacular creativity represents only one mode of creative cultural production historically embraced by people of African descent in the United States, not the whole of their creative universe.

Although, since the 1930s, Horace Pippin's work has been associated with the vernacular in African American culture by virtue of the labels used to describe it, discussion of it from this perspective has been based on simplistic views of what vernacularity actually means. In most cases, his relationship to the vernacular has been established through biographical analysis, trite allusion, and classification rather than an examination of his process of creativity. For example, the famed art collector Albert C. Barnes set the tone for much of the later discussion that would attempt to ground Pippin's art in the African American vernacular in the essay that he produced for the catalog accompanying the first formal showing of Pippin's art. In describing Pippin's work, Barnes alluded to the fact that his paintings "have their musical counterpart in the spirituals of the American Negro" (quoted in Stein 1993, 2). Other commentators have been more explicit in their evocations of the vernacular in discussing Pippin's art. Alain Locke, the intellectual and spiritual father of the Harlem Renaissance, described Pippin as "a real and rare genius, combining folk quality with artistic maturity so uniquely as almost to defy classification" (quoted in West 46). David C. Driskell, the dean of African American art historians, has continued this tendency to locate Pippin's art in the African American vernacular. Driskell claims that "Pippin relied strongly on the lore of local people, including their interpretations of the Bible, as well as the history he read and the memories of his own experiences at home and abroad" (xii). In most instances, discussions of the relationship of Pippin's art to the African American vernacular focus not on his process but on the images that he created that would seem to reveal influences of various aspects of the African American vernacular experience on his art.

Although there is little doubt that Horace Pippin was not only knowledgeable about African American vernacular forms and traditions and represented them in his art, this aspect of his work makes him neither a vernacular artist nor unique among artists who work within the African American tradition of creative cultural production. In many ways, Pippin's placement in categories that describe him as a vernacular artist obscures the fact that, despite his social background and lack of formal training in techniques of Western painting, his art is deeply grounded in literate Western traditions of visual representation, especially in a formal sense. Historically, many African American artists creating in diverse media—whether they are academically trained or simply possessed of extraordinary artistic talent, or both—have appropriated Western forms and processes of artistic representation to embody cultural ideas and images evocative of the black experience in the United States. Moreover, these artists have frequently inscribed in their created products, both consciously and unconsciously, creative forms and performances associated with the African American vernacular. In attempting to understand uses of the vernacular by African American artists, scholars have employed various analytic approaches, especially in examinations of written texts. However, they have focused most often on the ways in which the vernacular finds new meaning in creative contexts and, more recently, in developing theoretical models for understanding the African American tradition of textual production.[9]

Although all of these approaches have proven useful in providing an understanding of the intricate and complex ways in which African American modes of creative cultural production inform each other, they tend to focus on the products and results of an active engagement with the vernacular rather than the processes by which artists appropriate the vernacular in producing creative texts. Moreover, the bulk of this scholarship involves the study of written literature, a scholarly endeavor where neither formal training nor vernacular engagement determines the classification of either artists or artistic products; that is, whether a creative writer spends years studying his or her craft in college or writing workshops or simply embarks on a writing career without any formal training in the creation of a chosen genre has no bearing on the status of the artist or the created product. A similar observation can be made about vernacular engagement on the part of creative writers; that is, whether a writer produces a short story modeled after a folktale, creates a poem in black dialect, or simply incorporates vernacular forms or performances associated with vernacular traditions in a novel, the writer will not be considered a vernacular artist nor will his or her creations be considered folk literature. From the perspective of a discourse of folkness, the treatment of creative writers in this regard reveals the extent to which the production of texts in writing is already considered Western regardless of the expressive form embraced or the level of language used by the artist.

The difference in the scholarly discourses and approaches that have developed to discuss vernacular engagement by creative artists who produce written text and those artists who create visual ones is illuminating. Critics of written texts seem to accept the fact that the very ability to write implies formal training or, at the least, sufficient exposure to literate forms of expression to be able to create within the Western tradition. On the other hand, most critics of the visual arts do not accept the ability to produce visual texts as implying training, formal or otherwise—as is evident in the use of a term such as *self-taught,* for example. However, this perspective denies the reality that the learning of aesthetic forms and process occurs in vastly different ways in different cultural communities. Moreover, as Gerald Davis has argued, what individuals often learn through their membership and participation in cultural communities is not necessarily how to construct specific aesthetic objects but rather "technologies of aesthetic construction" that, once learned, can be utilized in the production of various aesthetic products (296). Art historians and other scholars who tend to be concerned with created objects rather than the processes by which individuals learn to construct aesthetic objects in cultural community seldom consider these processes of learning in evaluating and classifying artists such as Pippin.

Despite an emphasis in Western art history on the importance of formal training to the development of artistic ability, this perspective is not shared cross-culturally. For example, as Davis has pointed out, many African Americans embrace certain notions about artistic ability that are important to an understanding of how it is viewed within the culture. Specifically, he notes that many African Americans hold a belief in the possibility that, without the benefit of formal training, certain individuals possess "God-given talents" to perform in expressive media that may or may not be recognized as traditional within their community (297). Moreover, African Americans who embrace this notion believe that individuals who possess such talents are spiritually blessed and thus mandated to perfect and use them both for the glorification of God and the good of their community. To these African Americans, there is no greater gift than a "God-given talent" and no greater waste of human potential and spiritual energy than the failure to utilize that talent to its fullest. Because they generally accept the perfection of a God-given talent as a spiritual necessity, most African Americans tend to place little significance on whether an individual perceived as possessing such a talent uses it to gain success in Western arts through academic training, pursues it in the production of artistic forms more generally associated with modes of cultural production in African American communities, or uses it in the production of seemingly idiosyncratic forms. The important consideration for most African Americans is that the individual uses his or her talent in positive and productive ways, that is, in ways that enhance rather than threaten the well-being of the community.

The esoteric notion of "God-given talent" is useful to an understanding of how individuals in African American communities would most likely respond to seemingly idiosyncratic artistic performances in diverse media by members of the community. The notion has also been noted as an influence on the artist's conception of his or her talent and work. For example, art historian Judith McWillie has noted in her study of a number of contemporary African American vernacular artists that "the idea of being 'anointed,' beyond being talented," constitutes an important aspect of their self-conception (10). She argues that, in her work with what she calls Afro Atlantic artists, the association between creating art and doing "spiritual work" was made so frequently that it must be seen as an important connecting strand linking them to one another. The extent to which Pippin viewed his creative abilities in overtly spiritual terms is difficult to ascertain from the biographical narratives. However, a reporter for the *Baltimore Afro-American* described Pippin as a "profoundly religious man" and indicated that his religion was an important influence in his everyday life. This description echoes sentiments shared with Judith Stein (1993, 10) in her interviews with neighbors and friends who knew him. We also know from an often-reported remark that he made when asked about the value of art classes that he attended that he held a rather organic view of artistic talent. He is reported as having responded that "To me it seems impossible for another to teach one of art" (Rodman 4). In addition, Julius Bloch wrote in his journal after a meeting with the artist that Pippin expressed to him a strong belief that "his talent came to him from God, who directs his work and when he has difficulty with it, he prays at night, and the next morning help comes and the problem is clearer and nearer solution" (quoted in S. Wilson 6).

Regardless of the source of Pippin's artistic ability, it is clear that he used it to represent various aspects of the African American vernacular experience in many of his works. Although his ability and pronounced tendency to engage the vernacular probably derive at least in part from his mastery of technologies of aesthetic construction learned from his participation in black communities throughout his life, I would argue that his engagement of the vernacular was in many ways part of a highly conscious process in which he attempted to represent African American experience and identity in terms of forms and performances that he viewed as unique to the African cultural experience; that is, like many other African American artists, he incorporated various vernacular forms and traditions in his created texts in order to represent accurately, and, he believed, authentically, the African American cultural and historical experience. However, because he was a member of the group with which these traditions are associated, his methods of appropriating the vernacular have been assumed to be subjective and based entirely on personal experience. Therefore, his seeming intricate and intimate knowledge of vernacular forms and performances have led to an assumption that, in creating art, he performed the traditions that he sought to represent artistically. I want to argue, however, that close scrutiny of his method of engaging the vernacular can offer an alternative way of envisioning his relationship to the African American vernacular.

In other words, I want to suggest that Pippin's engagement with the African American vernacular representation can best be understood by examining closely his process of creativity vis-à-vis the vernacular. For example, from all accounts, Horace Pippin maintained a lifelong desire to document his experiences and memories as an African American in the ways that he had available to him. If we can judge from the glimpses of his life contained in the biographical narratives, Pippin displayed an early interest in using his artistic ability to capture images and memories evocative of everyday experiences (S. Wilson n.p.; Rodman 6–7). For example, as a public school student, he reported that he was often forced to stay after school for illustrating his lessons with images that brought them alive. In the various jobs that he held from farmworker to hotel bellboy, he routinely sketched images of the activities and people who surrounded him. During his stint in the army in World War I, he kept an illustrated diary in which he sought to chronicle the experiences of his all-black regiment. Although he destroyed all but a few pages of this diary after his injury, which he later regretted doing, he still maintained an incredible desire to record and preserve his experiences and those of his fellow soldiers for posterity. In an effort to recapture these images, he attempted to put in writing his memories of his early life during the period after the war when he believed that he would never be able to produce visual art again. Although he worked laboriously to write his autobiography, he was able to produce only a five-page manuscript because of his disability and/or his lack of verbal agility. Of this effort, he later observed that "One winter, I tried to write my story of some of my experiences but did such an unsuccessful job that I gave it up" (Rodman 80). Although unsuccessful as a writer, Pippin persisted in his effort to find a way of inscribing his memories of his life experiences. Despite his disability, his tenacious desire to capture his experiences led him back to visual art. He notes that after his failed attempts to produce a written biography, "I started to make drawings on wood panels ten years after my discharge. Still my arm and shoulder were so weak I could not work long at a time, but I kept trying. One day I decided to get some oil paint and I started the picture in my mind, 'The End of the War Starting Home,' and made others" (ibid.). As Pippin worked at his art, his maimed arm became increasingly stronger and he began working feverishly to re-create the pictures in his mind on canvas.

What I want to suggest is that Pippin's artistic process was always influenced by what might be called a documentary impulse. His view of his process as essentially documentary is clearly revealed in an anecdote recorded by Edward Loper, another painter who befriended him. In response to a query from Loper, Pippin is reported to have exclaimed: "Ed, you know why I am great? . . . Because I paint things exactly the way they are. . . . I don't do what these white guys do. I don't go around here making up a whole lot of stuff. I paint exactly the way it is and exactly the way I see it" (quoted in Stein 1993, 16). In attempting to name the process by which Pippin engaged the vernacular, I want to suggest that his response to Loper represents a serious assessment of the process that informed his uses of the vernacular in the creation of visual images. As such, I want to argue that his statement to Loper can be accepted as an expression of both an artistic and an anthropological sensibility—a combination of sensibilities being increasingly recognized as coterminous in the production of cultural knowledge and meaning. In other words, I want to suggest that a productive way of highlighting Pippin's relationship to the vernacular is to envision his engagement with the vernacular from an ethnographic perspective. Viewing Pippin's work from an ethnographic perspective provides a means of understanding in a more objective manner the process by which he transformed his memories and observations of the everyday and the ordinary—the vernacular, if you will—into powerful visual images evocative of the unique lifestyle and perspective shared by people of African descent.

An ethnographic approach seems particularly useful when Pippin's description of his process is viewed in light of recent critical appraisals and discussions of ethnographic practices. Johannes Fabian (1992, 85), for example, argues that "seeing and observation [have been] the most important or at any rate the most reliable sources of ethnographic knowledge. 'Saving the oral' then requires making it visible." In attempting to "save the oral" by "making it visible," I want to argue that the anthropologist who uses ethnographic inscription and the artist who uses creative texts, written or visual, to inscribe oral performances share a similar process or, at the least, achieve a similar result. Clifford Geertz, who defines the ethnographer as one who "'inscribes' social discourse," offers another useful perspective for thinking about the relationship between art and ethnography (19). He argues that in inscribing social discourse, the ethnographer "turns [social discourse] from a passing event, which exists only in its own moment of occurrence, into an account, which exists in its inscriptions and can be reconsulted." Although Geertz emphasizes the written nature of ethnographic inscription, the enduring quality of such inscriptions suggests certain affinities between artistically rendered visual representations and written ethnographies. In addition, James Clifford, who defines ethnography as a more general process that he calls "culture collecting," offers further justification and support for an ethnographic approach in examining Pippin's work. In Clifford's view, "To see ethnography as a form of culture collecting . . . highlights the ways that diverse experiences and facts are selected, gathered, detached from their original temporal occasions, and given enduring value in a new arrangement" (231). Clifford notes further that culture collecting is a process carried out by cultural "insiders or outsiders" and represents a form of cultural appropriation productive of new understandings of cultural phenomena (232).

In proposing an ethnographic approach in examining Pippin's work, Geertz's view of ethnography as "interpretation" provides another possible level of analysis—one that allows for a more complex view of his artistic accomplishments (15). As Geertz observes, ethnographies are not simply literal representations of observed culture experiences, but rather interpretations of the observed and recorded. Moreover, he claims that ethnographies are also "fictions: fictions, in the sense that they are 'something made,' 'something fashioned'—in the original meaning of fictio— not that they are false, unfactual, or merely 'as if' thought experiments" (ibid.). To become aware of the fictional quality of ethnography, according to Geertz, "is to realize that the line between mode of representation and substantive content is as undrawable in cultural analysis as it is in painting" (ibid.). The difficulty of drawing such a line, argues Richard Nonas, an anthropologist turned artist, is "the inevitable otherness of art itself." Art's otherness, Nonas suggests, derives from the fact that "all art inevitably starts with an outside and an outsider" in the sense that artists always stand outside of their representations (164). The fact that both artist and ethnographer approach their representational tasks from the outside assigns them, according to Geertz, to a mission to "clarify what goes on . . . to reduce the puzzlement . . . to which unfamiliar acts emerging out of unknown backgrounds naturally give rise" (16). In this sense, the written ethnographic document comes to serve as a context for ordering random conversations, observations, and, especially for the ethnographic folklorist, performances recorded over a period of time.

In suggesting an ethnographic approach to Pippin's art, I am neither claiming that we should ascribe to him the literal status of an ethnographer—certainly not in the scientific sense implied by this designation— nor suggesting that Pippin's purpose in creating visual images was identical to that of an ethnographer who sets about to describe cultural practices in writing. Instead, I am suggesting that his process, which involved an attempt to represent the cultural lives of his subjects from their point of view, shares processual and representational features in common with ethnographic practice. In addition, I am suggesting that, in reading the images that he created, we embark on what Fabian has described as a "special kind of ethnographic work," the decoding of inscribed "oral performance" as represented textually. In pursuing this special kind of ethnographic work, according to Fabian, we must attempt to "listen and match recorded sounds and [visual] symbols with communicative competence, memories and imagination" in our effort to apprehend cultures and lives as represented textually (1992, 86).

In an important sense, I would argue that Pippin's work has always been read ethnographically and that it is these implicit ethnographic readings that have led to problematic classifications of his art; that is, the labels that have been used to describe Pippin as an artist and to categorize his work have assumed that his art is based on firsthand knowledge of African American culture and performance practices and thereby provides easy access to the cultural Otherness of African Americans. In one sense, the kind of critical reading of his work that I am suggesting does not disrupt this reading to an appreciable degree. In another, more profound, sense, however, it is intended to alter our reading of Pippin as an artist and creator of cultural knowledge by transforming our conception of him from that of an ethnographic subject to that of an ethnographic agent. It is as an object of ethnographic investigation rather than as a producer of ethnographic knowledge that he has been forced to become, in the minds of his critics, the embodiment of the very aesthetic that he attempted to represent in his art as evidenced by the focus on his biography.[10] In effecting this transformation, we are able to confound meanings deeply inscribed in labels such as "naive," "primitive," "folk," and "self-taught" that are used to describe him as an artist. From an ethnographic perspective, we can envision him as a stable, creating, and controlling presence in the production of knowledge about the African American vernacular experience rather than one whose art is guided and controlled by an aesthetic associated with the vernacular. In the process, we embrace the possibility of being able to rethink how his art can be read as the expressive embodiment of both aesthetic and cultural knowledge.

When Pippin's art is envisioned as the expressive embodiment of ethnographically derived insights, those aspects of his art that have seemed most revealing to his critics as evidence of his naïveté take on new meaning. In the past, Pippin's critics, in their efforts to represent him as a true naïf, have tended to interpret his concern with creating images characterized by balance and symmetry, his inclusion of seemingly innocuous details, his tendency toward skewed perspective, his use of dramatic colors, his attention to the mundane and everyday, as well as his repetition of imagistic fields as indicative of a naïve sensibility and the absence of an aesthetic or social consciousness in producing his art.[11] When viewed as art deeply grounded in observation and even participation in the events and forms that he represents on canvas, Pippin's work can be examined as a reflection of a mature and well-defined intentionality that emerged from his attempts to represent the integrity and nuances of African American life as he saw it and as he believed it existed in the minds and actions of African Americans; that is, his art can be examined as a product of his belief that this integrity resided in the details, the small revelations of cultural performances and the displays of cultural and artistic competence that defined and characterized what it means to be an American of African descent in the United States.

The documentary or ethnographic impulse that informs Pippin's artistic process is nowhere better revealed than in his concern with representing the vernacular as emerging and functioning in particular contexts rather than as isolated artifacts. In bringing the vernacular into view, his created images reflect a concern with contextualizing vernacular performances in ways that imbued them with situated meaning. His ability to use his art as a context for creating meaningful representations of vernacular cultural experiences and processes is revealed nowhere more tellingly than in his domestic interiors, in which he characteristically incorporates various created forms evocative of the vernacular arts. A quilter quietly performing her art by the fireside, a brightly colored quilt covering children in bed, a woven rug foregrounded on the floor, or doilies prominently displayed on table tops characteristically appear in his images representing interior scenes. The presence of these creative endeavors and created objects reveals in rather dramatic ways Pippin's attempts to contextualize these objects and to reveal something about the artistic processes and competence of African Americans and the desire for aesthetic order and pleasure characteristic of African American domestic life. Moreover, his placement of these aesthetic objects in settings that open invariably to reveal impoverished lives, evidenced by gaping holes in walls created by crumbling plaster, allowed Pippin to comment on the socioeconomic status of African Americans of his day and to simultaneously reveal that, despite these conditions, African Americans nevertheless filled their lives with aesthetic pursuits.

Despite frequent characterizations of Pippin as a humble and unassuming man lacking aesthetic and social sophistication, his art, when viewed from an ethnographic perspective or as the expressive embodiment of a vernacular aesthetic, reveals a mature social consciousness as well as an astute eye for nuances of African American culture and life in both historical and contemporary manifestations. As an African American growing up in a segregated society and one who participated in a segregated military that left him bitter and a confirmed pacifist, Pippin was well aware of the distorted images of African American culture and life that existed both within and outside of the United States. As a cultural insider, Pippin also was aware of the ways in which stereotypical images of African Americans negatively influenced the well-being of individuals and

the group. From his familial and cultural background he had developed a
view of African American life in which order and integrity prevailed, faith
and fun pervaded everyday existence, and people acted bravely and hon-
orably. As a talented artist, he realized that he possessed the communicative means to perform in an expressive medium that would bring to the
world alternative images of the African American experience—images
that reveal something of the lifestyle of millions of African Americans who
had no communicative means of their own.

In creating visual images reflecting his sense of the African American
cultural experience, Pippin embraced a process that reveals a strong desire
not only to record the "picture in his mind" accurately, but also to tell the
story in as much ethnographic detail as possible. In producing many of his
paintings, he lends a new meaning to the concept of "thick description" in
that he routinely applied multiple layers of paint to his images, constantly
reworking them until he felt that he had captured the reality of the event
portrayed.[12] For example, he claims that it took him three years and "at
least a hundred coats of paint" to produce his first painting, *The End of the
War Starting Home* (Rodman 11). In addition to the constant reworking of
images, Pippin's art reveals a pronounced tendency toward narrativity in
that he routinely created narrative cycles in which he produced a number
of paintings on the same or a complementary subject with only slight, but
often meaningful, changes in the original image. From an ethnographic
perspective, we might suggest that Pippin's tendency to create images
that tell a story in multiepisodic fashion represents his attempt to create
visual images that reproduced the style of African American oral narra-
tors. The African American oral narrative tradition in which convention-
alized characters serve as a focus for creating narrative cycles based on the
exploits of a central figure such as Brer Rabbit or John is well known
(Roberts 1989). However, this technique of episodic narration is characteristic of African American storytelling even in the creation of personal
narratives. Pippin's tendency to appropriate this style of narrative representation in his art is probably more responsible for the claim that he created "visual narratives," in Richard Powell's terms, than any single painting (138). Although his individual images often tell a compact, yet dense,
story, his series allowed him to embellish his narratives and, through
imagistic repetition, to critique and enhance our sense of the situations
depicted as well as the meanings that they hold for an understanding of
African American culture and history. His episodic paintings, when read
as extended narratives, would seem to belie the often-repeated claims of

his critics that his early works generally reveal an absence of critical social conscience.

For instance, his "Cotton in the Cabin" series, one of his earliest, has often been read as his perpetuating the "happy darky" tradition. Not surprisingly, scholars also frequently point to this series as emblematic of his engagement with the vernacular. This series of paintings, according to art historian Judith Wilson, was inspired by an image of a cabin in the opening and closing credits of the 1932 movie of the same name (147–48). The movie itself was based on a book chronicling the growing hostility between Southern planters and poor white tenant farmers and presented African Americans as only peripheral figures. Pippin's inspiration for these paintings may very well have been the movie because he spent only a couple of months in the South while in the army. Bearden and Henderson, however, suggest another source for the "Cotton in the Cabin" series (358). They claim that these images reflected Pippin's attempt to visualize the narratives about Southern black family life that he heard from his adult relatives and other transplanted Southerners that he met during his lifetime. We have no confirmation from Pippin about his sources, but it is conceivable that various experiences contributed to the productions of this series of paintings in different ways. On the one hand, the movie could have provided the inspiration for the series. On the other hand, it is virtually inconceivable that Pippin would not have heard stories in the 1930s about the cotton-growing South from African American migrants to the Philadelphia area, a major destination for thousands of black Southerners who fled these regions during the period of the Great Migration that reached its height in the 1920s.

What is certain is that, in the "Cotton in the Cabin" series, Pippin creatively transformed his sources and produced at least four paintings that he differentiated by adding numbers to the original title. In his interpretation of the thematic of the Southern cabin, he envisions African Americans as the occupants and prominently depicts them as engaged in various everyday activities around its exterior. Through an accumulation of realistic detail, the cabin takes on all the aspects of home. Although in all of the images the cabin is situated on the edge of a field of cotton ripe for picking, the first three paintings depict evening scenes and foreground various aspects of African American domestic and family life, including an elderly woman relaxing in the yard, a mother tending to her children, and a scene of evening entertainment with a banjo player. When viewed as isolated and singular images, the leisurely attitudes assumed by the figures in these paintings invite comparison with the happy darky tradition of representing Southern African Americans. However, when these three images are read as part of an episodic narrative that includes the fourth in the series, a more critical commentary on the nature of African American life in the cotton-growing South is revealed to be Pippin's purpose in creating this series.

In *Cotton in the Cabin IV*, Pippin created a daytime scene in which an African American male appears to be bringing a basket of cotton to an African American woman seated at a loom. In the center of the painting, a figure that appears to be a white Southern belle is seated with hands folded in what appears to be a flower garden. The belle, who is attired in a fashionable white dress and bonnet, both the same color as the cotton in the background, seems curiously out of place in the bustling work environment of the African Americans. When this image is included as another episode in Pippin's cabin narrative, the series of paintings can be read as a poignant statement about the relationship of African American workers to a planter class in the cotton-growing South. The fact that Pippin chose to depict the scenes of carefree black family life as nighttime activities is surely no accident. In the kingdom of cotton, the evenings were the only times that African Americans had for themselves and the kind of life-affirming activities that he depicts in the first three paintings. The daytime, as *Cotton in the Cabin IV* suggests, was one in which the production and refinement of cotton totally occupied African Americans. As a result of the endless labors of African American workers, cotton production provided Southern white planters the kind of leisure symbolized by the belle's idleness and her conspicuous affluence.

In concluding that Pippin did not inscribe social commentary in his "Cotton in the Cabin" series, his critics also tend to ignore another painting, *Old King Cotton*, that he imagistically aligns with this series and infuses with biting social commentary. A relationship between *Old King Cotton* and the series is suggest by the presence of the cabin on the edge of a field of cotton and an African American woman seated at a loom wearing the same colored kerchief as the woman in *Cotton in the Cabin IV*. This painting is usually ignored as part of the series because it was executed in response to an invitation from *Vogue* magazine for an image to accompany its "cotton festival layout," a fashion spread (Stein 1993, 30–31). *Vogue* rejected the image, however, claiming that it was too difficult to reproduce the brilliant colors that Pippin had used. Instead, the magazine used *Cotton in the Cabin IV* in the same issue, but in a layout focusing on new artists. In their caption for the Pippin painting, the editors wrote that the work revealed that the artist "combines a primitive sophistication of design with clean, happy colors" (quoted in J. Wilson). *Vogue's* stated reasons for rejecting *Old King Cotton* may very well have been based on technological inadequacy at the time (Stein 1993, 31). It is also conceivable, however, that the editors sensed that Pippin's colorful images masked obvious social commentary that they believed would offend some readers.

In *Old King Cotton,* Pippin depicts a scene in which a faceless African American woman sits at a loom weaving strands of cotton that run from the loom through a dress worn by a Southern belle figure in the center of the painting through the dresses of three colorfully dressed white women of fashion standing in front of a cotton field in full flower. Although colorfully arrayed, the three fashionably dressed white women display body language and pained facial expressions that suggest discomfort with their position in the whole affair. It is very possible that the *Vogue* editors, upon viewing this image, recognized that Pippin's painting, in all of its colorfulness, suggested vividly one of the ways in which Northerners were complicit in the exploitation of black labor in the South.

Ethnographically speaking, Pippin's "Cotton in the Cabin" series creates a fictional narrative that chronicles a moment in the history of African Americans by realistically and honestly, from Pippin's point of view, interpreting for his viewers not so much the place of the Southern cabin in the lives of African Americans as cotton, a major source of black exploitation during this era. By using his art to visualize the cabin as a site of home and work and by texturing that site through the incorporation of subtle details productive of a deeper understanding, he renders a kind of thick description that brings the viewer inside a reality experienced daily by millions of African Americans. In working from the remembered experiences of others, Pippin creates a historical narrative that artistically renders the past meaningful. In the process, he imbues the experience with enduring meaning in a new arrangement intended to evoke contemporary understanding.

Pippin's engagement with narrative creation in his art remained an enduring aspect of his process. In addition to creating narratives that linger on a single dominant image, he created narrative series in which he progressively develops different narrative moments based on the activities or history of his subject. His earliest works, which were based on his personal memories and interpretations of his experiences in World War I, illustrates this process. As was to become a common practice for Pippin, the images that he created to chronicle the World War I experience attempt to represent the collective memories of those who served. In her study of Pippin's war paintings, Judith Wilson describes these images as having a "documentary flavor" (61). In *The End of the War Starting Home* as well as other paintings on World War I such as *Gas Alarm Outpost: Argonne, Shell Holes and Observation Balloons: Champagne Sector, Dog Fight over Trenches,* and *Outpost Raid: Champagne Sector,* Pippin chronicled the experiences of war endured by his regiment and emphasizes the technologies of warfare introduced in World War I. His first completed painting, *The End of the War Starting Home,* as many of his critics have noted, does not depict an event that Pippin could have witnessed because he was recuperating in a French hospital from his injury when the war ended. Nevertheless, in this painting he imaginatively re-creates a scene of surrender in which German soldiers stand on the battlefield surrounded by scenes of carnage and destruction. Although he was not physically present at the surrender, he undoubtedly heard numerous stories about it from other veterans with whom he routinely interacted at the local American Legion post, where he was an active member. In addition, though based on an imagined scene, he incorporated many of the symbols of war that he recorded in his illustrated diary and that were to reemerge in other paintings based on his World War I experiences.

In producing images of war, Judith Wilson has noted Pippin "shifts from a documentary to a protest mode during the 1940s" (64). However, his paintings of scenes related to World War I represent more than nostalgic remembrances of an old soldier. In an important sense, they literally inscribe the experiences of the thousands of African Americans who risked and sacrificed their lives in the defense of democracy—a story that Pippin strongly believed deserved telling, as indicated in his earlier written efforts. Like millions of other African Americans who expectantly joined the war effort in the belief that their sacrifices would change white American attitudes, Pippin returned home not only with images of the destructiveness of modern warfare indelibly printed in his mind, but also sharing in the disappointment and frustration of other African Americans soldiers who, upon their return to the States, encountered entrenched racism. Although his biographers often claim that Pippin harbored no bitterness about his injury or the aftermath of the war, they also frequently note that he became a confirmed pacifist—a pacifism strongly influenced by his Christianity. According to one of his earliest biographers and critics, Selden Rodman, Pippin's repressed feelings about the war erupted in his drawings and painting in various ways (10). Rodman writes that the images that Pippin created of war

> reveal at once what the tight consciousness of the narrative, with its platitudes, its clichés and its traditional patriotism, manages most effectively, to conceal. The war had been a shattering experience to Horace Pippin. He would not have admitted it. He may not have "known" it. But the drawings, and to a far greater degree the war paintings that were to following in twelve years, cannot be denied. He had seen the desolation of earth, the ruin of cities, the inhumanity of man (ibid.).

In various ways, Pippin's memories of these scenes of war made their way into his World War I visual narrative. His World War I series envisions war in all of its environmental and human destructiveness. The French landscape that Pippin described as "very pretty" upon his arrival emerges in his images depicting the aftermath of war as a virtual wasteland. Soldiers, though prominently depicted in some of the images, often appear in poses that make them seem insignificant and even helpless in the face of modern technologies of war, especially the bombers that fly over their heads and the gas masks that become extensions of their faces.

The apparent absence of overt social commentary in Pippin's World War I paintings may have resulted from his unwillingness to transform his and his fellow soldiers' memories into mere political statement. He demonstrated no such reticence in his World War II paintings, however. Although they necessarily do not focus on actual combat (he had no first-hand knowledge), they reveal Pippin's strong pacifist beliefs and his growing social consciousness concerning entrenched racism. In World War II–inspired paintings such as *Mr. Prejudice, Deep Are the Roots,* and *Barracks,* Pippin emphasized not only the important role of African Americans in national defense, but also the lingering racial prejudice both in the military and at home that constantly undermined and made a lie of the goals articulated as the reason for these wars. His painting *Barracks* is typical of the kind of biting social commentary that character-izes his World War II series. Although this painting is usually accepted as a part of his World War II series because it was created in 1945, it depicts a scene very likely executed from memory that he carried with him from World War I. In this painting, he creates a scene in which African American soldiers lounge on their bunks, sleeping or attending to rou-tine tasks while their guns rest idly by their sides. In a subtle visual move,

Pippin depicts the two soldiers foregrounded in this painting in World War I puttees, thereby suggesting that nothing had changed for African American soldiers. In so doing, he evokes the racism that continued to infect the military during World War II by denying the combat abilities of African American soldiers.

In *Mr. Prejudice,* Pippin drops all pretense at subtlety and represents in more overt terms his view of the destructive consequences of racism both in the military and in society. In the center of this painting stands Mr. Prejudice holding a huge anvil, which he is using to pound a wedge in an attempt to split the symbolic "V" for "Victory" of World War II. The image of Mr. Prejudice is flanked on one side by Miss Liberty and on the other by a hooded Klansman. Just beneath these figures are various service workers and, at the bottom, stand figures representing the clergy as well as soldiers wearing World War II uniforms reflecting their branches of the military. Continuity of attitude is represented by an African American soldier dressed in World War I puttees standing in the center of the groups of soldiers. The painting is perfectly balanced by the different racial groupings with the African American service workers, clergy, and soldiers standing to the right under Miss Liberty and the white service workers, clergy, and soldiers standing to the left beneath the hooded Klansman. Although the African American figures and the white figures in the painting are depicted as being loosely connected, the tenuous connection is threatened by Mr. Prejudice's constant hammering away at the symbolic "V." This painting, which angered some of Pippin's patrons, represented a strong statement about racism in the military and in American society. Although the painting has been lauded as a brilliant visual and symbolic representation of America's history of exploitation of and racism toward African Americans, his patrons tended to see it as a threat to their own view of him as a "naïf," as well as to the economic viability of his art.

The concern of Pippin's patrons that *Mr. Prejudice* represented an apparent turn to social realism and overt political commentary was never realized. In his work prior to and after *Mr. Prejudice,* he remained faithful to his ethnographic project of representing, in a more descriptive and narrative fashion, various aspect of African American history and culture. In his other narrative series, he continued to mine various aspects of African American historical memory and cultural life in an effort to order and make meaningful the experiences of African Americans. For example, his celebrated series of African American domestic interiors take viewers on a visual tour through the homes of ordinary African Americans

as they go about the business of everyday living; in such paintings as
Domino Players, in which he depicts two women seated around a table playing dominos while a young boy looks on and an elderly woman sits near
them piecing a quilt; *Interior,* in which he depicts an evening family scene
in which the mother sits in front of the coal-burning stove smoking a pipe
while one child cradles a doll in the center of the floor and another pores
over her school lessons; *Sunday Morning Breakfast,* in which a mother
serves a meal to two children seated at the table as the father sits near the
table either putting on or taking off his shoes; *Asleep,* which depicts two
children sleeping in a single bed near the stove; *Saying Prayers,* which
shows two children kneeling in an attitude of prayer in nightshirts with
their head in their mother's lap; and *Saturday Night Bath,* which portrays a
mother scrubbing a child in a washtub in front of the stove.

Pippin's domestic scenes, which open to viewers the interior of
African American homes and reveal his ability to interject subtle social
commentary into his visual renderings of subject matter, show Pippin at
his ethnographic best. These images bring the viewer into a large common room that seems to be the hub of family activity and life. At the same
time, the multiplicity of activities that occur in this single room suggests
the cramped quarters in which many African American families found
themselves in the North during the period of intense Northern migration.
The economic condition under which these families lived is indicated by
the walls of the room, which invariably display areas in which the plaster
has fallen away, indicating the deteriorating conditions of these homes.
Despite these conditions, the rooms are depicted as extremely neat, order-
ly, and warm, symbolized by an ever-present coal-burning stove.

Although, during his career as an artist, Pippin turned his talent to
the creation of images in diverse genres including still lifes, portraits, and
biblical scenes, his most enduring works depict some aspect of the African
American cultural and historical experience. The sources for many of his
historical works are not known precisely, but some of the images that he
created on these subjects were undoubtedly based on his own or the
remembered experiences of others that he acquired over time. For example, his historical works include several celebrated series depicting various
moments in the lives of heroic figures such as Abraham Lincoln and John
Brown whose contributions to the African American struggle for freedom
circulated as legends in African American communities during Pippin's
day. Although his sources for the Abraham Lincoln series merely hint at a
source in legend, his John Brown series is most often attributed to his

efforts to render visually narratives told him by his mother, who his biographers claim was present at Brown's hanging. Memory obviously served Pippin well in producing some of his paintings, whereas other works were based on direct observation. For instance, local residents recall seeing Pippin as he set up his easel on the streets of West Chester, where he captured outdoor scenes such as *Harmonizing*, an image that documents the doo-wop craze of the 1940s.

By viewing Pippin as an artist who stands outside of his created images, an analytic perspective can be achieved that reveals the profound depth of his insights concerning his culture and society during and between the world wars. From an ethnographic perspective—which allows us to view Pippin as an artist who used his knowledge and experiences of African American cultural attitudes, beliefs, and performative practices in producing art—we are able to focus attention on his created images and the meanings that they inscribe. As I have attempted to demonstrate, the scholarly tendency to conceptualize him a priori as a vernacular artist results more from his pronounced tendency to turn to the everyday experiences of African Americans for inspiration and subject matter than from his process of creativity. As a result, Pippin has not only been denied objectivity in his efforts to represent the African American cultural and vernacular experience visually, but has also all too often been viewed as the embodiment of the very aesthetic that he sought to represent on canvas.

That an African American artist would make the cultural and historical experiences of African Americans a primary focus of his creative works should not be surprising. However, although many of the visual images that Pippin created during his career demonstrate a pronounced interest in documenting visually aspects of the everyday and remembered experiences of African Americans, his process of engaging the vernacular and creating images on canvas would seem to have more in common with literate modes of visual representation than with African American traditions of vernacular expression. In many ways, the critical and classificatory approaches that have been used in discussions of Horace Pippin as an artist emerge out of a historically problematic discourse of folkness as it has impacted on the study of African American creative cultural expression. Within an oppositional discourse of folkness as it has been rehearsed in the United States, cultural difference has historically served as a more important basis for classifying the creative cultural production of artists who cannot claim a European cultural heritage than has their process of creativity. This perspective not only perpetuates a problematic comparative approach, but it also denies the complexity of creative cultural production within specific cultural communities in the United States.

NOTES

1. Since the late 1930s, art critics and historians have used one or another of these terms to describe Horace Pippin and/or his art. As Judith McWillie notes in *Another Face of the Diamond*, labels used to describe African American artists such as Pippin tend to be highly arbitrary and reflect "the intellectual and economic investment of those who appropriate the work" (7).

2. With the exception of exhibition catalogs for one-man shows of Pippin's art and brief newspaper and magazine notices, the vast majority of discussions of him as an artist are found in biographically oriented texts that offer portraits of a number of individuals whose works are associated with nonacademic Western traditions.

3. The following authors (see Works Cited) who discuss the life and work of Horace Pippin in some detail take a biographical approach: Stein; Bearden and Henderson; Lewis; S. Wilson; and Rodman. In addition, a biographical approach is the most common one used in the numerous short magazine and newspaper accounts that most often serve as public announcements of upcoming or ongoing exhibitions of Pippin's work.

4. The controversy concerning Pippin's discovery as an artist is summarized in Stein, *I Tell My Heart: The Art of Horace Pippin*. Most of Pippin's biographers, however, repeat the story that N. C. Wyeth and Christian Brinton discovered Pippin. The most common version of this "discovery narrative" is that they saw one of Pippin's paintings hanging in the store window of a local merchant while walking down the street in West Chester.

5. For relevant discussion of the problematic history and use of such terms, see Abrahams; Davis; Fabian 1983; Roberts 1993; Torgovnick. In addition, many of the essays collected in Michael D. Hall and Eugene W. Metcalf Jr., *The Artist Outsider: Creativity and the Boundaries of Culture*, critique one or another of these terms as applied to art and artists. Although all of these terms have somewhat different histories of use, they share a common purpose in that they all represent attempts, from an academic and/or Eurocentric perspective, to name nonacademic and non-European traditions of creative cultural production.

6. For a discussion of the history of primitivism and the ways in which it has been figured in diverse media and scholarship by Europeans and Euro-Americans over time, see Marianna Torgovnick, *Gone Primitive: Savage Intellects, Modern Lives*.

7. Several studies examine and critique the ways in which American folklorists operationalized a European paradigm for the study of folklore in the United States, among them Dundes; Bell; Roberts 1993; and Zumwalt. In all of these studies, the European equation between folk and peasant is discussed as a problematic that attended early efforts to institutional the European model of folklore in America, even though these scholars do not agree on the importance of the equation.

8. William Wells Newell, one of the architects of American folkloristics and the first editor of the *Journal of American Folklore*, outlined the field of American folklore in the first issue of the journal. In his outline, he identified African Americans, Native Americans, Cajuns, and Mexican Americans as the groups whose folklore would be the focus of collection and study in the United States. Although he also noted that folklorists should continue to collect and study "Relics of Old English Folk-Lore (ballads, tales, superstitions, dialect, etc.)," he did not identify in specific terms the population among whom this work would be carried out.

9. A number of scholars have offered theoretical models for apprehending the nature of African American textual production based on vernacular concepts and terms. In literature, the best-known works are Houston A. Baker Jr.'s *Blues, Ideology, and Afro-American Literature* and Henry Louis Gates Jr.'s *The Signifying Monkey: A Theory of African-American Literary Criticism.*

10. The process that I am describing here is one that appears to be fairly general in the study of artists who make representing the vernacular in culture a major focus of their work. Two prominent examples in the American tradition would be Mark Twain and Zora Neale Hurston. In both cases, these artists have been transformed through a biographical emphasis into the aesthetic embodiment of the vernacular traditions that they sought to represent in their works.

11. S. Wilson, Lewis, Bearden and Henderson, and others have identified one or all of these as basic elements of Pippin's style and suggest that these are characteristics of vernacular art.

12. Clifford Geertz uses the term "thick description" to describes an ethnographic process in which the ethnographer observes and records the layers of events and other meaningful signs and symbols in order to be able to interpret cultural behavior and forms.

WORKS CITED

Abrahams, Roger D. "Phantoms of Romantic Nationalism in Folkloristics." *Journal of American Folklore* 106 (1993): 3–37.

Baker, Houston A., Jr. *Blues, Ideology, and Afro-American Literature: A Vernacular Theory.* Chicago: University of Chicago Press, 1984.

Bearden, Romare, and Harry Henderson. *A History of African American Artists.* New York: Pantheon Books, 1993.

Bell, Michael J. "William Wells Newell and the Foundation of American Folklore Scholarship." *Journal of the Folklore Institute* 10 (1966): 7–22.

Clifford, James. *The Predicament of Culture: Twentieth-Century Ethnography, Literature, and Art.* Cambridge: Harvard University Press, 1988.

Davis, Gerald. "Elijah Pierce, Woodcarver: Doves and Pain in Life Fulfilled." In *The Artist Outsider: Creativity and the Boundaries of Culture,* ed. Michael D. Hall and Eugene W. Metcalf Jr. Washington, D.C.: Smithsonian Institution Press, 1994. 290–311.

Driskell, David C. "Introduction." In *I Tell My Heart: The Art of Horace Pippin.* Exhibition catalog edited by Judith E. Stein. Philadelphia: Pennsylvania Academy of Fine Arts, 1993. xii–xiii.

Dundes, Alan. *The Study of Folklore.* Englewood Cliffs, N.J.: Prentice Hall, 1965.

Ellison, Ralph. *Going to the Territory.* New York: Random House, 1986.

Fabian, Johannes. *Time and the Other: How Anthropology Makes Its Object.* New York: Columbia University Press, 1983.

———. "Keep Listening: Ethnography of Reading." In *The Ethnography of Reading,* ed. Jonathan Bayarin. Berkeley: University of California Press, 1992. 80–97.

Gates, Henry Louis, Jr. *The Signifying Monkey: A Theory of African-American Literary Criticism.* New York: Oxford University Press. 1988.

Geertz, Clifford. *Interpretation of Cultures.* New York: Basic Books, 1973.

Hall, Michael D., and Eugene W. Metcalf Jr., eds. *The Artist Outsider: Creativity and the Boundaries of Culture.* Washington, D.C.: Smithsonian Institution Press, 1994.

Lewis, Samella. *Art: African American.* Los Angeles: Hancraft Studios, 1990.

Lippard, Lucy R. "Crossing into Uncommon Grounds." In *The Artist Outsider: Creativity and the Boundaries of Culture,* ed. Michael D. Hall and Eugene W. Metcalf Jr. Washington, D.C.: Smithsonian Institution Press, 1994. 2–18.

Locke, Alain. "Horace Pippin, 1888–1946." *Horace Pippin Memorial Exhibition.* Philadelphia: The Art Alliance, 1947.

McWillie, Judith. "Introduction." *Another Face of the Diamond: Pathways through the Black Atlantic South.* New York: INTAR Latin American Gallery, 1988.

Newell, William Wells. "On the Field and Work of a Journal of American Folklore." *Journal of American Folklore* 1 (1888): 1–4.

Nonas, Richard. "The Snake in the Garden." In *The Artist Outsider: Creativity and the Boundaries of Culture,* ed. by Michael D. Hall and Eugene W. Metcalf Jr. Washington, D.C.: Smithsonian Institution Press, 1994. 162–70.

Powell, Richard. *Homecoming: The Art and Life of William H. Johnson.* Exhibition catalog. Washington, D.C.: Smithsonian Institution, 1991.

Roberts, John W. *From Trickster to Badman: The Black Folk Hero in Slavery and Freedom.* Philadelphia: University of Pennsylvania Press, 1989.

———. "African American Diversity and the Study of Folklore." *Western Folklore* 52 (1993): 157–72.

Rodman, Selden. *Horace Pippin: A Negro Painter in America.* New York: Quadrangle Press, 1947.

Stanford, Theodore. "Call Pippin Greater Than Tanner." *Baltimore Afro-American,* May 13, 1994.

Stein, Judith. "Brushing with Greatness: The Search for Horace Pippin's Paintings." *Philadelphia Inquirer Magazine,* January 16, 1994.

———, ed. *I Tell My Heart: The Art of Horace Pippin.* Exhibition catalog. Philadelphia: Pennsylvania Academy of Fine Arts, 1993.

Torgovnick, Marianna. *Gone Primitive: Savage Intellects, Modern Lives.* Chicago: University of Chicago Press, 1990.

West, Cornel. "Horace Pippin's Challenge to Art Criticism." In *I Tell My Heart: The Art of Horace Pippin.* Exhibition catalog edited by Judith Stein.

Philadelphia: Pennsylvania Academy of Fine Arts, 1993. 44–52.

Wilson, Judith. "Scenes of War." In *I Tell My Heart: The Art of Horace Pippin.* Exhibition catalog edited by Judith Stein. Philadelphia: Pennsylvania Academy of Fine Arts, 1993. 56–69.

Wilson, Sarah J. "Horace Pippin: A Chester County Artist." West Chester, Pa.: Chester County Historical Society, 1988.

Zumwalt, Rosemary L. *American Folklore Scholarship: A Dialogue of Dissent.* Bloomington: Indiana University Press, 1988.

The Gendered Subject of Human Rights: Asian American Literature as Postcolonial Intervention

Leslie Bow

> Sister Katherine said that just because something was imaginary did not mean
> it could not have consequences in the real. She told us to write that down,
> and that when we were older we would understand.
>
> —FIONA CHEONG, *The Scent of the Gods*

In 1995, the *New York Times* pronounced the emergence of a new South Africa, this time, in Asia.[1] Burma, now known as Myanmar, was reported to be the target of an international divestment campaign on the basis of its human rights and environmental abuses.[2] This shift from South Africa to Burma as recipient of the dubious honor of greatest human rights abuser arose from the events of 1988, in which the military fired on a crowd of prodemocracy demonstrators culminating in the detention of an estimated three thousand political prisoners, including the house arrest of the National League for Democracy (NLD) leader, Aung San Suu Kyi in 1989.[3]

Although the events of the 8/8/88 democracy movement in Yangon (Rangoon) were displaced in the American media by reports of the massacre in Tiananmen Square the following year, the Burmese democracy movement gave the media one thing that the Chinese movement did not: a living and breathing goddess of democracy in the form of Aung San Suu Kyi, the Western-educated daughter of assassinated national independence leader Aung San. Like the papier-mâché goddess erected in Tiananmen Square, Aung San Suu Kyi quickly became the emblem of what Burma lacked, and a potent symbol of the collective desire of a people. After casting about for an appropriate analogy for Aung San Suu Kyi (Bhutto? Aquino?), the British press hit upon "Burma's Gandhi" in an attempt to describe a platform familiar to the West: nonviolent protest, democracy, human rights (Kreager 321).

These representations of Burma in the 1990s reinforce what has consistently been taken as Asia's difference from the West. As Rey Chow has suggested in regard to Tiananmen Square, coverage of the Burmese democracy movement was likewise a spectacle of Asian lack—of democracy, freedom of expression, the right of assembly—and an occasion in which Americans could indulge in reports of their national symbols reproduced for global consumption, whether of hastily constructed models of the Statue of Liberty on the streets of Beijing or of the Gettysburg Address recited word for word in English outside the American embassy in Yangon.[4] The construction of such differences, as Lisa Lowe has noted, serve specific American interests, not only justifying U.S. imperialism but producing the very idea of American national self-conception.[5] Most recently, reports of Asian lack of basic freedoms and civil liberties serve as a reminder of what the United States is proud to export along with its now triumphantly touted brand of capitalism. For example, a democracy such as Singapore, once lauded as a model of postcolonial modernization and now enjoying Asia's highest standard of living after Japan, has gained media attention in the United States for abrogating social freedoms. Although Michael Fay's caning in Singapore in 1994 was not an event comparable in magnitude to the events in Burma, it was nonetheless heavily covered in the U.S. media; his punishment was the occasion for comparison to Asian philosophy and governance, in this case, as a means of evaluating the American domestic "crisis" over juvenile crime.[6] The American public was both entertained and shocked to hear about Singapore's "draconian justice" in which graphic descriptions of flogging supplemented reports of bans on chewing gum or smoking in public, and of fines for such offenses as littering (U.S. $625), failing to flush a public toilet (U.S. $94), and eating on the subway (U.S. $312) (Branegan 36).[7] The caning incident both assured Americans that they have what Asia wants—individual freedom—and reminded them of what they once had and lost: discipline.

In spite of the seeming contrast between such representations of Asia invoked by Aung San Suu Kyi's quiet courage while under house arrest, Harry Wu's cribbing notes in the margins of a dictionary in a Chinese prison, or an American bad boy unduly punished, an underlying similarity emerges: all three representations depend on the figure of an individual who suffers the abuses of a regime in the name of abstract rights. Such images portray not just the violation of democratic rights, but the violation of democratic rights as *human* rights.

With the Cold War dead, the war on drugs taking an uncomfortably domestic focus, and fears of Asian economic competition complicated by reports of Toyotas being manufactured in Kentucky (and now diminished by the Asian economic crisis), human rights has emerged as a dominant framework in which the United States places Asia. A testament to the strength of such a narrative, the emphasis on human rights succeeds in reconciling for an American public the economic and political situations of countries as various as Burma, Singapore, China, and Vietnam. For example, in spite of their shared history as former British colonies, Burma and Singapore have taken opposite courses. Under the leadership of a military junta since 1962, Burma was named a "least-developed country" by 1987. In contrast, held up as an economic success, Singapore is known as one of Asia's four "dragons" along with South Korea, Hong Kong, and Taiwan. Governed by single parties whose tenure has lasted more than three decades, both Burma and Singapore have been called to account for alleged violations, though obviously to different degrees. At best, this concern over human rights abuses in Asia represents an increased awareness of the repressive methods of state control, a vigilance acknowledged to be the shared responsibility of global powers. At worst, it is merely a form of spectacle suitable for entertainment—one season's *The Year of Living Dangerously* starring Sigourney Weaver becomes next season's *Beyond Rangoon* starring Patricia Arquette. But as labor standards and political freedoms are increasingly linked to trade and international diplomacy, human rights issues become levied as strategic bargaining chips, as not-so-subtle forms of punishment and reward.[8] The selective sanctioning of nations on the grounds of human rights violations has been criticized as a form of Western hegemony as much as it has been hailed as an effective means of policing repressive regimes. "The Western community of nations presided over by the United States," Edward Said writes, "has given itself an internationalized and normative identity with authority and hegemony to adjudicate the relative value of human rights" (1993, 197). Human rights is not merely a theory of universal citizenship based on equality, but, as critics of the Helms-Burton law have charged, a means through which the United States furthers its own interest.

Underlying the critique of human rights as a mask of cultural imperialism is a postmodern suspicion of universalist doctrine. Such cautions become especially urgent as the movement toward economic globalization provokes warnings about the erosion of state influence.[9] As Judith Butler has noted in regard to normative political philosophy, any position that "seeks to establish the metapolitical basis of a negotiation of power relations . . . is perhaps the most insidious ruse of power" (6). Such a recognition does not preclude the fact that metapolitical philosophy itself may be called upon to interrogate insidious ruses of power. In asking its participants to speak on human rights, the Committee of the 1992 Oxford Amnesty Lectures noted the apparent contradiction between political commitment and postmodern philosophy. Its invitation to prospective lecturers posed the question, "Does the self as construed by the liberal tradition still exist? If not, whose human rights are we defending?" (Johnson 2). But philosophical suspicion of human rights' dependence on humanist ideals does not obviate the need for vigilance of violations such as state-sponsored torture, a violation that is, as Amnesty International notes, a "calculated assault on human dignity and for that reason alone is to be condemned absolutely" (1984, 7). To paraphrase from Fiona Cheong's novel *The Scent of the Gods*, just because the liberal subject is imaginary does not mean that it cannot have consequences in the real.

In affirming the universal rights of the individual, human rights discourse offers a specific ideologically invested rhetorical frame that can be deployed as a form of political persuasion "in the real." This is particularly evident in Asian American literature, which, like the media, is a site where representations of Asia are reproduced for American consumption. Thus, one could question literature's investment in this recent narrative on Asia particularly in regard to countries that, like Burma and Singapore, have been in the public eye for human rights violations; do such representations merely serve to reproduce, as Chow suggests, Asia's difference from the West? Just as figures such as Aung San Suu Kyi become a means of accessing Asia in American culture, Asian American literature could be said to create analogous figures of political advocacy, but for potentially alternative purposes. Both Wendy Law-Yone's *Irrawaddy Tango* (1993) and Fiona Cheong's *The Scent of the Gods* (1991) deploy the rhetoric of human rights in order to critique methods of governmental repression justified by the construction of national crisis. In representing violations such as torture and detention without trial, the authors expose methods of state control as a means of commenting on the contemporary national politics

THE GENDERED SUBJECT OF HUMAN RIGHTS   41

of their "home" countries. *Irrawaddy Tango* suggests a fictive solution to an ongoing historical conflict in Burma by appealing to the individual's sovereignty as protected by the discourse of human rights. *The Scent of the Gods* draws an allegorical parallel between home and state in order to reveal how the mandate to modernize was positioned as antithetical to individual rights; the novel shows the loss of civil liberties to be foundational to the "fledgling nation." The emphasis is not so much, following Lowe's premise, that these fictional representations are constitutive of an Orientalized Asia that in turn create, sustain, or resist certain conceptions of Asian Americans. Rather, Asian American writers' placement in the United States enables them to produce critiques of postcolonial state politics that employ First World conceptions of individual rights. Moreover, as if in comparison to American strategies of ethnic homogenization, both novels connect postindependence promotion of internal ethnic disunity to securing the hegemony of single-party rule.

The overseas focus of both American novels appears to testify to both the "postnational" trend in American studies and what Sau-ling Wong has called the denationalizing direction of Asian American studies as it has shifted from domestic, immigrant models of minority group interaction with the dominant culture to emphasize global migrations and postcoloniality. Marking a distinction between American minority and transnational modes of inquiry produces the perception of a paradigm shift in Asian American studies. For example, although Susan Koshy acknowledges that "*trans*national is not antithetical to the national" in her critique of Wong's terminology, she nonetheless enforces such a distinction in a temporal argument that situates "old" sociological paradigms associated with early Asian immigration and dependent on linear models of acculturation against what she sees as the complex, nonstatic Asian migrations taking place in the era of transnational capital (340). In suggesting that the discipline has failed to produce theories of literary canonicity that exceed an originary appeal to pluralist inclusion and panethnic commonality, she argues that scholarship has failed to account for "the effects of transnational forces on Asian American ethnicity" as they appear in "newer" literary productions (331). My goal here is not to reproduce the distinction between immigrant and diasporic, "new" and "old" paradigms, but to suggest one avenue through which literature reveals a mutual investment between American national and Asian postcolonial concerns; in this case, the works do not necessarily produce an account of Asian American ethnicity alternative to that located in the inaugural moment of the discipline, although they might well imply this. Rather, they suggest that what travels transnationally is not labor or capital but rhetoric. What one witnesses in Law-Yone's and Cheong's depictions of Asia is the deployment of "universal" notions of individual rights in service of commentaries on current Asian national leadership. Significantly, such narratival configurations are not only nationally inscribed but gendered according to First World precepts about injury, women's rights, and individual redress. The force of both writers' commentaries depends on constructing a female subject of state reprisal—the repression of political dissent is depicted as the regulation of female sexuality. In keeping with the work of international feminist scholars who explore the role of gender representation in reproducing and securing nationalist imaginaries, Asian American women's literature reveals that gender difference is a means of signaling mechanisms by which affiliations are formed and consolidated, often against territorial, ethnic, or national allegiances. Interrogating the conflict between ethnic group interests and national unity via a gendered appeal, both works raise pressing questions about human rights' necessary subject.

> Officials tortured an ally of Aung San Suu Kyi to death as part of a campaign of arrests, torture and intimidation targeting opposition leaders, a dissidents' group said Tuesday. Hla Than, 52, died at a hospital Aug. 2 from internal injuries he suffered during torture in prison, where he has spent the past six years, the Washington-based National Coalition Government of the Union of Burma said, citing unidentified sources in Burma.[10]

> "[W]e don't like hurting other people. We refrain from killing. We refrain from doing what you might call unpleasant things." (Colonel Ye Htut, State Law and Order Restoration Council, Myanmar)[11]

Under house arrest for a period of six years until July 1995, Aung San Suu Kyi became a mobilizing force for a people living under military-controlled dictatorship since 1962 when General Ne Win came to power in a coup d'état against the civilian government of Prime Minister U Nu. The catalyst for international attention for her party, the National League for Democracy (NLD), Aung San Suu Kyi is the embodiment of Burma's prodemocracy platform, a single subject who voices collective desires, suffers the abuses of the regime, and receives the accolades of activism as well. Awarded the Nobel Peace Prize in 1991 while still incarcerated, she

continues to speak on behalf of the NLD platform, which advocates freedom of assembly and speech, and condemns the junta's continuing measures against democracy supporters. In *Irrawaddy Tango,* Burmese
American Wendy Law-Yone portrays a more ambiguous national heroine
than Aung San Suu Kyi, one who solves the political ills of her country in
a way that her real-life counterpart cannot—she assassinates the military
dictator, who is also her husband. As the embodiment of the abstract subject of political torture, Tango bears a specifically gendered relationship
to the state; the novel's critique rests on configuring state power not as
the failure of benevolent paternalism but as conjugal abuse.

In the course of creating "Daya" as a counterpart to Burma, Law-
Yone provides a utopian solution to what was in 1993 and continues to be
a political impasse: the National League for Democracy won the 1990
election but the military junta known as the State Law and Order
Restoration Council (SLORC) refuses to relinquish the reins of power. As
the daughter of the late Edward Law-Yone, a leading journalist impris-
oned after General Ne Win's coup, Law-Yone has firsthand knowledge of
methods of Burma's domestic repression. In representing the rise of a
despotic and eccentric general whose xenophobia and strong-arm tactics
give rise to increasing dissent near the end of his rule, her novel references specific elements of Burma's postcolonial history to suggest one
avenue of political change. Rather than providing a forum for the stu-
dent-led democracy movement, the novel addresses another form of organized dissent in its portrayal of ethnic insurgent armies along Burma's
borders, the hill tribes who have sought autonomy in one form or another since Burmese independence in 1948. Yet, one aspect of the novel's
representation of dissent in Daya and Western media attention to Burma
remains constant; both center on the figure of a woman who becomes the
singular subject of state reprisal, a body whose actions must be forcibly
controlled for the continuance of the national status quo.

In the case of U.S. media representations of Aung San Suu Kyi, one
could ask, what does it mean that a single subject comes to both incorporate and displace the more graphic image of the fired-upon masses? It is
the same question one could pose about the image of the lone Chinese
man standing down a row of tanks during Tiananmen Square, an image
that has become iconographic. It is clear that the most generally accepted
concept of human rights requires an individual for whom attention, concern, and then outrage can be channeled into activism. As the central figure for the NLD, Aung San Suu Kyi is the body through which political

protest is made intelligible. Literary representation deploys similar strate-gies as a mode of rhetorical persuasion—the center of *Irrawaddy Tango*'s not-so-thinly veiled critique of Burmese politics is its portrayal of the state-sponsored torture of its female protagonist, Tango. As in the media's emphasis on Aung San Suu Kyi, the novel's commentary is produced not through a direct appeal to a collective movement, whether prodemocracy or ethnic insurgency, but through an appeal to the figure of a woman. Although Aung San Suu Kyi's political legitimacy was first derived from her position as the daughter of Aung San, assassinated leader of the anti-imperialist coalition, the Anti-Fascist People's Freedom League, and her activism might be marked as a form of filial inheritance, Burmese state politics have not particularly relied on gendered images to secure the country's national self-image. As a case in point, Burmese officials would no doubt fail to see the irony in the fact that their delegate to the 1995 Fourth World Conference on Women in Beijing was a male army general. The gendered convergence in American media and literary representa-tions of Burma thus speaks to the power of the women-as-nation allegory so often invoked in the service of postcolonial nationalism.

In its strategic use of gender, *Irrawaddy Tango* dialogues with other Asian American women's writing in figuring women's political alliance as a matter of sexual betrayal. Despite one reviewer's characterization of the novel as an account of a woman's "sexual adventures," it is not merely a form of female picaresque but deploys sexuality to signal shifting collec-tive allegiances (Trescott C1). As critic C. Lok Chua notes, Tango is a cross between Eva Peron, Patty Hearst, and a black widow; her marriage to the dictator is clearly the Faustian bargain of an ambitious small-town girl with "potential," and her subsequent counterinsurgency only seems to come about via another sexual alliance as mistress of the leader of an oppressed hill tribe. But, as important, the novel's emphasis on the single, tortured female body reveals the gendered structure of the novel's politi-cal appeal as it resonates with contemporary discourse on human rights—it exposes the dictator's irrational despotism as it is waged not against a national body or ethnic group but against his wife. In the novel, the mili-tary's unfitness to rule appears as abusive dominance in the home, hence as a violation of women's rights.

This domestic-as-national parallel seems to rely on the discourse on domestic abuse popularized after the women's movement in the United States, linking the novel's First World placement to its international advo-cacy. For example, as if to suggest "battered woman's syndrome" as a form of popular psychology, the novel portrays the dictator's crisis of mastery as a series of possessive behaviors and physically enforced demands for obedience followed by extravagant promises of contrition and future reform.[12] The fictional general's beatings of his wife initiated by charges of infidelity are significantly couched in terms of national representation as Tango's desirability comes to represent a form of international recognition:

> "I saw the way that American son of a bitch had his big hand on your flesh, there where the back of your waist was bare. Did it feel good? Tell me how it felt and don't lie. Did it make you itch? Did you feel that nerve running down the center of your crotch swelling and twitching? Were you thinking what it would be like to have a huge American prick up you for a change?" . . . I'd give him the lowdown he wanted. I'd describe step by step, from foreplay to climax, the imagined infidelity. (104–5)

The accusation of infidelity initiates a false confession of betrayal, the purpose of which is not to provide information but to provoke his desire through the process of narration, a function only fulfilled as long as the narrative remains avowedly fictive. As an act, Tango's confession is without content—like rape, it has to do not with substance but with transmission: rape, we are told, is not about sex, but about (his) power. The "confessions" prefigure the scenes of political torture by unmasking the idea that the need for information during interrogation is the motive for cruelty; as Elaine Scarry writes about the structure of torture, the content of the prisoner's answer may be inconsequential, but "the fact of his answering is always crucial."[13] The episodes end in a reminder that power is ultimately the ability to control meaning: he jerks her head back by the hair to pose the question, "Love me?"—an inquiry that, given its context, has but a single answer.

The use of this discourse on wife battery as gendered political appeal allows Law-Yone to reflect on complex notions of victimization and resistance, shifting from the battered woman as a single agent to a national or ethnic minority population undergoing despotic and irrational mistreatment. The novel depicts domestic violence throughout the trajectory of Supremo's violent rise to power as it is linked to suppressing ethnic insurgency; Tango's belated recognition, "My God, I'd married a maniac," might also be the national sentiment.[14] The dual meanings of the word *domestic* conjoin: just as the police are often reluctant to interfere in domestic disputes, roughing up groups within one's national borders is not a global, but an internal, affair. Just as Burma's policy of isolationism places its treatment of ethnic insurgency beyond the realm of international intervention, the parallel suggests, batterers' enforcement of social isolation secures their partners' dependency and prevents interference in the relationship. Tango's mixture of quiescence, calculation, disgust, and accommodation provides a partial answer to why there seems to be no more than token resistance to political despotism: one can only hope that certain accommodations will prevent the escalation of mistreatment. It is thus that the novel sets up a suggestive link between what in the discourse of battery has been called the "learned helplessness" of women's social conditioning and the inability to resist despotism. Law-Yone's conjugal-national parallel resonates through explanations of why battered women do not leave based on a conditioned acceptance of naturalized masculine authority; the power of the despot is likewise always already legitimated by the fact that he occupies the position of authority.[15] Of course, to ascribe lack of resistance to the pathology of a people, as the narrator does, is akin to blaming the victim for her own abuse. Political rule, after all, is a condition of military backing, not merely a failure to act decisively, or the "learned helplessness" of a diverse people. The analogy ends as the answer to why there has been almost a half century of authoritarian rule in Burma can be conveyed through a simple explanation about the use of force. The novel makes these tactics of power clear in reporting the apparent lack of resistance to Supremo's rise to power in a "quiet" coup—Tango's assessment that "nobody resisted" is ironized by her subsequent acknowledgment that all members of the cultural elite had been "detained." Law-Yone's fictional representation of the coup resonates with General Ne Win's takeover in 1962, an event reported by her father, Edward Law-Yone, editor and founder of the *Nation* prior to his own five-year "detention" as a political prisoner.

It is perhaps not such a great leap to suggest that the methods of submission employed by the state easily mesh with forms of conjugal violence: feminist work on domestic abuse in the late 1980s in fact engaged studies of state-sponsored torture to describe the psychological and physical tactics used by domestic batterers.[16] Both discourses rely on sedimented First World conceptions of individual sovereignty, injury, and pop psychology; Law-Yone's novel plays on these conceptions in its graphic representation of sexualized state violence. In employing such a discourse, the novel potentially reinforces both humanist constructions of self and traditional parallels between women and nation even as it engages a gendered form of advocacy. The accusation of treason after Tango's capture as "rebel queen" marks her political betrayal as indistinguishable from adultery; her torture comes at the hands of agents of a husband whose authority is that of the state. What is treason, the novel seems to imply, but infidelity on a larger scale? If, as Deniz Kandyoti suggests, women are controlled "in the interests of demarcating and preserving the identities of national/ethnic collectives," the female body is the site of policing transgressions of affiliation and loyalty (382).[17] Thus, the instrument of Tango's political punishment is fittingly represented as a reflection of her "crime" of infidelity: she is raped with the barrel of a gun in a version of Russian roulette. Reflecting the Maoist axiom that political power grows out of the barrel of a gun, the novel's use of a substitute penis to represent the instrument of state power associates masculinity with a naturalized but arbitrary hierarchy of rule. In this case, Tango's sexual violation with a weapon carries further national resonance: if the word for Daya also signifies "wound," an injury in which the skin or other external surface is pierced or broken, her penetration evokes the nature of the crime, the penetration of the national body by ethnic insurgents along its border. The punishment for abetting the violation of national sovereignty is thus the violation of the boundaries of the individual subject, but with specifically gendered resonance. Amnesty International defines torture as an act intended to destroy one's humanity; the intention behind torture is the dissolution of the subject through the infliction of pain (1973, 30). A means of embodying the authority of the state, rape is a specific form of torture that reduces the female subject to her defining bodily orifice, confirming the subject position that woman inhabits as the negation of man. In substituting the phallus with a symbol of state power, rape as torture confirms Scarry's point that "Pain is a pure physical experience of negation" (52).

Scarry begins with the premise that physical pain not only transcends signification through its incapability of being shared, but actively destroys it, "bringing about an immediate reversion to a state anterior to language, to the sounds and cries a human being makes before language is learned" (4). This deconstructive process represents "the loss of the world" as pain obliterates meaning. The novel's depiction of Tango's torture reveals that political power is the ability to control meaning, not just in the sense that official propaganda can be exposed as a form of doublespeak, but that absolute power is the power to subvert meanings assigned to signifiers. "We're shaving you so you won't worry about getting hurt,"

Tango is told in prison. "We don't hurt nuns; good Buddhists never hurt nuns, see?" (173). Such an assurance is rendered meaningless as, prior to her rape, she is told both "Didn't we tell you we don't fuck nuns?" and "Especially we don't fuck whores!" (177). The distinction between nun and whore, purity and defilement no longer matters; the torturer's power is not just the ability to reassign meanings within systems of classification, but to render such classification superfluous. Similarly, when common household objects are used as weapons, as instruments of pain, they become divorced from their referents, demonstrating the ease with which the mundane can be rendered diabolical. When Tango becomes the assassin and makes use of such innocent items as duct tape and an electric fan to kill, the token of her power is not only the violence of her act but the fact that, like the torturer, she transforms the banal into an agent of pain. The novel configures narration as a form of political power, revealing that torture indicates not merely the state's power to induce pain, but, as Scarry notes, to unmake the world. While incarcerated, part of her punishment is to anticipate varieties of torture from a fellow prisoner apparently driven mad by torture, a narratival form of punishment meant to induce extreme dread. The woman's story of involuntary orgasm during genital torture with electric shock implies that the torturer has the power to undo meaning, to transform pain into pleasure, erasing agency: "you can't avoid what happens, Little Sister. You have—how to say it? A climax. A low moment for a woman. But what can a woman do? Nothing" (177).[18]

The novel's portrayal of torture elicits horror and sympathy for the abused female body, thereby appealing to human dignity as a fundamental right. Significantly, it reflects the translation of global human rights violations into terms familiar to an American audience. If the effectiveness of agencies such as Amnesty International depends, as Scarry notes, on their "ability to communicate the reality of physical pain to those who are not themselves in pain,"[19] this familiarity in part explains how the discourse of wife battering can work to expose foreign political repression. Simply, the appeal is effective if offenses against female political prisoners are defined as somehow *more* heinous than those against men. Given that women are perceived to be more embodied, they may be more easily imagined as threatened *in* their bodies by playing on traditional conceptions of sentimentality and women's vulnerability. Moreover, women's association with the domestic, "nonpolitical" realm signals the state's violation more acutely. But there are more complex resonances: the novel's collapsing of distinctions between treason and adultery, political torture and domestic abuse allows Law-Yone to engage the concept of individual and collective rights simultaneously. The belief that "women and children have an absolute right to live free from bodily harm" (Jones 5), for example, is one way the concept of *group* rights has entered an American lexicon. *Irrawaddy Tango* appeals not just to the abstract human subject of human rights, but to an individual who is also part of a collective group— a woman.

Tango is apparently tortured for advocating the sovereignty rights of an ethnic minority. In making her a spokesperson on behalf of "the Jesu," Law-Yone has chosen to model her fictional hill tribe on the Karen, a Christian ethnic group on Burma's eastern border with Thailand who have been involved in a secessionist war with the central government since 1948. Although the Shan have also been involved in an armed struggle for sovereignty, like the Kachin, their human rights cause in the West may be compromised by their alleged involvement in drug trafficking.[20] By modeling the Jesu on the Karen, Law-Yone focuses on an ethnic group whose secessionist claim can be represented most forcefully as the right to religious freedom. This choice of ethnic group among the many represented in the hill regions thus does not muddle the question of who should have "rights"—the Karen can be represented as freedom fighters rather than drug smugglers. The emergence of human rights as a concern in Southeast Asia might have given the long-standing armed insurrection new urgency had it not been supplanted by mass demonstrations for democratic reform, an event the novel vaguely refers to as a "spectacle of protest and massacre" (247). The Karen's armed struggle against the central government has garnered little attention in the West aside from some media coverage of the threat of their forced repatriation from refugee camps in Thailand. Ironically, one way the Karen came into Western perception was through their conscription of children into the army, a circumstance implicitly portrayed as a violation of human rights— a form of child abuse.[21] Such a portrayal only highlights the ease with which appeals to moral universals can be deployed in support or criticism of specific political causes. My point is not to draw one-to-one correspondences between historical events and literary depictions, but to highlight the similarity between fictional and media representations of, in Scarry's terms, the lives of those "whose name[s] can barely be pronounced" (9) as a means of accessing an Asian "over there" in terms that are very much "over here."

By invoking the body in pain to highlight both the ethnic right to self-rule and the more general stance against despotism, the novel affirms the individual necessary to the concept of human rights as it is currently understood and that each human subject has intrinsic worth because of his or her uniqueness. The idea of sovereignty and self-rule as human rights cannot be reconciled to liberal ideals, a point debated by delegates to the United Nations charged with ratifying a Universal Declaration of Human Rights in 1948.[22] That the novel ultimately makes its appeal to the Karen-as-Jesu sovereignty movement through Tango may suggest that gender is a form of group identity perhaps more easily reconcilable to the concept of individuality than racial or ethnic group affiliation. This reconciliation is echoed in Hillary Rodham Clinton's anxiously anticipated comment at the 1995 Fourth World Conference on Women in Beijing: "If there is one message that echoes forth from this conference, let it be that human rights are women's rights and women's rights are human rights, once and for all."[23] Virginia Woolf's famous dictum on women's ambivalent allegiance to patriarchal nationalism—"[A]s a woman, I have no country. As a woman I want no country. As a woman my country is the whole world" (197)—signals a similar belief in woman as global citizen whose naturalized humanitarian concerns transcend borders. Intended as a statement against the recent record of human rights abuses of the conference's Chinese hosts, the first lady's direct condemnation was internationally applauded, indicating that issues referenced in the speech such as bride burning, the rape of POWs, female infanticide, domestic violence, genital mutilation, and coerced abortion or sterilization somehow obviated previously contentious debates on cultural practices versus the rights of women-as-individuals transcendent of context. That such issues maintain the appearance of universals suggests that liberalism can encompass women's rights as a form of group rights more easily than ethnic or racial rights, except perhaps in cases of genocide. "Woman" can appear as a collective entity unvexed by issues of territorialization, allowing for a subject who is not wholly individualized.[24]

Yet, the novel's portrayal of human rights as a method of soliciting international attention is both self-conscious and cynical, a cynicism that extends to the efficacy of coalitional identity politics in the United States. What brings Dayans, "that most minor of minority groups," into the American spotlight is not the spectacle of protest but "another disaster, far more newsworthy than anything the internal affairs of our country could have generated: the disappearance of an American rock star in the wilderness of our northern jungles" (247). Law-Yone comments on the fact that political concern is based partly on self-interest, and that recognition of the collective must be concretized through individuation—or better, celebrity. In this ironic aside on the hapless rock star—not the massacre—as the reason for Daya's return to international visibility, one cannot help but think of media focus on Aung San Suu Kyi, indicating perhaps that the politics of caring keeps a cause in public memory better than disembodied issues. But this is, in effect, a strategy the novel deploys as well; the sovereignty issues of the Jesu—"self-rule, religious freedom, human rights" (128)—are conveyed to the reader and the fictional world through a single female spokesperson. Tango resists this role as collective representative in a direct repudiation of the very appeal in which the novel engages:

> I didn't want to be an activist or a born-again crusader for human rights and other civil liberties or to go on the torture circuit. . . . Even for a good cause, I wanted no part of it. Even if the point was to educate the humanitarian American public on inhuman practices in other parts of the world. Even if the public could then get involved by writing to their congressman or calling an 800 number to pledge support. (248)

While this resistance to public confession might be read as an individual's logical response to trauma, it is more significantly a rejection of democratic politics as it appears to be practiced in the United States as a form of identity politics—a rejection of, as Lauren Berlant has noted, the moment in which "private life" becomes indistinguishable from notions of citizenship and civic responsibility. In repudiating the salutary and politicizing effects ascribed to consciousness raising through public confession, Tango refuses, as Wendy Brown puts it, "the steady slide of political into therapeutic discourse" (75). In her resistance to using experience to mobilize for change, the novel foregrounds the ineffectiveness of coalitional democratic representation for influencing diplomatic policies in the "Turd World." The novel portrays coalitional politics as mindless caterwauling: from within the United States, Dayan exiles are "neutralized" as one of many special interest groups naively lobbying Washington for attention and aid in the manner of Berlant's infantile citizen who optimistically believes in the utopian promises of the system. Although Tango's outsidedness upon immigration to the United States echoes Asian American portrayals of expatriate alienation, it is also part of the novel's refusal to locate the United States as a model political system and an expression of impatience with its perhaps undeserved reputation as global interventionist.[25] In spite of—or perhaps because of—the National League for Democracy's support within and outside of Burma, the novel refuses to portray the democracy movement as an effective form of resisting a military regime. References to such a movement are noticeably absent, aside from Tango's belittling comments to the effect that "nonviolent protest" is deemed an "idiot phrase," and the cry "What do we want? Democracy! When do we want it? Now!" a "mindless chant." Moreover, the acronym for the novel's "Foundation for Asian Democracies" is "FAD." In keeping with Lowe's situating Asian American literature as a site where the contradictions of American national promise are uncovered, the novel exposes the contradiction between American democratic rights as the fantasy of each citizen's equal influence on state policy and the United States as arbiter of human rights in the international realm.

Given that *Irrawaddy Tango*'s critique of the military junta is not identical to an appeal to general democratic rights, does the novel's solution, as Barbara Harlow would claim for resistance literature, "insist on the collective historical consequences of individual experience" (119)? The novel raises the question of whether Tango's act of violence represents a collective, political action or is simply an act of revenge. At one level, the novel seems to ask the reader to understand Tango's behavior as a psychological response to trauma; she murders not as a show of solidarity with the Jesu rebels or the Dayan people; rather, either her return to the site of trauma is a step in healing—a point she consciously rejects—or the assassination is a form of payback. One might easily inscribe Tango's actions in the familiar terms of the talk-show confessional she abhors—"Women who kill: victims who turn the tables on their abusers." Her question as she awaits the judgment of the rioting masses outside, "But I'd killed the beast out of revenge—nothing but revenge. Had I really serviced a nation?" (286), references the personal-as-political link invoked by the epigraph, ". . . either I'm nobody, or I'm a nation." Yet, the epigraph asks that the novel be read allegorically, whereas its protagonist resists collective association. Although its emphasis on a lone heroine may be dictated by narrative convention, one consequence is that the novel can individualize tyranny as well.[26] Unlike Jessica Hagedorn's critique of the Marcos regime in *Dogeaters*, which condemns the tripartite collusion between big business, elected officials, and the military in the country's governance, Law-Yone's attention to character may present Daya's problems as too simply located in the actions of a single power-hungry individual, rather than in the systematic intertwining of civil and state methods of control. The open-endedness of the novel rests not on interpreting the collective implications of the individual's act of transgression, but in translating this act in terms of political systems. Ironically, Tango's act of individual aggression inscribes her within an American national ethos and her final thoughts are of Washington, where she has previously marked her alienation from American national symbols. Still, *Irrawaddy Tango* stands out as a model of postcolonial commentary that resists advocating what the Third World is always presumed to lack; interestingly, it questions the current democracy movement precisely at a moment in which "democracy has . . . replaced development as the 'buzz-word' of the 1990's" (Qadir, Clapham, and Gills 415).

Law-Yone's *Irrawaddy Tango* is clearly a commentary on the past despotism of General Ne Win and the ongoing abuses of a military-controlled state. The work might indicate that Law-Yone is no fan of the democracy movement; elsewhere she has suggested that what is lacking in Burma is not active resistance but a common agenda and unity among the many opposition groups—NLD leaders, fugitive students, and ethnic insurgents. As she rightly predicted in 1989, the NLD's call for multiparty elections did not assure a transfer of power (Law-Yone 1989). Rather than invoking the revered figure of Aung San Suu Kyi, known in Burma simply as "The Lady," the novel offers a self-serving heroine who, in knowing both how to fuck and how to kill, is no lady. In the end, it is not so much the nature of the solution envisioned that marks the novel's political commentary. Its message—"assassinate the dictator, free the people"—is not the most original vision of change; dispatching a fictive hit woman to resolve a historical dilemma is not a blueprint for Burma's remaking. In transforming the national body into the body of the oppressed individual, the single body in pain who bears the brunt of state-sanctioned violence, the novel may ironize the work of human rights relief agencies, but ultimately it does not dispute their ability to focus public attention. *Irrawaddy Tango*'s invocation of the discourse on battered women to expose methods of political repression inverts the relationship established by feminist studies, which draw on reports of the treatment of political prisoners as an analogy to domestic abuse. The image that remains from the novel is not the shot-upon crowd, nor, in the end, the embattled ethnic insurgents. Rather, a wife is being beaten.

Such an argument is not meant to deflate the effectiveness of the appeal or to suggest the trivialization of a national call to action; rather, it highlights the ways in which Asian American literary expression utilizes the tactics of postcolonial nationalism linking gender and nation, but to subversive effect. International feminists have suggested some of these tactics in critiquing the ways in which, for example, images of emancipated women are made to signify postindependence modernization (Kandyoti), feminine sexuality is used to promote national industry (Heng), or political parties use women's issues to broaden their appeal (West). In this case, however, what I would foreground is the novel's First World investment, its use of what have become normative values in the United States concerning women's rights in the service of its Asian postcolonial commentary. Law-Yone's work thus exemplifies the gendered politicism of Asian American women's writing as it interrogates the juxtaposition of competing collectivities: women, ethnicity, nation. This interrogation reflects V. Spike Peterson's point that although women have been situated as ancillary to international relations theory through their association with the private sphere, this association places them as primary to the production of group loyalties, affiliations, and identificatory processes central to nationalist projects. Her taxonomy of the relationship between women and nation suggests, following Kandyoti, that women are often invoked to signify other group differences, "to delineate the boundaries of group identity" (132). Such is the relationship explored in Fiona Cheong's *The Scent of the Gods,* which exploits gender's connection to the domestic to reveal the state's intrusion into the private sphere as it legislates new group loyalties upon Singapore's independence. The narrator's innocent rumination on the wooden fence separating "the family's property from the rest of the country" (122), that "a wind was coming soon which was going to blow on the fence just hard enough to topple the fence over" (135), metaphorizes the novel's concern with the erosion of the border between public and private. Just as Homi Bhabha has noted that the "recesses of the domestic space become sites for history's most intricate invasions" (9), the novel exposes the methods by which state-mandated affiliations are created and upheld by drawing allegorical resonance between civic duty and gendered associations with submission and self-preservation.

He who is subjected to a field of visibility, and who knows it, assumes
responsibility for the constraints of power.
—MICHEL FOUCAULT, *Discipline and Punish*

It was May 1969. . . . The government had begun to take care of everything. . . . We had peace now. We had progress. . . . There was to be
no more poverty in Singapore, no more slums.

—FIONA CHEONG, *The Scent of the Gods*

If *The Scent of the Gods* suggests a national allegory in its treatment of
domestic space, it is the continual violation of the realm of the "private"
that provides the force of Cheong's commentary on postindependence
Singapore, violations that signify an encroachment on the freedoms of
the individual. The divisions in Cheong's fictional family mirror the
potentially volatile divisions of the state as ethnic loyalty competes with
national duty at the moment that kinship and family begin to cede their
functions of socialization to the public sphere. Yet, the family is not simply a microcosm of the state, nor is *Scent*'s bildungsroman an allegory of
Singapore's rapid modernization and development. From 1965 to 1990,
Singapore went from being a small island with no natural resources to a
metropolitan city-state with the highest gross national product in Asia
after Japan. Dubbed the "Orient with plumbing," Singapore has been
taken as model society whose rise is largely attributed to the postindependence policies of the ruling People's Action Party (PAP) led by Prime
Minister Lee Kuan Yew from 1959 to 1990. Given its success, Singapore
was held up as a model for economic development not only in the Third
World, but in the West as well. Although the protagonist of Cheong's
novel remarks in hindsight, "In a few years Prime Minister Lee would
prove himself" (107), the work is not a celebration of Lee Kuan Yew's policies, nor is it entirely a condemnation of his three-decade tenure. Rather,
in depicting the year of Singapore's expulsion from the Federation of
Malaysia in 1963, the first anniversary of the republic in 1966, and the subsequent leadership of 1969, the novel reflects a 1990s concern with the
erosion of civil liberties. Like *Irrawaddy Tango, Scent*'s postcolonial commentary depends on a parallel between the repression of individual rights
and the containment of feminine sexuality.

The Scent of the Gods reveals how the longevity of the PAP was secured
both through legislated means of civil control and through the rhetoric
of impending crisis, which secured voluntary compliance with the official
mandates of modernization and "multiracialism" in the years following
Singapore's "forced" independence from Malaysia. Instilling allegiance
through the rhetoric of crisis legitimates authority and consolidates
power, a point the novel mirrors in both the domestic and the national

spheres. From the grandmother's point of view, "divine protection" provided by ancestors in the face of unspecified malevolence justifies traditional ethnically based filiation. Just as grandma portrays the family as besieged by willful gods whose intentions remain cryptic, Singapore cultivated the image of a besieged Chinese isle within a hostile Malay region and of a democratic isle threatened by communist expansion. The novel reflects the PAP's potentially contradictory task in 1965: to invoke fear of the *overseas* Chinese influence among Singaporeans and to promote the progress-oriented interests of its English-educated Chinese population without seeming to encourage "Chineseness" as the cornerstone to Singaporean identity. Hence, the official discouragement of ethnic tribalism through the promotion of "multiracialism" served the purpose of differentiating two types of Chinese—red and loyal. Like other Asian American texts, the novel exposes the general dynamic in which the production of an ethnic margin constitutes the legitimacy of the center. Paralleling yet distinct from Lowe's discussion of Asian American racial formation as it serves the purposes of American national self-definition, in this case the concept of difference exploited by the state could not simply fall along racial or ethnic lines, but according to loyalties to political and economic systems.

As the novel reveals, the success of such ethnic management against the construction of an external enemy contributed to the longevity of the PAP and a highly stable polity that some now characterize as soft authoritarianism. Following both academic and mainstream media critiques of the loss of democratic rights in the wake of rapid modernization and three decades of single-party rule, the novel questions the methods of securing, as Esha, the narrator, notes, "peace and progress." Although concerns over state influence on the dissemination of information and the general impression of lack of journalistic freedom, for example, may be a far cry from the methods of state control now employed in Burma, as Singapore's publicized use of corporal punishment reveals, the state has developed a significant civil apparatus for dealing with both dissenters and lawbreakers. The PAP has been particularly successful in using the legal tools of democracy as instruments of control: the deregistration of radical unions, the withdrawal of newspaper licenses, the threat of defamation suits, and selective prosecution for tax law violation.[27] Although representations of prohibitions and penalties do not suggest that they are violations of human rights, other criticisms of Singapore law focus on the Internal Security Act, an "emergency" measure allowing for detention without trial that originated out of fear of communist subversion.

In portraying the disappearance of Esha's Uncle Tien, who goes into hiding and presumed exile rather than face arrest when suspected of involvement with the Barisan Socialis, or Socialist Front, the novel highlights the use of the Internal Security Act in quashing internal dissent, a measure that meant, as Li Shin explains to Esha, "If the government suspected someone of being a Communist, that person could be arrested and sent to jail" (50). Originally the only party with the potential support to challenge the PAP, the Barisan Socialis had broken from the more moderate PAP in 1961 in order to campaign against a federation with Malaysia that had outlawed communism. Through the Internal Security Act in 1963, one hundred Barisan leaders and supporters were arrested and held without trial in what was dubbed "Operation Cold Store." This sweep and the Barisan's boycott of the 1968 election effectively eliminated the development of a viable two-party system in Singapore, allowing for a PAP ascendancy that continues. At the time of the novel's publication, "detainees" from Operation Cold Store were still being held.[28] As Geraldine Heng has shown, this authoritarianism has extended to women; the measure was deployed against the women's movement in the 1987 detention of two founding members of the feminist organization AWARE.

In recalling the PAP's most blatant violation of human rights in the figure of Tien, the novel reveals the accusation of subversion to be a blanket charge to suppress dissent, an irony heightened by the implication that Tien merely supports the academic and personal freedoms associated with liberal democracy. In foregrounding the loss of civil liberties that occurs in the name of guaranteeing democracy, *The Scent of the Gods* links postcolonial history to a contemporary concern with human rights in global politics. Its portrayal reveals these losses to be not aberrant but foundational to the formation of the state. Yet, *Scent*'s commentary is not simply to be deduced from a straightforward representation of historical events. Rather, its historical content is understated, filtered through the limited consciousness of a child moving toward adolescence. A form of bildungsroman, the novel is not overtly analytic; Esha's beliefs are still unformed and much of her thought is focused on moments in which she comes to some awareness of sexuality. History may appear at times as a backdrop to these flashes of recognition, but because Esha's maturation is always portrayed in conjunction with events that highlight reaction to governmental policy, it is clear that Cheong's specifically gendered genre is the means of articulating her political commentary. In contrast to Shelley Sunn Wong's reading of the bildungsroman as a narrative of progressive incorporation into and identification with majority culture and thus an ideologically suspect genre for Asian American women writers, the bildungsroman is the vehicle for Cheong's critique of the connection between maturity and the acceptance of the state's disciplining authority.

Female maturation is characterized by constraint; Esha is subject to a new set of prohibitions that are meant as both safeguards and messages to others about oneself: she must keep her knees together, keep her shirt on, and learn to walk like a girl. In witnessing the public humiliation of a schoolmate forced to stand in front of the class without her panties in punishment for displaying mildly pornographic images of "naked British people chasing one another around" (140), she learns that sex is not just secret but is, like masturbation, a punishable offense. Such warnings about self-discipline and proper behavior are meant to convey one message: to overstep the boundaries of decorum is to invite violation. Esha's interior reflection and the political terrain converge in the representation of Auntie Daisy's rape and subsequent pregnancy. Esha witnesses Daisy's virtual incarceration in the house when bars are placed over her window, bars she is told that "*Auntie Daisy herself* had asked for" (161; emphasis added). The identity of the rapist remains unknown and the blame falls on her aunt for her previously "free" behavior. Esha recognizes that the grown-ups need to blame Auntie Daisy for the rape because they cannot deal with a "horror without a source"; it may also be implied, however, that a horror without a source has potential uses: an undefined evil makes all the more urgent the necessity to discipline one's own behavior and to submit to protection for one's own good. Whereas the judicial response to rape often hinges on the issue of consent, within the framework of Cheong's gendered political allegory the question of consent bears relevance to Singapore's current state of affairs: Does Daisy consent to the curtailment of her freedoms? Are the bars designed to keep others out also meant to keep her in?

The fact that neither the woman nor the girl becoming a woman can object to measures taken in the name of her own defense resonates with sociologist Chua Beng-Huat's statement concerning the government's characterization of repressive measures as forms of civic responsibility: "Politically, the conflation [of government and society] rationalises and justifies all state interventions as preemptive actions which 'ensure' collective well-being and, as such, are measures of good government rather than abuses of individual rights" (663). Just as Daisy and Esha suffer the restriction of their movements based on a "caring" paternalism, so the populace appears to consent to a restriction of freedoms based on the assurance of the benevolent caretaking abilities of the state. The family's justification of Esha's seclusion in a convent after she gets her period is echoed without overt judgment by Esha herself: "In Great-Grandfather's house the family had to be protected. That was the law. It had always been. It would always be" (247). Her innocent commentary on gender role conformity implies that what now appears as sacrifice—a request to modify individual behavior—is justified by the payoff of future security: "Men were going to treat me according to how I behaved. One day when I was older, [Grandma] said, I would understand what she meant, and I would be grateful that she had taught me the proper graces" (9). As Grandma and the government both recognize, such feelings of gratitude can only be produced by transforming the representation of restriction from punitive to merely regulatory. The gendered contrast between Li Shin's desire to be a soldier and Esha's lessons in feminine behavior reveals the roles to be directed toward an identical purpose, that of instilling self-discipline. The roles are complementary and reciprocal—a duty to protect implies those who need to be protected. The idea of consensual behavior modification (the family's request of Esha) may be distinct from the threat of detention (the government's threat to Tien), but they operate under the same logic; an appeal to national citizenship and collective survival justifies the suspension of individual freedom.

If Esha is to stand in some measure as a reflection of Singapore's postindependence population, Cheong represents her as neither eager to acquiesce nor entirely passive or duped by authority. This balance is enacted through her portrayal of Esha's growing consciousness of sexuality: though she does not rebel against it, Esha reads beyond the adults' representation of sex-as-threat enough to understand that she is only receiving the authorized narrative. Thus, in seeing her cousin's penis, his "almost grown-up birdie," for the first time, she is astonished at its soft helplessness. Its presence ruptures its prior characterization—what previously she cannot look at or discuss is revealed to be nothing fearful at all. Unlike *Irrawaddy Tango*, in which the penis-form becomes an instrument of state power, the analogy here is that, like the unseen but potentially threatening communists, the penis serves as the sign through which the appeal for modifications in behavior is elicited, a sign whose effectiveness is only assured by its nebulousness. As she matures, Esha is implicitly and explicitly warned about the dangers of sexual contact and the need for self-discipline just as the "grown-ups" are warned to submit to government curfews purported to protect them. Yet, in spite of attempts to convince her that sex is dangerous, Esha becomes emotionally aware of not just the beauty and deep intimacy of the sexual act, but the power it wields over others. Cheong's gendered commentary thus plays on the very beliefs in women's vulnerability that international feminists have noted serve post-colonial national cohesion; as Cynthia Enloe notes, nationalist men often represented women as a resource in need of protection from outside influences, particularly from "progressive" Western exports such as feminism. Here, however, the nuanced connection between gender and nationalism relies on the analogy between communism and sex as they signal both illicit temptation and physical violation.

But it is not merely through grafting political resonance on to Esha's observations that Cheong's critique is derived; Esha's ability to comprehend the motivations of the adult world is limited, her knowledge is partial. Depicting a period where "meaningful answers were not spoken" (3), Cheong renders poetic the divide between feeling and perception as a commentary both on coming of age and on the climate of a specific postcolonial moment: "[T]here were things you knew," Esha thinks. "There were things you did not know, too, but some things you knew" (38). The narrative is retrospective but rarely allows for retrospective awareness—the clarity of an adult perspective based on historical hindsight—to intrude upon the partial consciousness of the child's narration. For Esha, meaning is always elusive and deferred until an unspecified moment in the future, a moment the adults assure her will come, if only as the rationale for keeping her now in ignorance: "[Grandma] was telling me something I was not expected to understand yet. . . . Someday all that I had kept of hers, all that she had passed to me, would be taken out, unraveled, and given away, and it would become useful. How this was to happen, I did not know" (100). One reviewer's comments reflect discomfort with the novel's insistence on maintaining the tension between knowing and not knowing, between historical "fact" and the consciousness of an eleven-year-old, seeing Esha's lack of "strong perceptive reasoning" as a failure of character development (Baras B7). Yet, this evaluation fails to see that partialness is the point—and not only because Cheong's choice of narrative voice can be seen as a commentary on the way perception is conditioned and delimited by those in authority. Her use of the faux naïf is not like Hisaye Yamamoto's or Sandra Cisneros's coming-of-age fiction in which the reader is invited to read beyond what slips past the child-women's awareness. Rather, Cheong's choice of point of view—Esha's lack of "perceptive reasoning"—carries specific historical resonance. The narrator's (and ultimately the reader's) incomplete information on the deaths of her parents and Li Shin, the rape of Auntie Daisy, and the disappearance of Uncle Tien produces a climate of anxiety and confirms her subordinate place in the household. Her lack of access to the complete story parallels the situation of a populace whose acquiescence is assured by a state of uncertainty, neither knowing if communists might infiltrate the island nor, conversely, if the home will be infiltrated by the state. This connection between national and domestic space is likewise reinforced by Li Yuen and Esha's growing suspicion of adults, which results in alliance between them, a circumstance reflecting the reconfiguration of alliances and loyalties along ethnic lines in the early stages of independence. The children's perpetual state of unenlightenment breeds paranoia about whom to trust: "We were only two of us, now. Anyone else could be an enemy, and we did not know what the grown-ups might do" (233). Although taught to obey the authority of adults, Esha and Li Yuen begin to draw a clear division between spheres, just as the adults themselves draw tighter ranks around the household against multiple, vaguely specified threats—the Malays, would-be rapists, Chinese Communists, vengeful gods, and visits from government men. In language pregnant with hints of conspiracy, Li Yuen warns, "Grandma hears everything" (189), as a caution about monitored behavior and the potentially punitive forces of the lawgiver; for the adults, it is becoming increasingly clear that "[n]o one escaped the government's eye" (81). Although the absence of definitive information in the faux naïf certainly reflects a postmodern concern with the bias of knowledge production, in portraying the effect of siege mentality in parallel spheres, Cheong's use of limited consciousness as the narrative's point of view carries additional political meaning by reproducing the climate of the times.

As Sister Katherine confirms in a lesson about the equator, the imaginary does have consequences in the real; in *Scent*, several "imaginaries" are instrumental in securing the hegemony of the current regime, most notably that of a Singaporean citizen where there were once only Chinese, Malays, and Indians, and of the ever-elusive communist presence that unified through the threat of siege. In exploring the effect of government policy on one Chinese family, *Scent* reveals the ways in which national identity as "imaginary community" is often secured through the projection of both external and internal threats that define common affiliation; the novel's original title, *Soldiers,* underscored this point but was rejected as unmarketable by the publisher.[29] In signaling the politically invested interests in which identifications are formed and consolidated, the novel engages the theoretical dynamics noted by numerous scholars concerned with difference as a constitutive element in national cohesion, a dynamic reflecting Stuart Hall's assertion that Englishness, for example, "was always negotiated against difference . . . in order to present itself as a homogenous entity" (22).[30] Thus, in discussing the novel as a form of historiography, I am less concerned with whether the threats of communist infiltration and ethnic disunity were actually imminent than with the uses to which such claims of crisis were put. What becomes clear in the hindsight of the novel's writing is that the "Red scare" served both as a source of common interest for a populace divided by generation, ethnicity, and class and as the PAP's initial justification for the abrogation of civil liberties and the implementation of social controls in the civic realm.

Scent exposes the ways in which the "Red scare" served the purpose of nationalism, but it does so without condemning the abuse of power as clearly as does *Irrawaddy Tango;* its nostalgic tone reflects an ambivalence about what sacrifices are necessary for progress. In regard to her family's deliberate forgetting of her ambiguously murdered cousin, Esha reflects:

> I understood why the names had to disappear, put out like flames of unwatched candles that might burn down a house. It was not punishment for the dead. It was protection for the living.
>   But Li Shin I had loved. (226)

The family's manipulation of history is not overtly questioned; she "understood why" future security requires a willful disregard of the past. Nonetheless, even as the novel portrays the state itself as more threatening than the increasingly nebulous enemy, her comment seems to support strategic "forgetting" in the political realm where individuals are sacrificed for the collective good. Love is the surplus of such forgetting, a sentimental excess of the drive toward futurity. Intimacy, Cheong suggests, is an attachment that has no place unless redirected toward the affiliations produced and regulated by the state. Although the government claims that policies enacted in the years following independence such as multiracialism, bilingualism, integrated government housing, and modernization are responsible for producing "social harmony," one can as easily say that they have succeeded in turning Singapore into the embodiment of the Panopticon in which discipline is enforced, if not by constant surveillance, then by the internalization of surveillance. The enforcement of social control in Singapore does not appear as absolute tyranny because, as Foucault writes in regard to the Panopticon, its end is not power itself but the strengthening of social forces "to increase production, to develop the economy, spread education, raise the level of public morality; to increase and multiply" (208). If acceptance of the loss of democratic rights in the name of the public good and social evolution becomes internalized, it is because technologies of power are not merely repressive but productive and the loss comes to represent a fair exchange for a higher standard of living. And, given the thirty-four years of single-party rule in Singapore, as David Brown notes, "Once government equates the maintenance of social and political stability with its own dominance and legitimacy, then the concept of democracy becomes redefined so that it begins to refer, in effect, merely to the degree of public acquiescence of government and its policies" (1008). It remains to be seen whether the affluent middle class will initiate the call for more freedoms, or whether its own dependence on the state will preempt a move for greater democratic participation. In light of this contemporary context, *Scent* lays out for critique the suspension of individual rights in the name of the collective; its depiction of Singapore's history highlights transgressions ironically justified by the need to guarantee a political system meant to ensure those rights.[31]

As the means of their advocacy, both *The Scent of the Gods* and *Irrawaddy Tango* represent the years following independence as the source of contemporary political conflicts linking 1960s postcolonial nationalism to a 1990s concern with human rights as it had become part of an American cultural idiom. In highlighting tactics that secured the rule of specific regimes, the works represent postindependence history as continuous with the policies of the present, past repressions with contemporary abuses of power. Both novels focus on human rights abuses as if to highlight Weber's definition of the state as the agent of a set of institutions specifically concerned with the enforcement of order, and as such, the holder of a monopoly of legitimate violence. The works point to complementary methods of social control; what Foucault would call the "traditional, ritual, costly, violent forms of power" employed by SLORC have been superseded in Singapore by a "subtle, calculated technology of subjection" based on corporatist population management (220). An appeal to human rights gestures toward one agency of potential policing not bounded by the state, and one effective for soliciting international attention. But, just as standardized measures of time and space can be said to represent a move toward globalization, the philosophy of universalism underlying human rights is itself subject to questions of influence.[32] The Oxford Amnesty Lecture Committee's question, "Whose human rights are we defending?" is itself a response to philosophical suspicion of a subject transcendent of history. But, as Judith Butler notes,

> To take the construction of the subject as a political problematic is not the same as doing away with the subject; to deconstruct the subject is not to negate or throw away the concept; on the contrary, deconstruction implies only that we suspend all commitments to that to which the term, "the subject," refers and that we consider the linguistic functions it serves in the consolidation of and concealment of authority. (14)[33]

The invocation of human rights and its necessary subject implies not a suspension of commitment but a call to intervention, one overtly intended to oppose oppressive authority. If the idea of human rights is recognized as a necessary fiction, a "contingent foundation" on which activism is mobilized, the question becomes not "What is the status of the subject of human rights within postmodernity?" but "How can this individual subject be deployed as part of a collective appeal?" Moreover, Richard Rorty invites us to reconceive "universal" notions of justice as matters of loyalty, asking, "Should we describe such . . . moral dilemmas as conflicts between loyalty and justice, or rather, as I have suggested we might, as conflicts between loyalties to smaller groups and loyalties to larger groups?" (47). Hence, human rights would no longer assume the aura of transnational morality, but be recognized as an expression of loyalty to Western conceptions of justice. *Irrawaddy Tango* raises the question of whether an appeal to activism based on a woman's torture is equivalent to an appeal to ethnic sovereignty rights or national reform; its portrayal mirrors American coverage of Burma's ongoing state of affairs, which depends on a female subject positioned in opposition to a military-controlled state, an appeal meant to extend beyond the single body. The fact that Burma's national self-image has not been particularly gender-invested only reveals the extent to which specific configurations of gender difference can be mobilized within the United States in service of critiques of Asian leadership. For example, like the novel, Hollywood's 1995 portrayal of the democracy movement in *Beyond Rangoon* engages a female point of view to depict its protagonist's political involvement in Burma as a response to gendered trauma—the loss of a child, attempted rape, and murder. The protagonist's psychic healing culminates in a commitment to humanitarian, non-national activism as she joins a doctors-without-borders-type outpost in the jungle.[34] In contrast, as Geraldine Heng has shown, Singapore's ruling party harnessed gender representation to postindependence mandates for national unity, from its conditional support of the women's movement to its utilization of eroticized sexual allure in the form of the "Singapore girl" to sell its national airline.

As international feminist scholars have cautioned, yoking gender to the promotion of nationalist imaginaries does not always reflect the best interests of Third World women, particularly as such representations often fall into traditional appeals to women's reproductive duty or women as "nationalist wombs."[35] Women are also called upon simply to symbolize the nation's relationship to modernization, to signal degrees of either progressiveness or precolonial authenticity. As Aiwah Ong has pointed out, even feminist studies of women in development fall into a reductive binarism by evaluating gender inequality along this single opposition between modernization and tradition. The only distinction, she writes, is that "feminists mainly differ over whether modernization of the capitalist or socialist kind will emancipate or reinforce systems of gender inequality found in the Third World" (82). Moreover, as Kandiyoti notes, women's symbolic use as boundary markers between national, ethnic, or religious collectives may jeopardize their emergence as full-fledged citizens (382). Thus, it is important to emphasize that the gendered advocacy of these two Asian American novels does not reflect a feminist commitment to Asian women as much as an understanding of how the gender tropes that saturate American culture can be put to use. One could argue that Law-Yone's appeal to the injured female body plays on traditional ideas of women's victimization by reinforcing limited concepts of empowerment from injury.[36] Similarly, Cheong's coming-of-age narrative relies on gender-differentiated models of agency and passivity to parallel the state's methods of soliciting loyal citizenry: feminine submission to protective custody becomes the analogue to masculine conscription.

These literary representations linking women and political advocacy speak to the potency of gendered metaphors in American national consciousness and their potential efficacy in eliciting sympathetic awareness of what inevitably is shown to be the patriarchal heavy-handedness of

Asian governance. Although this certainly reverses colonialist portrayals of
a feminized Orient, both novels may reinforce the notion of Asia's
absolute difference from the West—Law-Yone through representations of
barbarous and inept Asian military rule and Cheong through implicit
comparisons between Asian "guided" and Western "free" democracies. In
reproducing Asia through differentiation, as Lowe suggests, these portrayals may sustain the narrow characterization of the always alien Asian
American subject. Significantly, however, both works' emphasis is not on
the contestation of Asian inclusion or exclusion in the United States.
Rather, in keeping with Lowe and other Americanists' general thesis on
American nationalism produced out of confrontations with difference, the
works reveal the processes of ethnic management to be endemic to the
nationalist enterprise—here, under postcolonialism. Moreover, Cheong
reverses presumptions about the West's construction of the East to show
how Singaporean nationalism itself relied on distinctions between East
and West to secure its sense of Asian ethnic cohesion. Here, gender difference becomes the vehicle for exposing how postindependence regimes
constructed ethnically differentiated internal and external "enemies" as
predicates of national unity and the legitimacy of their own rule.

As gender is positioned as a sign that secures group cohesion, it mediates the formation of collective identifications in the state's re-formation of
affiliations and roles and becomes a means of defining group loyalties. As I
argue elsewhere, the rhetorical connection between women's sexual transgression and national betrayal is one bridge across the presumed divide
between ethnic American and transnational perspectives in Asian
American studies.[37] Just as Third World nationalists may position feminism
as an imported Western corruption of indigenous tradition or female figures as betraying national collectives, so too have ethnic cultural nationalists represented gender concerns as a betrayal of ethnic American solidarity and continuance. More pertinent to my argument here, gendered discourses familiar to an American readership (spousal abuse, women's rights
as civil rights) work to intervene in postcolonial Asian politics. This is certainly in keeping with Lowe's view of literature as one site where "the individual invents lived relationship with the national collective" as he or she
becomes "immersed in the repertoire of American memories, events, and
narratives" (5). As the sedimented contradictions between citizenship as
the democratic promise of inclusion and the material realities of racial
hierarchy erupt in Asian American cultural productions, Lowe notes, these
productions become contestatory sites of American national culture. I

want to suggest that this immersion can also produce not a contestation with national culture but a strategic replaying of its normative values. This staging or narratival deployment of ideas saturated with First World precepts appears in the gendered narratives of other Asian American women writers: Le Ly Hayslip's appeal for an end to the American embargo against Vietnam, Jessica Hagedorn's indictment of the Marcos regime, Helie Lee's call for Korean reunification. Thus, an emphasis on the uses of gendered appeal is one means of displacing the distinction between exilic and immigrant sensibilities in Asian American art, given that it focuses instead on an interrogation of how U.S. investments influence representations of "home" or vice versa.[38] This is not to imply Asian American cultural enfranchisement as much as a familiarity with, for example, gendered rights as a tool for advocacy; there is, of course, a certain irony to my point given the tradition of valuable scholarship showing that civil rights have not historically extended to or do not currently extend to, populations within the United States marked by class, race, or sexuality. Asian American positioning suggests an immersion in—and an ability to manipulate—First World ideologies and discourses, an ability particularly significant for writers who continue to have stakes in reenvisioning the governance of their home countries.

Highlighting literature's investment in the national thus speaks to Sau-ling Wong's compelling caution about the shift in focus from domestic to diasporic perspectives in Asian American studies, a movement that potentially elides the class and coalitional history of Asian Americans that motivated the formation of the discipline. Certainly, as Koshy notes, new Asian American literary production cannot be conceptualized simply within national boundaries; however, rather than a strategic forgetting of, in her terms, "outmoded identity politics," it is important to recognize how literature advances political advocacy in terms reflective of the rhetoric of rights intrinsic to the inception of the field. Of consequence is not so much that the texts I discuss here inscribe modes of Asian American subjectivity, although they may well do this, but that their narratives are partly authorized by, in Wong's words, their authors' "land of residence." Conversely, if Asian American literature is singularly situated as American minority literature, it can be erroneously positioned in opposition to postcolonial literature as interventionist political allegory. This opposition is implicit in reviews that found Scent's historical contextualization an awkward intrusion; one concluded that Cheong was "not as brilliant as Tan or Kingston." Such an assessment suggests that an association with the canon of "minority" literature, at least in mainstream perception, leads to a misreading and would relegate the history of social upheaval in such texts to a backdrop for narratives of identity quest. This association would position *Scent*'s bildungsroman not as the vehicle for commenting on political developments, but as a genre merely concerned with maturation and the "intensity of a young girl growing up in a lush and beautiful land," as one review noted, or the cultural conflict between tradition and modern values.[39] Although less an issue for *Irrawaddy Tango*, emphasis on the novel's use of the picaresque ("a woman's sexual adventures") can displace a reading based on Tango's relationship to the state as a shifting collective alliance motivated by sexual activity. Rather, in both novels "identity quest" becomes the vehicle for revealing the role of the state in conditioning the bounded expressions of identity and structures the authors' national commentaries. Both reconcile hard-and-fast distinctions between "minority" American literature and postcolonial literature by revealing that the gendered configurations of ethnicity, family, and nationality that figure into expressions of hyphenated identity are also vehicles for postcolonial critique. Both means of situating Asian American literature converge in a specifically gendered rhetoric that comes to structure political advocacy.

Wong's call for historicizing the push to globalize Asian American cultural criticism can be seconded by a need to historicize literature's simultaneous investment in global activism and domestic values. With this assertion of investment comes a necessary caution: although my discussion of the "universal" concept of human rights highlights literature's appeal to a transnational means of governance predicated on the rights of the Enlightenment subject, such appeals may carry implicit Western ideological agendas even as they advance ideals that seemingly transcend American national interests. Far from rendering Asian American literature postnational, an emphasis on a national rhetoric of gendered rights reveals the literature to be imbued with potentially hegemonic First World values.

Scarry has noted that Amnesty International's effectiveness depends on its "ability to communicate the reality of physical pain to those who are not themselves in pain" (9). Although the novels engage situations of differing urgency, both narrate the body's pain and the trauma of loss as a reminder that the "collective task of diminishing pain" does not end with independence from colonial domination. In Burma, the status quo is uneasily maintained as SLORC (now self-designated the State Peace and Development Council) continues to isolate Aung San Suu Kyi and disrupt assembly outside her home. Ironically, the ethnic secessionist struggle for Kawthoolei, a Karen homeland, now lives on in fiction after suffering a historical setback: Radio Myanmar reported the fall of the Karen National Union central headquarters in Manerplaw, forcing thirty thousand Karens across the border into refugee camps in Thailand in early 1995.[40] *Scent*'s portrayal of the PAP's implementation of "emergency" measures such as curfews or the Internal Security Act in the years following independence reveals the crisis surrounding communist subversion to be the initial justification for the suppression of internal dissent, which continues into the present. The tactic of invoking national crisis to elicit consent for state mandates continued into the early 1980s: as Geraldine Heng and Janadas Devan note, in 1983 Prime Minister Lee Kuan Yew charged educated (ethnic Chinese) women with a failure to regenerate the population in proportions equivalent to the moment of the nation's founding; theirs was a dereliction of the patriotic duty to reproduce a genetically superior workforce to secure Singapore's future.[41] Both novels' representation of postcolonial Asian politics invokes the increasingly influential discourse of human rights as a reminder that the past is only rendered accessible in the terms of the present; and in doing so, they situate Asian American literary production as a medium of timely global commentary. As the treatment of political dissidents increasingly narrates the individual's relationship to the state, it becomes more urgent to understand the ways in which "universal" concepts such as human rights transcend neither history nor context, but are deployed in the interest of specific political agendas.

NOTES

I would like to thank Russ Castronovo, C. Lok Chua, Tassie Gwilliam, Frank Palmeri, and Mihoko Suzuki for their astute and careful comments on earlier drafts of this article.

1. *New York Times Magazine,* April 2, 1995. See also Joye Mercer, "Morality in Investing," *Chronicle of Higher Education* 29 (March 1996): A49–51.

2. In electing to retain the use of "Burma" rather than "Myanmar," the name chosen in 1989 by the military junta, the State Law and Order Restoration Council (SLORC), I follow the lead of the author whose text I am discussing. My decision is also based both on readers' familiarity and on political considerations in spite of the fact that the name change has been widely adopted by the media. Maureen Aung-Thwin and Thant Myint-U note that "Burma" is "merely another way of

saying Burma in Burmese" (75). Journalist Michael Fredholm marks his choice to retain "Burma" more politically, stating that "Myanmar" means "strong" in Burmese, the language of the Burman ethnic majority, and therefore the name change is not accepted by all ethnic groups (7). However, original citations using "Myanmar" have not been changed.

3. The number of political prisoners is an estimate; SLORC has acknowledged the detention of 1,200 people between September 18, 1988, and August 18, 1989, according to Amnesty International (1989).

4. As the *New Yorker* noted, "Some demonstrators carried the American flag, and at one point, a group of students came to the front door of the Embassy and recited the Gettysburg Address word for word in English" (Sesser 80–81). It is unclear whether the use of English, American history, or the feat of memorization was more astounding to the American journalist.

5. In suggesting that the American citizen has been defined in opposition to the Asian immigrant, Lisa Lowe's *Immigrant Acts* uncovers the ways in which Asian immigrants "have been fundamental to the construction of the nation as a simulacrum of inclusiveness" (5). As Asian subjects in the United States are constructed partly as a response to U.S. economic and military interests in Asia, she writes, legal definitions of belonging are likewise constituted by various projections of Asian difference.

6. Detractors of Fay's punishment ranged from President Clinton, who called the sentence "extreme," to those who saw flogging as a form of torture. Still others seemed far more outraged at the *lack* of outrage expressed by a complacent citizenry: as one journalist put it, "[Michael Fay is] going to be thrashed and bloodied in a foreign land, and America doesn't seem to care" (Elliott 19).

7. In addition to corporal punishment, there is a mandatory death penalty for murder, and, according to W. Timothy Austin, trafficking in fifteen grams of heroin or more brings the death penalty, as does dealing in illegal firearms. There are regulations on hair length for men as well as prohibitions against fruit or flower picking on public land, noise after 10 P.M., and sidewalk or street dancing. Failure to report a change of address within two weeks could incur a fine of five thousand dollars, five years' imprisonment, or both (915).

8. During the 1996 conference on trade and economics between twenty-five leaders of Asia and Europe, for example, members of the Association of Southeast Asian Nations (ASEAN) and China, Japan, and South Korea lamented that Europeans "only want to preach to them about human rights" rather than talk business (*New York Times*, March 1, 1996).

9. See, for example, Masao Miyoshi's "A Borderless World? From Colonialism to Transnationalism and the Decline of the Nation-State," which views transnational corporatism as a form of neocolonialism. In contrast, economists have noted that fears of the death of the state in global restructuring are overstated. See Hirst and Thompson, Wade, and Weiss.

10. *Miami Herald,* August 7, 1996, 9A.

11. *New York Times,* September 17, 1996, A8.

12. The term comes from Lenore E. Walker's influential study *The Battered Woman.*

13. Scarry notes that what the torturer desires in compelling confession is not information but confirmation that "intense pain is world-destroying" (29).

14. Given the excesses of Burma's General Ne Win during his twenty-six-year term as leader of the military-dominated Burma Socialist Programme Party until his resignation in the face of mounting protests in 1988, Law-Yone's depiction of "Supremo," head of the "People's Party Council," required potentially little embellishment to convince of this irrationality. For example, in keeping with his belief in numerology, Ne Win wreaked havoc on Burma's economy by changing the denomination of larger bills to reflect his lucky number, nine, rendering the previous bills worthless. He once canceled an official state visit to France after interpreting an accident in his welcoming motorcade as an inauspicious omen (Fredholm 243–44). Like other colonial independence movements, Burma's independence was furthered through an uneasy anti-imperialist coalition among diverse ethnic and political groups who experienced different treatment under British rule. The territories of the Karen and the Shan, for example, were administered as separate from the interior; both tribes' resistance to the new state arose from the feeling that they experienced greater autonomy under British control (Silverstein). Perceiving that the newly independent state privileged the Burman ethnic majority under its state policy of "burmanization," and unable to reconcile themselves to the administration of the centralized state after independence, both the Karen and the Shan continue to wage active warfare, now against SLORC. But, despite this long-standing history of opposition, these groups have mounted a relatively ineffectual challenge to the sovereignty of the state or the rule of the military regime (Law-Yone 1989). It is this history of increasingly token resistance that elicits condemnation from *Irrawaddy Tango*'s narrator, Tango: "Help was not forthcoming from any quarter as far as this eye could see—not from outside, not from inside the borders. Not from the only other men with the guns—those eternally bickering separatist groups . . . who couldn't set aside their petty quarrels long enough to gang up on [the general] for the ultimate kick in the head" (261). Her comment recasts insurgent armies with a long history of political causes— "self-rule, religious freedom, human rights" (128)—as squabbling siblings who, in addition to their failure to join forces to oust a despotic ruler, seem more significantly to lack a self-help movement, a point later resonant with Tango's disparagement of experientially based coalition politics in the Unites States.

15. Walker's *The Battered Woman* is one source of the phrase "learned helplessness." An obvious problem with this concept is that it marks the battered woman as tangentially complicit in her victimhood via a conditioned passivity. This complicity also makes problematic translating the idea of "learned helplessness" into political analogy; along the same lines, links have been drawn between Burmese Buddhism and the longevity of Ne Win's rule. It has been said that the Burmese believe that the power of a ruler is a function of the merit he is born with; hence Ne Win's authority could be seen to be derived from the merit he had accumulated from a previous existence (Sesser 76). Of course, such an assessment may reveal as much about the West's fascination with Buddhism as about the existence of culturally conditioned passivity.

16. Reports parallel methods of eliciting compliance, including beatings,

burning with cigarettes, sleep deprivation, social isolation, and the withholding of medical care; these converge most forcefully in methods of sexual torture—the insertion of objects into vagina or rectum, coerced sex acts, and rape. Mary Romero draws a direct comparison between tactics used on American POWs in Korea and battered women in "A Comparison between Strategies Used on Prisoners of War and Battered Wives." Diana Russell cites A. D. Biederman's schematic "debilitation, dread, and dependency" to draw an analogy between tactics used to break down the resistance of prisoners of war and those used by batterers. See also Boulette and Anderson's discussion of the "Stockholm syndrome" and Tifft's use of Elaine Scarry's discussion of torture.

17. I am indebted to an anonymous reviewer for this reference.

18. This is an imperfect example of what Scarry might see as torture's deconstructive ability; after all, the inverse of pain is not pleasure, but the cessation of pain.

19. Scarry writes, "When, for example, one receives a letter from Amnesty in the mail, the words of that letter must somehow convey to the reader the aversiveness being experienced inside the body of someone whose country may be far away, *whose name can barely be pronounced,* and whose ordinary life is unknown except that it is known that ordinary life has ceased to exist" (9; emphasis added). Her comment unwittingly reveals that international agencies such as Amnesty International locate the West as an implicit center for human rights activism.

20. The U.S. Drug Enforcement Agency (DEA) has viewed Khun Sa, former leader of the Shan United Army, as an opium drug lord. Khun Sa claimed to be fighting for an independent Shan state, but the DEA alleged that he had raised a personal army to protect his heroin business (Reuters World Service, May 15, 1995). In contrast, the Karen apparently fund their activities by taxing goods smuggled into Thailand (Sesser 74). Based on SLORC's record of human rights abuses, the United States is now reluctant to lift its arms embargo on Burma even to fight the "war on drugs" in the region between Burma, Laos, and Thailand known as the Golden Triangle and cut drug-enforcement aid after the events of 1988 (see Falco and Reuter). Ethnic groups claim that the government was using anti-opium herbicides on insurgent armies' food supply (Law-Yone 1989 and Sesser).

21. For example, this from *Time*: "Gentle in gesture and speech, the Karens do not seem capable of nurturing hatred. Nor do the guerrillas seem capable of dispatching their children to the front lines to fight, and die, alongside the men. But they do" (Stanley 41).

22. Members of the Soviet bloc of nations objected to a liberal construction of freedom that ignored group rights—the right to speak one's own language, ensure the protection of one's national culture, or guarantee the rights of national minorities. The USSR put before the delegates a draft amendment reflecting group rights that was subsequently rejected (*Yearbook of the United Nations 1948–49* 535).

23. The statement is also reflected in Article 14 of the Beijing Declaration and Platform for Action disseminated by the United Nations, September 15, 1995.

The conference's keynote address was delivered by Aung San Suu Kyi via a smuggled-in videotape (*New York Times*, September 6, 1995, A4).

24. Of course, one would only have to look at specific instances to show how this distinction cannot be sustained. Jenny Bourne points out as much in her discussion of how Jewish feminist identity politics in Britain fails to take a stand on Zionism.

25. Ironically, feminist studies of domestic abuse speak of solutions to battery in terms of political systems. For example, Romero compares the tactics of domination used by wife batterers to those employed by the Chinese captors of American POWs in Korea order to suggest that "deprogramming" victims "ought to include the resocialization to feminist values within a supportive and *democratic* environment" (545; emphasis added). If, like the political despot, the male batterer inappropriately uses violence to maintain inequities in power, studies suggest that, among other strategies, stopping domestic violence lies in equalizing the gender hierarchy that legitimates masculine entitlement in order to remedy the lack of consensual decision making found in more "democratic" relationships. See Tifft.

26. Law-Yone notes, "If you grow up in a society like the one I was trying to describe, the whole notion of introspection is different. Especially in a Buddhist society, the idea of self, the individual as the ego, is just not prevalent. . . . On the other hand it takes a certain kind of introspection to be an interesting character. Especially in the Western tradition, the whole direction has been toward telling secrets. . . . In Asia it is your job as an artist not to challenge, not to subvert, but to reproduce reality and make it palatable. The self is not important, it is the community that is important" (quoted in Trescott). Law-Yone makes clear that she locates herself against this nonpolitical, nonconfrontational character of writing in Asia, thus situating her writing within a tradition of advocacy marked as Western (personal interview, December 28, 1996).

27. See Chua Beng-Huat. This fear of libel suits may or may not extend to fictional representations of the regime. For example, *The Scent of the Gods* was available and reviewed in Singapore at the time of its publication; Cheong recalls her trepidation in anticipating official response but was not officially "scolded" for her portrayal in government-owned newspapers. She attributed this lack of response both to the literariness of the representation and to the relative newness of fiction about Singapore produced in the West (personal communication, June 12, 1998). As Shirley Lim notes, creative political critiques may be unlikely if only because, as part of the English-educated elite working in government-controlled institutions, Singapore writers have interests "inextricably bound with governmental, bureaucratic aims" (541).

28. Chia Thye Poh, arrested in 1966 for allegedly advocating armed struggle against the PAP government while a member of parliament representing Barisan Socialis, was released in November of 1998 after being held in internal exile on the island of Sentosa.

29. Personal communication, May 13, 1998.

30. Reflecting Homi Bhabha's recognition that "the production of discrimi-

natory identities . . . secure[s] the 'pure' and original identity of [colonial] authority," this structure of argument appears in numerous writings on the relationship between nationalism and alterity (112). For a discussion of the relationship between racialization and American national identity, see the work of Rayna Green, Lisa Lowe, Toni Morrison, Michael Rogin, Carroll Smith-Rosenberg, and Robyn Wiegman.

31. In commenting on the irony produced by defying democratic principles to ensure democracy, the novel reveals that the PAP dealt with this contradiction by drawing a distinction between Western "free" democracy and Asian "guided" democracy. Li Shin repeats the PAP line: We were not like America. America was a free democracy, he said, because American people did not like being guided. "How come we don't want a free democracy?" I asked. "Because we're Asians," he said. "We don't always believe the same things as Americans" (50).

32. For example, Immanuel Wallerstein notes the dual use of ideologies of universalism underlying not only human rights as a form of international law, but science communities and principles of citizenship within sovereign states as well: "[I]t is precisely because there is in reality a hierarchy of states within the interstate system and a hierarchy of citizens within each sovereign state that the ideology of universalism matters. It serves on the one hand as a palliative and a deception and on the other as a political counterweight which the weak can use and do use against the strong" (171).

33. Rey Chow also notes that human freedoms are themselves contingent. Freedom of the press, she writes in regard to American coverage of Tiananmen Square, is not "a basic existential condition to which all are entitled (though this is the claim that is made) but a network of demands, negotiations, and coercions that are themselves bound by historical determinants constructed on slaughter and bloodshed" (85).

34. The film reinforces the representation of the individual-as-collective in its depiction of the moment Aung San Suu Kyi single-handedly stands down a line of government soldiers during a mass demonstration.

35. The phrase is Enloe's. See also Heng and Devan, Peterson, and West.

36. See, for example Wendy Brown's exploration of the limitations of Catharine MacKinnon's theory of sexuality as the eroticization of gender inequality. MacKinnon's concept of gender, she suggests, forecloses prospects for radical social change if there is no agency for subjects seemingly wholly constituted by dominant power. Brown's comments are suggestive for Asian American coalitional democratic participation, but such an inquiry is beyond the scope of this essay.

37. Leslie Bow, "Betrayal and Other Acts of Subversion: Feminism, Sexual Politics, Asian American Women's Literature." Unpublished manuscript.

38. See, for example, Campomanes. His positioning of Filipino American literature as exilic literature may blur an important distinction between the political statuses of the exile and the émigré. As Edward Said notes (1984), immigration suggests the possibility of choice rather than banishment. Said, however, does not go further to stress political exile as a condition of banishment as a punishment enforced by the threat of violence where return is rendered impossible. For example, Wendy Law-Yone's stakes in representing false charges of conspiracy against

the state are linked to her condition of exile. In addition to witnessing her father's detention and his subsequent participation in former Prime Minister U Nu's government in exile, she herself was held at secret-police headquarters in Rangoon in the late sixties after trying to leave the country illegally to meet her American husband, an act she recognized as "defiance amounting to treason" (1994, 41). Moreover, Campomanes's distinction may also unwittingly imply that immigrant literature is characterized by an uncomplicated relationship to national culture.

39. Few reviews discuss Singapore's political climate. Although Howard Coale's review opens by acknowledging governmental repression, calling Singapore "a Stepford country" and an "Asian version of 1984," he validates the fact that the novel "manages to avoid being overtly political." See also Baras and Christine Bell, "In Times of Trouble: A Search for Identity," *Los Angeles Times,* January 28, 1992, E6.

40. The *New York Times* estimates the number at fifteen thousand. Many Karen remain in Thailand fearing harsh treatment upon repatriation, but their welcome is increasingly strained as Thailand seeks business opportunities with Myanmar (BBC Summary of World Broadcasts, May 8, 1995, and May 13, 1995). Despite fears that the Thai government would reverse its twenty-year policy of granting haven to Karen refugees, Thailand agreed not to force repatriation of 2,300 unarmed Karen. See Seth Mydans, "In Thai Camps, Fear of Burmese Troops Grows," *New York Times,* March 3, 1997, and "Thailand Says Refugees Can Stay," *New York Times,* March 4, 1997.

41. "Cabinet ministers began to exhort graduate women to marry and bear children *as a patriotic duty.* Obediently taking their cue from the government, two (nonfeminist) women's organizations accordingly proposed, in a disturbing collusion with state patriarchy, that women be *required* to bear children as a form of National Service—the equivalent, in feminine, biological terms, of the two-and-a-half year military service compulsorily performed by men for the maintenance of national defense" (Heng and Devan 348).

WORKS CITED

Allman, T. D. "The Failures of Singapore's Success." *Asia* (May–June 1983): 20–27.

Amnesty International. *Report on Torture.* London: Duckworth with Amnesty International Publications, 1973.

———. *Torture in the Eighties.* London: Amnesty International Publications, 1984.

———. *Myanmar (Burma) Prisoners of Conscience: A Chronicle of Developments since September 1988.* November 1989.

Aung-Thwin, Maureen, and Thant Myint-U. "The Burmese Ways to Socialism." *Third World Quarterly* 13:1 (1992): 67–75.

Austin, W. Timothy. "Crime and Control." In *The Management of Success: The Moulding of Modern Singapore,* ed. K. S. Sandhu and P. Wheatley. Singapore: Institute of Southeast Asian Studies, 1989. 913–27.

Baras, Jonetta Rose. "Writer Debuts in Tan Tradition." *Washington Times,* November 3, 1991, B7.

Bell, Christine. "In Times of Trouble: A Search for Identity." *Los Angeles Times,* January 28, 1992, E6.

Berlant, Lauren. *The Queen of America Goes to Washington City: Essays on Sex and Citizenship.* Durham, N.C.: Duke University Press, 1997.

Bhabha, Homi K. *The Location of Culture.* New York: Routledge, 1994.

Boulette, Teresa, and Susan Anderson. "Mind Control and the Battering of Women." *Community Mental Health Journal* 21 (1985): 109–18.

Bourne, Jenny. "Homelands of the Mind: Jewish Feminism and Identity Politics." *Race and Class* 23:1 (1987): 1–24.

Branegan, Jay. "Is Singapore a Model for the West?" *Time,* June 18, 1993, 36.

Brown, David. "Crisis and Ethnicity: Legitimacy in Plural Societies." *Third World Quarterly* 7:4 (1985): 988–1008.

Brown, Wendy. *States of Injury: Power and Freedom in Late Modernity.* Princeton, N.J.: Princeton University Press, 1995.

Butler, Judith. "Contingent Foundations: Feminism and the Question of 'Postmodernism.'" In *Feminists Theorize the Political,* ed. Judith Butler and Joan W. Scott. New York: Routledge, 1994. 3–21.

Campomanes, Oscar V. "Filipinos in the United States and Their Literature of Exile." In *Reading the Literatures of Asian America,* ed. Shirley Geok-lin Lim and Amy Ling. Philadelphia: Temple University Press, 1992. 49–78.

Cheong, Fiona. *The Scent of the Gods.* New York: W. W. Norton, 1991.

Chow, Rey. "Violence in the Other Country." In *Third World Women and the Politics of Feminism,* ed. Chandra Talpade Mohanty, Ann Russo, and Lourdes Torres. Bloomington: Indiana University Press, 1991. 81–100.

Chua Beng-Huat. "Arrested Development: Democratisation in Singapore." *Third World Quarterly* 15:4 (1994): 655–68.

Chua, C. Lok. "Constructing an Asian American Protagonist: Popular Culture, Bricolage, and Wendy Law-Yone's *Irrawaddy Tango.*" Unpublished manuscript.

Coale, Howard. "Porcelain Dreams." *New York Times,* November 24, 1991, sec. 7, 22.

Elliott, Michael. "Crime and Punishment: The Caning Debate." *Newsweek,* April 18, 1994, 18–22.

Enloe, Cynthia. *Bananas, Beaches, and Bases: Making Feminist Sense of International Politics.* Berkeley: University of California Press, 1990.

Falco, Mathea. "Don't Make a Deal." *New York Times,* July 17, 1994.

Foucault, Michel. *Discipline and Punish: The Birth of the Prison.* New York: Vintage Books, 1979.

Fredholm, Michael. *Burma: Ethnicity and Insurgency.* Westport, Conn.: Praeger, 1993.

Hall, Stuart. "The Local and the Global: Globalization and Ethnicity." In *Culture, Globalization and the World-System,* ed. Anthony P. King. London: Macmillan, 1991. 19–39.

Harlow, Barbara. *Resistance Literature.* New York: Methuen, 1987.

Heng, Geraldine. "'A Great Way to Fly': Nationalism, the State, and the Varieties of Third-World Feminism." In *Feminist Genealogies, Colonial Legacies, Democratic Futures*, ed. M. Jacqui Alexander and Chandra Talpade Mohanty. New York: Routledge, 1997. 31–45.

Heng, Geraldine, and Janadas Devan. "State Fatherhood: The Politics of Nationalism, Sexuality, and Race in Singapore." In *Nationalisms and Sexualities*, ed. Andrew Parker, Mary Russo, Doris Sommer, and Patricia Yaeger. New York: Routledge, 1992. 343–64.

Hirst, Paul, and Grahame Thompson. "Globalization and the Future of the Nation State." *Economy and Society* 24:3 (August 1995): 408–42.

Johnson, Barbara, ed. *Freedom and Interpretation: The Oxford Amnesty Lectures 1992.* New York: HarperCollins, 1993.

Jones, Ann. *Next Time, She'll Be Dead: Battering and How to Stop It.* Boston: Beacon Press, 1994.

Kandyoti, Deniz. "Identity and Its Discontents: Women and the Nation." In *Colonial Discourse and Post-Colonial Theory*, ed. Patrick Williams and Laura Chrisman. New York: Columbia University Press, 1994. 376–91.

Koshy, Susan. "The Fiction of Asian American Literature." *Yale Journal of Criticism* 9:2 (1996): 315–46.

Kreager, Philip. "Aung San Suu Kyi and the Peaceful Struggle for Human Rights in Burma." In *Freedom From Fear*, ed. Michael Aris. New York: Penguin, 1991. 284–325.

Law-Yone, Wendy. "Life in the Hills." *Atlantic* (December 1989): 24–36.

———. *Irrawaddy Tango.* New York: Knopf, 1993.

———. "The Year of the Pigeon." In *Without a Guide: Contemporary Women's Travel Adventures*, ed. Katherine Govier. Toronto: Macfarlane Walter and Ross, 1994. 41–60.

Lim, Shirley. "The English-Language Writer in Singapore." In *The Management of Success: The Moulding of Modern Singapore*, ed. K. S. Sandhu and P. Wheatley. Singapore: Institute of Southeast Asian Studies, 1989. 523–43.

Lowe, Lisa. *Immigrant Acts: On Asian American Cultural Politics.* Durham, N.C.: Duke University Press, 1996.

Miyoshi, Masao. "A Borderless World? From Colonialism to Transnationalism and the Decline of the Nation-State." *Critical Inquiry* 19 (summer 1993): 726–51.

Ong, Aiwah. "Colonialism and Modernity: Feminist Re-presentations of Women in Non-Western Societies." In *Inscriptions.* Santa Cruz: University of California, Santa Cruz, Center for Cultural Studies, 1989. 79–93.

Peterson, V. Spike. "The Politics of Identity and Gendered Nationalism." In *Foreign Policy Analysis: Contiguity and Change in Its Second Generation*, ed. Laura Neack, Jeanne A. K. Hey, and Patrick Haney. Englewood Cliffs, N.J.: Prentice Hall, 1995. 167–86.

Qadir, Shahid, Christopher Clapham, and Barry Gills. "Sustainable Democracy: Formalism vs. Substance." *Third World Quarterly* 14:3 (1993): 415–22.

Reuter, Peter. "Myanmar's Drug Habit." *New York Times*, April 3, 1995.

Romero, Mary. "A Comparison between Strategies Used on Prisoners of War and Battered Wives." *Sex Roles* 13:9–10 (1985): 537–47.

Rorty, Richard. "Justice as a Larger Loyalty." In *Cosmopolitics: Thinking and Feeling beyond the Nation,* ed. Pheng Cheah and Bruce Robbins. Minneapolis: University of Minnesota Press, 1997. 45–58.

Russell, Diana. *Rape in Marriage.* New York: Macmillan, 1982.

Said, Edward. "The Mind of Winter: Reflections on Life in Exile." *Harpers* (September 1984): 49–55.

————. "Nationalism, Human Rights, and Interpretation." In *Freedom and Interpretation: The Oxford Amnesty Lectures 1992,* ed. Barbara Johnson. New York: HarperCollins, 1993. 175–205.

Scarry, Elaine. *The Body in Pain: The Making and Unmaking of the World.* New York: Oxford University Press, 1985.

Sesser, Stan. "A Rich Country Gone Wrong." *New Yorker,* October 9, 1989, 55–96.

Silverstein, Josef. *Burmese Politics: The Dilemma of National Unity.* New Brunswick, N.J.: Rutgers University Press, 1980.

Stanley, Alessandra. "Burma: Junior Rambos." *Time,* June 18, 1990, 41.

Tifft, Larry L. *Battering of Women: The Failure of Intervention and the Case for Prevention.* Boulder, Colo.: Westview Press, 1993.

Trescott, Jacqueline. "Tango of Emotions: In Wendy Law-Yone's Fiction, a Revelation of Dreams." *Washington Post,* March 16, 1994, C1.

Wade, Robert. "Globalization and Its Limits: Reports of the Death of the National Economy Are Greatly Exaggerated." In *National Diversity and Global Capitalism,* ed. Suzanne Berger and Ronald Dore. Ithaca, N.Y.: Cornell University Press, 1996. 60–88.

Walker, Lenore E. *The Battered Woman.* New York: HarperPerennial, 1979.

Wallerstein, Immanuel. *Geopolitics and Geoculture: Essays on the Changing World-System.* Cambridge: Cambridge University Press, 1991.

Weiss, Linda. "Globalization and the Myth of the Powerless State." *New Left Review* 225 (1997): 3–27.

West, Lois. "Feminist Nationalist Social Movements: Beyond Universalism and Towards a Gendered Cultural Relativism." *Women's Studies International* 15:5–6 (1992): 563–79.

Wong, Sau-ling. "Denationalization Reconsidered: Asian American Cultural Criticism at a Theoretical Crossroads." *Amerasia Journal* 21:1–2 (1995): 1–27.

Wong, Shelley Sunn. "Unnaming the Same: Theresa Hak Kyung Cha's Dictee." In *Writing Self, Writing Nation: A Collection of Essays on Dictee,* ed. Elaine H. Kim and Norma Alarcón. Berkeley: Third Woman Press, 1994. 103–40.

Woolf, Virginia. *Three Guineas.* London: Hogarth Press, 1938.

Yearbook of the United Nations 1948–49. Lake Success, N.Y.: United Nations/Department of Public Information.

Can the Settler Speak? Appropriating Subaltern Silence in Janet Frame's *The Carpathians*

Penelope Ingram

The questions of whether a subaltern[1]—or, indeed, for the sake of argument, any formerly colonized subject—can recover a "lost origin," of whether she or he is silent or has a voice, and of whether she or he is placed or displaced by recuperative historiographies and narratives not only relate to the "native," the so-called Third World Other, but are also of particular concern to "settlers," the white inhabitants of those countries, such as Australia, Canada, and New Zealand, which Alan Lawson has called, however problematically, the "Second World." At issue for both "Second" and Third World is the *possibility*, it would seem, of the recovery of an autochthonous tradition and culture.[2] Although the feasibility of this recovery may seem slightly greater in the case of some Third World countries (though by no means all, and surely even those possessing what would seem to be an easily definable indigenous population, such as the case of the Indians in India, must no doubt encounter competing claims of belonging, be they ones of language, caste, or religion, between different cultural groups), it would appear a virtual impossibility for the countries of Lawson's Second World, whose settlers' claims to autochthony must be always already usurped by the *actuality* of the already/still-resident indigenous population, who are themselves in the process of attempting their own cultural recuperations.

In the case of either the native or the settler, perhaps the most immediate concern is whether or not a "lost origin" or an "authentic" voice is indeed recoverable. The first part of this essay will examine the question of the subaltern's silence or voice. Is there a position outside the history of colonization where the native exists in absolute difference, as the truly "authentic" Other? Is this difference/authenticity, if established, recoverable? Or does any attempt at identifying a native voice (an act seemingly indistinguishable from that of retrieving an authentic voice for the native) necessarily reproduce the epistemic violence of imperialism by erecting an ideal voice and full subjectivity in the place of an always already silenced one? Is any attempt at a recovery of, or even simply a belief in, an authentic origin again merely an ascription of false presence onto a fundamentally uninscribable, hence essentially unknowable, subaltern? Or can the subaltern's "voice" paradoxically be heard only in his or her silence? In sum, is the space that the subaltern is said to inhabit, and/or that she or he may seek to recover, a space of erasure or one of resistance?

In order to further explore these questions in relation to settler cultures' quests for indigeneity, in the second part of the essay I will examine a novel, *The Carpathians*, by the New Zealand author Janet Frame. In my reading of that novel I will demonstrate how the silence of the Maori subalterns enables the production of an "indigenous" voice for the settler, a voice that is unsignifiable and untranslatable, one that would seem to emerge from that very place of undecidability where the "real" subaltern's silence is lodged. In Frame's text, then, it is not the subaltern or the native who recovers a voice, or indeed a "lost origin," out of indeterminate silence, but the settler.

I

I have suggested that there is something compatible between the act of recovering the voice of the subaltern and indeed that of recovering or discovering a "lost origin." These two concepts—insofar as the subaltern comes to represent the trace—have become entangled through Derridean deconstruction where origin relates to the deconstruction of the metaphysics of presence through the example of the *différance* of the sign. However, in postcolonial discourse, though the terms *origin* and *trace* clearly derive from Gayatri Chakravorty Spivak's deconstructivist framework, they take on a meaning more politically concrete whereby the trace refers to the voice of the subaltern and origin becomes part of a discourse of national and cultural identity. Thus, in spite of a deconstructive vocabulary, such postcolonial discourse can in fact be seen to reproduce certain metaphysical conceits. Before I examine the specific debates about voice and origin that have arisen in relation to the subaltern subject, however, I will explore the relationship between voice and origin with regard to the precarious positionality of the settler, a precariousness that is duly acknowledged in Simon During's description of the postcolonial settler subject as the "post-colonizer" (126).

There is, I would argue, a distinct, albeit problematic, connection in settler texts between the recovery of a "lost origin" and the recovery of the voice of the subaltern. The relationship between the two acts reveals itself in many settler texts where the act of recovering the voice of the subaltern becomes inseparable from the act of making the subaltern speak, or indeed speaking for the subaltern, in order that the settler might establish his or her *own* relation to origin. Indeed, it is precisely this connection between the subaltern's voice and what I would see as the settler's "nostalgia for lost origins" (Spivak 1988, 307) that enables a new interpretation of the current debate around the question of the appropriation of voice or, as Linda Alcoff phrases it, "The Problem of Speaking for Others."[3]

The issue central to this debate concerns the practice of people with privilege speaking for those without and initially appears to rest on the question as to whether minority or indigenous groups have the right to make and disseminate their own representations of self and culture. Ultimately, however, this question becomes reinflected to that of whether or not indigenous groups and minorities have this right solely. In Canada, specifically, what this reinflection reveals is that what was originally a debate about racism and the appropriation of Native culture in white texts has become one in which whites accuse Native peoples and other minorities of attempting to impose censorship and restrict white freedom of speech.[4] Indeed, the original debate gets altered further by those critics who hail, affirmingly, the act of speaking for or as a Native person as a "literary strategy." In the case of the work of Diana Brydon, for example, cultural appropriation in white texts—what she calls "creole texts"—can be read as an attempt at achieving a "new globalism" that would seem to overcome the "problem" of difference by absorbing it, "seek[ing] a way to cooperate without cooption, a way to define differences that do not depend on myths of cultural purity or authenticity but that thrive on an interaction that 'contaminates' without homogenising" (196). What Brydon fails to address, however, is that these "creole texts" are, by her definition, authored by whites and not natives. (A text written by a native is always a native text; unlike whites who can "go native," native writers do not usually get the opportunity—and if they do, it is seldom sanctioned—

to "play" at being white.)[5] Thus, this "new globalism" with its overarching imperative "to define differences" only operates in one direction. Brydon's "strategy" of "contamination" is a literary strategy for white authors only and therefore reveals itself as nothing other than an attempt to improve the white literary gene pool, to add a touch of so-called native color to a culture that is desperate for an indigenous identity. It becomes apparent, therefore, that even in Brydon's seemingly sociopolitical assessment of such texts—texts that she claims are offered as an escape from the "impasse of the endless play of post-modernist difference" (ibid.)—the question of the appropriation of a native voice in white literary texts would seem to be inseparable from the settler's need to establish a cultural identity. In other words, whether one seeks cultural purity or contamination, the issue for the white settler would appear to be still, in Homi Bhabha's phrase, the "location of culture."

What such reinflections signify in terms of the argument of this essay is that the debate about who speaks for whom has become subsumed under the larger problematic of cultural belonging: the question of who gets to control and *produce* the nation's mythologies. As Stephen Muecke explains vis-à-vis the Australian situation:

> Within the issue of Aboriginal sovereignty there is more at stake than the use of lands; there is the right to control the production of Australia's mythologies. Most importantly our conception of "nationhood," and it appears that Aboriginality is the commodity which is being bargained for in exchange for aboriginal land and institutional power and control. "Tell us what you are really like," say the white institutions. "Dance for us once more and sing your songs. We will say to the world that this too is our *Australian* heritage: this is the nation which can stand proud amongst others because it has a timeless history in the Aboriginal peoples." (Benterrak, Muecke, and Roe 126)

The literary practice of white peoples speaking for native peoples is of course one that is fundamentally tied to questions of power, specifically those concerning the unequal access of indigenous groups to publishers, agents, and contracts by which to secure the means of representation, and as such this practice is also intimately bound to the issue of commodification. However, it would appear that what is at stake for the settler is not merely a desire for commercial gain, but also a profound, perhaps obvious, desire for spiritual gain, and in addition for a (far less obvious) genealogical gain. White settlers can be seen to be commodifying native culture not only because (for a number of related reasons) it is profitable, but because, in the act of inscribing indigenous culture in their texts, these white settlers are attempting to write themselves into origin, to become indigenous. As Terry Goldie observes:

> In their need to become "native," to belong here, whites in Canada, New Zealand, and Australia have adopted a process which I have termed "indigenization." A peculiar word, it suggests the impossible necessity of becoming indigenous. For many writers, the only chance for indigenization seemed to be through writing about the humans who are truly indigenous, the Indians, Inuit, Maori, and Aborigines. (13)

It would appear, then, that recovering the subaltern voice or making the subaltern speak is realized in white texts by writing for, or even—perhaps especially—as, the Other.

Obviously, neither the settlers' efforts at "indigenization" nor their attempts at naturalizing an imposed relation to the land and hence to origin are a late-twentieth-century phenomenon, as the idealization of the "primitive" or "noble savage" was a common practice in the literature of several First World countries in the Romantic era, and the use of the primitive as Other was arguably the trope par excellence of many modernist texts. But there is and was a specificity as to the way in which the white settler constructed in writing (as well as in other forms of representation) his or her relation to the New World, one that invariably involved depicting an *original* relationship to the land. Apropos of the South African situation, J. M. Coetzee explains that, "In the early, patriotic phase of Afrikaans poetry, in the first decades of this century, the task was explicitly laid upon the writer to find evidences of a 'natural' bond between *volk* and *land,* that is to say, to naturalize the *volk*'s possession of the land" (61). Margaret Atwood makes a similar claim about Canada: "the Canadian poet's task was to come to terms with the ancient spirit— that is, the Native spirit—of the land whites had not yet claimed at a deep emotional level" (59). The "not yet" of Atwood's sentence would appear to be the key phrase here, for it signifies the settler's belief in the *possibility* of becoming indigenous. John Newlove's 1968 poem "The Pride," quoted by Atwood, demonstrates how an attempt to naturalize a white relationship to the land through a becoming-Other is effected, here, through a physical decomposition of the Indian into the land: "dry bones a part / of the dust in our eyes . . . in / our breath, in our / ears, in our mouths /

in our bodies entire, in our minds, until/ at last / we become them / . . .
and they / become our true forebears, moulded / by the same wind or
rain / in this land we / are their people, come / back to life again"
(Atwood 59). Thus, the white settler not only usurps the place of the
extinct, "authentic" Indian, but actually becomes the Indian by osmosis.
The Indian presence remains as "forebear" but, crucially, as the forebear
of the settler-cum-Indian, thereby naturalizing, through a manufactured
genealogy, the settler's claim to the land. The settler in the poem does
not, however, become a "real" Indian, that is, the colonized, acculturated,
"modernized" (read inauthentic) Indian, but rather, as "we / are their
people, *come / back to life again*," the settler becomes the mythical, precolonial, authentic Indian. In other words, the settler achieves the impossible—the return to, or reclamation of, an authenticity and origin indigenous to someone else, one to which even the indigene is unable to return.

A fundamental paradox thus lies at the heart of the settler's desire
to become indigenous. The original relationship that the settler seeks
with the land becomes expressed as a desire to recover an authentic,
prelapsarian, precolonial, autochthonous culture. The settler associates
this mythical originariness with the indigene; thus, the indigene is
employed in this type of settler text (not the indigene's culture, but the
figure of an indigene pasted onto the imagined culture created in the settler's mind) because the indigene is thought to embody the supposed
authenticity of this precolonial time. The problem, of course, is that such
an indigene, and indeed such a culture, no longer exist because of colonization, and yet, paradoxically, it is precisely because of colonization—
the extended historical and physical presence of the white settler in the
country—that the white settler feels implicated in this quest for origin;
which is to say that the settler sees this lost authenticity as his or her origin (as part of the history of the *settler*'s country, conveniently forgetting
his or her own role in that history) and thus asserts his or her claim to it.
The irony, however, is that this authentic, precolonial origin is always
already obliterated precisely because of the settler's very presence on, if
never quite *in*, the land; for, as Kwame Anthony Appiah asserts in terms of
the African situation: "we are all already contaminated by each other . . .
there is no longer a fully autochthonous *echt*-African culture awaiting
salvage" (354).

In summary, it would appear that in settler texts the question of
speaking or writing *for* the Other has become inseparable from the act of
speaking or writing *as* the Other, precisely because the settler attempts

through the act of speaking or writing for/as Other to become indigenous, to write himself or herself *into* origin. This act would seem to be, at the very least, not just inappropriate but also impossible, for how can a settler attempt to create a relationship of origin to the land when that origin is always already tied to, indeed part of, someone else? At the same time, however, it would appear that the very concept of a lost, authentic origin recoverable by either settler or native is in itself doubtful. As Stuart Hall, in theorizing a subject who rather than seeking an identity in the past experiences his or her identity as one in process, argues:

> Cultural identity . . . is a matter of "becoming" as well as of "being." It belongs to the future as much as to the past. It is not something which already exists, transcending place, time, history and culture. . . . Far from being eternally fixed in some essentialised past, [cultural identities] are subject to the continuous "play" of history, culture and power. Far from being grounded in a mere "recovery" of the past, which is waiting to be found, and which, when found, will secure our sense of ourselves into eternity, identities are the names we give to the different ways we are positioned by, and position ourselves within, the narratives of the past. (112)

Clearly, it would appear futile for either the settler or the native to attempt to recover something from the past that—in the case of the settler, even if she or he could lay claim to it—does not exist. An originary cultural identity can never be located because it is always already changing and subject to change.

However, if we remain within a postcolonial paradigm that presumes the existence of a "lost origin" but one that can never be recovered, the settler, it can be argued, might still believe himself or herself to be at a cultural disadvantage; which is to say that, in the eyes of the settler, the native and the settler have an uneven relationship to this "lost origin," for though neither can recover it, the native, unlike the settler, may still bear the historical trace of its presence—even if only as absence. The fact that the accessibility of a recuperable, authentic origin has been called into question certainly makes the settler's project to *recover* his or her origin problematic, but it does not radically alter his or her perceived need to *establish a connection* of past belonging.

In referring to the native as bearing the absent trace of a lost origin that is unrecoverable, I am invoking the work of Gayatri Chakravorty Spivak, specifically her theory of the silent subaltern. The next part of this

essay will discuss Spivak's position and the challenge offered to it by
Benita Parry. After discussing whether or not the subaltern actually can
speak—an issue that, as I have outlined, is inseparable from, in Spivak's
phrase, a "nostalgia for lost origins"—I will be reinflecting Spivak's subaltern theory with regard to the stance she takes in her essay "Three
Women's Texts and a Critique of Imperialism" in order to proffer a new
way of reading the appropriation of voice and native culture in settler
texts, using Frame's *Carpathians* as exemplum. The settler subject position
that I identify in texts such as Frame's is different from that generated by
white settler "indigenization" theorized by critics such as Goldie, and
indeed is not sufficiently accounted for in either position taken by those
entering the debate about "speaking for/as the Other"; it is addressed
neither in a stance such as Parry's, which attempts to "hear the voice of
the subaltern," nor indeed in Spivak's exhortation to "acknowledge the
silence of the subaltern." Rather, the major trope that I identify in contemporary settler texts such as *The Carpathians* is the—seemingly at first
glance nonadvantageous—desire to *appropriate the silence* of the subaltern.

In her influential essay "Can the Subaltern Speak?" Spivak asserts
that the success of the imperial "project to constitute the colonial subject
as Other" was dependent on effecting "the asymmetrical obliteration of
the trace of that Other in its precarious Subject-ivity" (280–81), for, "in
the constitution of that Other of Europe, great care was taken to obliter-
ate the textual ingredients with which such an object could cathect, could
occupy (invest?) its itinerary" (280).[6] For Spivak, the native who is the
subject of imperial and colonial historiography is Europe's "self-consolidating Other" standing in for the "real" native, subaltern, the trace of
whose presence (presence itself being perhaps only a trace, neither
"pure" nor "real," as Spivak is quick to highlight the Subaltern Studies
Group's attempts to deconstruct the "metaphysics of consciousness" by
assigning it a negative rather than a positive value),[7] in the process of textualization, has been displaced, has been silenced, entirely.

Benita Parry questions Spivak's assigning of absolute silence to the
native, arguing that the voice of the native, and especially the native
woman, can be located at "those sites where women inscribed themselves
as healers, ascetics, singers of sacred songs, artizans and artists" (35). For
Parry, Spivak's ascription of silence to the subaltern actually *reproduces* the
erasure of the native's subjectivity and voice that Spivak identifies in the
narratives of imperialism by dismissing the "evidence of native agency"
(ibid.) and thus "deny[ing] to the native the ground from which to utter

a reply to imperialism's ideological aggression or to enunciate a different self" (36). For Spivak, however, because "it is only the texts of counter-insurgency or élite documentation that give us the news of the consciousness of the subaltern . . . the subaltern's view, will, presence, can be no more than a theoretical fiction to entitle the project of reading. It cannot be recovered" (DH 203–4).

Spivak applies Lyotard's notion of the *différend*—a term used to define a situation in which there is no possibility of adjudicating or bridging the distance between two parties, phrases, or genres in dispute—to the subaltern utterance, asserting that the voice of the subaltern is a silent one not because it does not exist but because it is inherently untranslatable.[8] Therefore, the kinds of production that seem attributable to the subaltern in imperialist texts, the cultural utterances of the kind that Parry suggests, do not issue unmediated from the subaltern *precisely because* we can read or interpret them. In other words, such utterances have already been translated or converted into an idiom intelligible to us, thus operating through identification rather than difference, even if the translator's presence is obscured: "the first-world intellectual masquerading as the absent nonrepresenter who lets the oppressed speak for themselves" (CSS 292). The voice of the subaltern exists for us, then, always already through another's (a self's) voice, in others' narratives, and as such "is never fully recoverable, . . . is always askew from its received signifiers . . . is effaced even as it is disclosed, . . . is irreducibly discursive" (DH 203). Thus, it is only a representation of the voice of the subaltern and not the "real" voice that we can detect in the sort of cultural productions Parry proffers, and even, as Spivak cautions, in subaltern historiographies. The "real" voice itself can only exist under erasure, in displacement, in silence. To attempt to make the subaltern speak, or uncover narratives where she or he has spoken, merely contributes again to his or her construction. Thus, for Spivak, the voice or subjectivity of the subaltern can be detected only as an "inaccessible blankness circumscribed by an interpretable text" (CSS 294), a presence represented only by absence.

Whether we view the native as Parry does as an independent agent, as a "historical subject and combatant, possessor of an-other knowledge and producer of alternative traditions" (34), or agree with Spivak that "all such clear-cut nostalgias for lost origins are suspect, especially as grounds for counterhegemonic ideological production" (CSS 307), we can understand better how these issues relate to the question of the white appropriation of native voice and culture by examining the ambiguous

positionality of those who are both complicit in and products of the
"axiomatics of imperialism," the white Creoles and settlers.[9] Indeed, we
can further explore both Spivak's and Parry's positions by turning to their
discussion of the Creole in Jean Rhys's *Wide Sargasso Sea*. In so doing, we
can apprehend how Spivak's redeployment of her theory of subaltern
silence comes to bear on my reading of Janet Frame's novel.

In discussing Charlotte Brontë's novel *Jane Eyre* in her essay "Three
Women's Texts and a Critique of Imperialism," Spivak, it would appear,
alters the position she had adopted in "Can the Subaltern Speak?" by
"recasting" the role of the silent subaltern to include the white Creole,
Bertha Mason.[10] In justifying what is, according to Spivak, perceived to be
a reading privileging Bertha at Jane's expense to those U.S. feminists who
possess what she considers "a basically isolationist admiration for the literature of the female subject" (TWT 262)—in other words, to those feminists who are predisposed to sympathize with the plight of Jane (TWT
263)—Spivak exhorts us not to participate in Caliban's erasure by mistak-
ing our role, as Jane/Ariel (because we are women and oppressed), for
the doubly oppressed Bertha/Caliban (the female subaltern), as "claiming to be Caliban legitimizes the very individualism that we must persis-
tently attempt to undermine from within" (TWT 264). Thus, according to
Spivak, to "wrench oneself away from the mesmerizing focus of the 'subject-constitution' of the female individualist" (ibid.) necessitates from the
beginning a reading of Bertha, the white Creole, as the Caliban to Jane's
Ariel. In other words, it requires us to acknowledge that Jane's "subject-
constitution" is itself reliant upon a subjugation of Bertha, the "native
female" who "is excluded from any share in this emerging norm" (ibid.).
However, Spivak, for her part, ignores the possibility that Bertha, the
white Creole, may have developed her own "subject-constitution" at the
expense of the "real" native female. Thus, by assigning the position of
Ariel to Jane and Caliban to Bertha, Spivak negates the possibility of a
reading where Bertha is Ariel with a "so-called privilege" (ibid.) to
unlearn vis-à-vis her relation to—in the text of *Jane Eyre*—a literally "inac-
cessibly blank," "native" Caliban. The arbitrary recasting that Spivak performs becomes even more problematic when she reads Rhys's text, for,
having established that the white Creole, Bertha, is the Caliban figure in
Jane Eyre, a reading that she continues to maintain throughout her analysis of *Wide Sargasso Sea* despite the narrative alterations wrought by that
text's significant reinflection of the original story, Spivak is unable to
address adequately the inherent inequality of position between the creole

and the native, and thus the "real" Calibans, the black Jamaicans in Rhys's text, appear to become subjected to a further silencing by Spivak's own reading.

Indeed, it is Spivak's seemingly unproblematic placement of the white Creole in the role of silent subaltern—the Caliban position—that for Parry undermines Spivak's theory of subaltern silence altogether; for, according to Parry, in order to demonstrate that the subaltern is always silent, "Spivak assigns to Antoinette/Bertha, daughter of slave owners and heiress to a post-emancipation fortune, the role of the native female sacrificed in the cause of the subject-constitution of the European female individualist" (37) and thus disregards the clear speaking voice of the "real" native in order to consolidate her own reading of the silent subaltern: "What Spivak's strategy of reading necessarily blots out," Parry argues, "is Christophine's inscription as the native female, individual Self who defies the demands of the discriminatory discourses impinging on her person" (38). Thus, for Parry, "a black female who in [*Wide Sargasso Sea*] is most fully selved, must be reduced to the status of tangential figure, and a white Creole woman [must be by Spivak] (mis)construed as the native female produced by the axiomatics of imperialism" (ibid.).

Parry fails to see, however, that for Spivak Christophine is tangential precisely because she too is the "native female produced by the axiomatics of imperialism." Thus, Christophine's "voice" is yet further evidence of her silence, for, as Spivak cautions us: "Attempts to construct the 'Third World Woman' as a signifier remind us that the hegemonic definition of literature is itself caught within the history of imperialism" (TWT 273). Hence, whatever voice a subaltern such as Christophine possesses is always already mediated through its representation in narrative, even in *rewritings* of imperialist texts:

> Christophine is tangential to this narrative. She cannot be contained by a novel which rewrites a canonical English text within the European novelistic tradition in the interest of the white Creole rather than the native. No perspective *critical* of imperialism can turn the Other into a self, because the project of imperialism has always already historically refracted what might have been the absolutely Other into a domesticated Other that consolidates the imperialist self. (TWT 272)

It would appear that here Spivak is consistent with her position in "Can the Subaltern Speak?"—suggesting that Christophine retains her uninscribability, her "inaccessible blankness," in Rhys's text. Indeed, for Spivak, the fact that the text of the white Creole, Rhys, cannot make the subaltern speak is evidence that such a text has revealed "the limits of its own discourse in Christophine" (TWT 271). Such statements appear to accord accurately with Spivak's theory of subaltern silence. However, a slight modification is evident in "Three Women's Texts," for it would appear that, according to Spivak, Antoinette/Bertha can *also* stand in the place of "inaccessible blankness," that she too can play the part of Caliban in the imperialist narrative:

> In this fictive England, [Antoinette/Bertha] must play out her role, act out the transformation of her "self" into that fictive Other, set fire to the house and kill herself, so that Jane Eyre can become the feminist individualist heroine of British fiction. I must read this as an allegory of the general epistemic violence of imperialism, the construction of a self-immolating colonial subject for the glorification of the social mission of the colonizer. (TWT 270)

Like Christophine, then, Antoinette/Bertha is constructed for an other's self-"consolidation," and, like Spivak's paradigmatically silent subaltern, the widow who performs the act of sati, Antoinette/Bertha is constructed also as a "self-immolating colonial subject." Thus, though Spivak has acknowledged that a white Creole is "caught between the English imperialist and the black native" (TWT 269), she fails to negotiate the *specificity* of Antoinette/Bertha's subjection and thus continues to read Antoinette/Bertha as being subjected to the same degree of epistemic violence as is Christophine.

Parry is critical of Spivak's assigning the position of native subject to Antoinette/Bertha because, as a white Creole, she is positioned in relation to "a specific settler discourse, distinct from the texts of imperialism" (37). For Parry, in the text of *Wide Sargasso Sea*, the white Creole (and we can apply this observation also to the white settler in other texts) cannot be seen as the native subaltern because she has a different relationship to empire. However, Parry also denies the possibility for the subaltern, Christophine, to be read as silent. For Parry, the presence of Christophine's voice is not further evidence of her silence, as in Spivak's reading, but rather is proof of her resistance, her position as "articulate antagonist of patriarchal, settler, and imperialist law" (38), and as such, is evidence that Spivak's reading, "by demonstrating a deliberated deafness to the native voice" (39), cannot accommodate the voice of the subaltern exactly where and when it is to be heard.

In my view, however, Spivak is not mistaken in suggesting that the white Creole (and, again, I would extend this to the white settler) is also constituted by the axiomatics of imperialism and as such can be figured as the "self-consolidating Other" of Europe. Nevertheless, in making this claim, Spivak fails to maintain the distinction between the undeniably more privileged position of the white Creole and that of the so-called doubly oppressed silent subaltern. Although they may both be interpellated by the imperialist narrative, and can perhaps both be defined as a "woman from the colonies" (TWT 270), they are not and cannot be interpellated in the same way when they have inherently different relations to the center of power.

Indeed, to see both the white native, Creole, and the black native, indigene, as silent subalterns because both are "native" is to engage in a fundamental misreading of the subaltern identity. Just as Jenny Sharpe has criticized Parry for confusing the subaltern with the native elite (138–39), I would extend the same criticism to Spivak for the position she takes in "Three Women's Texts."[11] In this case, however, the conflation of native and subaltern is even more problematic because the white Creole does not merely occupy the position of elite vis-à-vis the subaltern, she occupies the position of elite in relation to those natives who *themselves* are situated as elite in relation to the subaltern. Thus, in applying her theory of the silent subaltern to the situation of the white Creole, Spivak distorts the concept of the subaltern as an "identity-in-differential" (CSS 284), as defined in difference, in opposition, to the indigenous elite, expounded in both her own work and that of the Subaltern Studies Group.

Thus, although Parry is justified in criticizing Spivak for failing to notice how Antoinette/Bertha's native subject position is inherently different from Christophine's, I would argue that Spivak mistakes this not, as Parry suggests, by reading Antoinette's silence in place of Christophine's voice, but more problematically by reading it in place of Christophine's *silence*. Spivak fails to take into account how, by according Antoinette/Bertha the uninscribable position of silence in her reading of the white Creole's text, she reproduces and further silences, beyond their places "tangential" to the imperial narrative, the subaltern positions of Christophine and Tia.

What is most striking in Spivak's essay, then, is her justification of— indeed, her positing of—a white Creole's silence in a white Creole's text.

And, though she duly cautions us "Ariel" feminists, when we attempt to see Jane as Caliban, that if "we are driven by a nostalgia for lost origins, we too run the risk of effacing the 'native' and stepping forth as 'the real Caliban,' of forgetting that he is a name in a play, an inaccessible blankness circumscribed by an interpretable text" (TWT 264), she seems unable—indeed, unwilling—to extend this analogy more suitably to the position of the white Creole or settler. For Spivak, despite this warning, it would appear that the white Creole or settler is as legitimate in his or her claim to Caliban's "inaccessible blankness," as the nonelite native subaltern herself.

In reading a white Creole's text as what could be interpreted to be an example of recuperative subaltern historiography, Spivak conflates the subject position of the white Creole/settler with the silence of the native, a conflation that (aside from the difficulties in this reading that I outlined above), I would argue, cannot actually be supported in a reading of Creole/settler texts. A difference between the subject position of the settler and the silence of the native, I will argue, can be discerned in the text of the white settler precisely at the point at which she or he expresses a desire for "symbolic identification" with the silent subaltern. According to Slavoj Zizek, symbolic identification occurs when "we identify ourselves with the other precisely at a point at which he is inimitable, at the point which eludes resemblance" (109). Thus, it is the native's silence or "inaccessible blankness," his or her very inimitability, that the settler considers "authentic" or "original" and desires to identify with. Viewed in this way, the subject position of the settler cannot be conflated with the silence of the indigene because the desire to be the Other, the silent subaltern whose presence is marked only by an absent trace, always already informs the white settler's own "native" subject position. Thus, for Spivak to preemptively assign to the settler the role of silent subaltern is to fail to see how the white settler actually reveals his or her already not silent status through the textualization of such a desire in narrative.

The issue of speaking for/as the Other—the question of the white appropriation of native voice and culture—has direct bearing, therefore, on the debate over the possibility of the recovery of an indigenous voice, a cultural authenticity, or "lost origins" engaged in by Spivak and Parry. If we view the settler's desire to become indigenous as a form of symbolic identification, occurring at the point at which the native is "inimitable," then the act of speaking for/as the Other, and indeed assuming the identity and culture of the Other, can be seen to occur not through an appropriation of presence, voice, but through an appropriation of absence, silence. If we agree with Spivak's formulation that the subaltern has a voice, though one that can never be heard, and certainly never recovered except as a silent mark, an "inaccessible blankness," and that it is the absence of the voice and not the voice itself that is able to be witnessed, we might—in an obvious departure from the lesson of deconstruction that teaches that the trace itself is the mark of the absence or loss of origin—posit this place of unsignifiability as the site of pure "consciousness" and hence of authentic origin. If we view this silence, this blankness, as the mark of authenticity and absolute alterity, because it resists colonization and/or inscription, then it can be argued that this silence represents not merely the trace of origin ("trace" here signifying absence, not presence) but the origin itself. If "origin," sought by the settler and the native alike, is unattainable because always already lost—yet the subaltern can mark its place, can represent its "inaccessible blankness," and can stand in the place of an unknowable origin—then perhaps it is precisely this mark of erasure (not what the mark may be believed to represent, but this loss, the site of silence where the truly, fully present subaltern always already unknown to us speaks an untranslatable idiom) for which the settler has become "nostalgic." In other words, perhaps the settler desires a point of difference that can never be known or inscribed, a blank trace of origin that itself is the "origin," is *différance* (if it is from there that the subaltern speaks and is subsequently silenced), an escape from the "interpretable text," the place of the autochthonous Other.

Of course, such a desire by the settler presupposes that the place of "inaccessible blankness" that Spivak accords to the subaltern has a fullness of presence that is independent of its presence as the trace of an absent voice or origin. Hence, the paradox for the settler is that the act of achieving origin and becoming "authentic" can only occur through a textualization of the site of "inaccessible blankness," yet, by inscribing this space, the settler necessarily represents that which can only be figured as unrepresentable. However, though the settler perhaps never achieves the mark of origin, because she or he is always signifying the trace, the native's textual relegation to the realm of "inaccessible blankness" brings with it the attendant side effect of enabling the settler to inscribe his or her own history in that blank space and thus, quite literally, to write out of existence altogether the native subaltern. It can be argued, therefore, that the settler's desire for an indigenous relation to origin requires the settler to become the subaltern—to adopt the presence of the necessarily absent and to signify the trace of the necessarily silent, those markers that represent the native subaltern's *origin*ality. This act is different from those of "speaking for" or "speaking as" the Other, which signify either an intention to speak on behalf of the modernized, hybridized native or to adopt the voice of the authentic, precolonial "noble savage." It is, rather, an act of appropriating silence: speaking as the silent subaltern. The settler views the silence of the subaltern as desirable because it represents a past claim to originality even as it acknowledges the erasure of that origin itself. It is thus by appropriating the native subaltern's silence that the settler attempts to become indigenous. However, by appropriating the subaltern's silence the settler attempts not to appropriate the *indigene*'s origin, but the *claim* that the indigene has to origin.

It is this distinction that defines my position in contrast to Terry Goldie's, whose term *indigenization* actually signifies a "becoming-Other," that is, a becoming Aborigine, Maori, Inuit, Native, and so on, by assuming the attributes of the indigene's person and culture. What I define as "becoming-indigene," however, is the act by which the settler creates an indigenous culture, or more properly the trace of an indigenous culture, for himself or herself through the erasure of the *indigene*'s culture. Thus, the white settler is not engaging in a form of cultural cross-dressing like Archie Belaney, the Englishman who immigrated to Canada in the early twentieth century and literally "became" the famous naturalist "Grey Owl" of the Ojibway Indians (which I acknowledge contributes to an erasure of actual indigenes too, but in a different way), but rather is becoming indigenous by removing the indigene entirely, inscribing himself or herself in the blank space that signifies the claim to a lost origin and an erstwhile authenticity, and performing a kind of textual genocide that erects the white settler in place of the indigene. The white settler thus becomes the white indigene.[12]

II

Janet Frame's *The Carpathians* is a magical-realist, apocalyptic novel that, with its multilayered frame and unreliable "imposter" narratives, actively resists summary. Nevertheless, to attempt one: the novel tells the story of a rich, middle-aged, New York woman, Mattina Brecon, who, on one of her yearly trips to "see the natives," and indeed to consume their mythologies, journeys to the town of Puamahara in New Zealand in the hope of recovering the town's legend, the "Memory Flower." Upon her arrival, a number of strange events, including a natural disaster, the "midnight rain," precipitated by the "Gravity Star," a phenomenon that causes time and distance to be altered or erased, occasion first the disappearance of language and then the removal of the inhabitants of one of the town's streets. *The Carpathians*, I will argue, can be seen not simply to participate in the colonial myth of *Terra Nullius* (the doctrine that there is no claim upon the land prior to colonization), but also, through the annihilation of indigenes and settlers alike, to literally create *Terra Nullius* as a reality; for, as I will demonstrate, if the white settler is to return to origin in this novel, the "lost origin" must bear no trace of previous habitation.

In Frame's novel, the white settler's desire to occupy the site of "inaccessible blankness," the trace of origin that has heretofore been marked by a nonrepresentable Maori presence, is depicted through the representation of the Maori people as always already "contaminated" by Pakeha (European) culture. The Maori indigenes appear in the text as paradigmatically silent subalterns; their consciousness "is never fully recoverable, . . . it is always askew from its received signifiers, indeed . . . it is effaced even as it is disclosed, . . . it is irreducibly discursive" (DH 203). Hare and Hene Hanuere have no claim to authenticity for they are as estranged from their own language as the white settlers who are learning it for the first time, as Mattina, the quintessential seeker of "lost origins," discovers:

> "I'm interested in this land, in Maharawhenua itself, in Puama-hara, the story of the land memory, the Memory Flower. I guess you know it in the Maori language."
>
> Hene looked embarrassed.
>
> "I get by with English," [Hene] said. "It's the language I've always spoken. It's the younger generation that are speaking Maori. I'm learning, you know, it's not so easy when you've been brought up Pakeha, but it's coming back. The trouble is, it's been away so long."
>
> [Hene] smiled, at ease now. "We're all changing back now. It's strange, you know. Like someone you turned out of your house years ago, and now they've come home and you're shy, and ashamed of having turned them out and you have to get to know them all over again and you're scared in case you make a mistake in front of the young ones, for the youngest ones know it all. You know it's been lonely without our language." (26)

As Mattina's frustrated search for the origin of the "authentic" Memory Flower would appear to reveal, there is no sanctioning of a "nostalgia for lost origins" in *The Carpathians.* Even in their attempts to revive their culture by leaving Kowhai Street and living "the way of life of our people" (81) on the *marae* (a traditional Maori community), there is a strong sense that these efforts by the Hanueres to re-create a Maori culture are not a return to an authenticity—which exists here but is not recuperable now as "it's been away so long"—but an acknowledgment of an attempt to negotiate their culture in this already-colonized space. As Hene says to Mattina, who is attempting to sample some "authentic Maori culture," the *marae* is "*like a small English village* without the post office, the pub and the general store" (83; emphasis added). The culturally hybrid nature of the "authentic" *marae* is further evinced in the departure of the teenage Maori after the *hangi* (a Maori celebration) who escape to town in order to find "a little excitement," and also by the "shots and the sound of police sirens from the television" brought in to amuse the younger children (87). Thus, as Marc Delrez observes: "however promising the Maoris' renewed experiment in community, . . . there is a suggestion in the name of Mattina's native friends (Hanuere is a transcription in vernacular of their own Pakeha name, January) that they themselves may still be fumbling with identity, at a very early stage in a cycle of exploration" (100).

Indeed, Frame's *Carpathians* perfectly demonstrates Spivak's thesis that all "clear-cut nostalgias for lost origins are suspect, especially as grounds for counterhegemonic ideological production" (CSS 307). But, in Frame's Puamahara, it is not only the Maori who are revealed as necessarily inauthentic, for the settlers too are revealed to be "imposters." As Dinny Wheatstone, the most obvious, but certainly not the only, imposter says: "Locked within the language of my imposture I further bind myself with every word I use. . . . Complete imposture, I repeat, leads to nothingness in which one inhabits all worlds except the world of oneself" (51).

It is Dinny, the marginalized, "nonentity" imposter—that is, Dinny, the colonized—that takes over and effectively "writes back" to the center, not in this case merely colonial Britain, but more specifically imperial New York, that is, to J. H. B. (the external frame narrator) and Mattina with their ethnographic claims to a knowledge of the Puamaharian Other.[13] Indeed, Dinny's narrative quite forcefully challenges the validity of such ethnographic knowledge production implicitly tied to nostalgias for origin or authenticity, by demonstrating that there is no pure native perspective, no such thing as a true native informant. What Dinny's narrative succeeds in doing through her "seizing of the point of view" is to undermine the idea that master narratives exist and to demonstrate that there is no "authentic" or "original" view, no absolute point of view that is not always already hybrid or syncretic. Dinny's narrative demonstrates that even a settler's narrative of resistance, her "counterhegemonic ideological production," far from demonstrating a "nostalgia for lost origins" is, rather, going to bear the trace of its "contamination" by the colonizer and his presence.

But, in spite of the appearance of "contaminated" natives and "imposter" settlers whose existence would seemingly put into question the concept of a recoverable, authentic origin, the novel, rather than simply marking the trace of origin with an "inaccessible blankness circumscribed by an interpretable text" (CSS 294), instead prefigures the inscription of that "blankness." Frame creates a phenomenon called the "Gravity Star," which enables "the natural destruction of known language. A new language, a new people, a new world; and perhaps the end of known civilization as human cognition, no longer supporting and supported by the words of the former languages" (119). Thus, in a cataclysmic event, the midnight rain, where the residents of Kowhai Street revert to what is described as a primitive, prelinguistic state, while watching the fall of all the old languages, Frame puts the process of colonization in reverse, effecting an elaborate, theatrical decolonization, or stripping, of that key colonizing tool, language:

> the residents of Kowhai Street, under the influence of the Gravity Star and the legend of the Memory Flower had each suffered a loss of all the words they had ever known, all the concepts that supported and charged the words, all the processes of thinking and feeling that once lived within the now shattered world of their words. The people of Kowhai Street had experienced the disaster of unbeing, unknowing, that accompanies death and is thought by man to *mark the beginning of a new kind of being and thought and language that, in life, is inconceivable, unknowable.* (129; emphasis added)

That which marks the "beginning of a new kind of being and thought and language that, in life, is inconceivable, unknowable" can perhaps be seen to be the trace of a lost origin that—because we can never escape the contamination of the colonial moment and its legacy "in life"—can never be recovered. In Frame's text, however, such a trace initially does appear to be recoverable by the people of Puamahara, Maori and Pakeha alike, through a process of decolonization. The curious, wordless, "primitive" state that the Puamaharians find themselves in after the midnight rain—despite the view maintained by Ashcroft, Griffiths, and Tiffin that the "syncretic and hybridized nature of post-colonial experience . . . refutes the notio[n] . . . that [there can be a] return to some 'pure' and unsullied cultural condition" (41–2)—could be interpreted as Frame's attempt, against her otherwise sophisticated efforts in Dinny's narrative, to represent the "syncretic and hybridized nature of post-colonial experience," to return the "natives" of Puamahara "to some 'pure' and unsullied cultural condition," or "mythic past," an attempt, in the words of Aijaz Ahmad, to "rehabilitate that lost but ever-present Authenticity, always in pursuit of a past that never was" (18).

Frantz Fanon has suggested that

> [t]o speak is to exist absolutely for the other. . . . To speak . . . means above all to assume a culture, to support the weight of a civilization. . . . Every colonized people in whose soul an inferiority complex has been created by the death and burial of its local cultural originality—finds itself face to face with the language of the civilizing nation; that is, with the culture of the mother country. . . . To speak a language is to take on a world, a culture. (13, 14, 29)

Consequently, by removing the language of the colonizer through the phenomenon of the Gravity Star, Frame removes the entire colonial apparatus of knowledge production and clears a space for the creation of "a new language, a new people, a new world" (119)—in other words, for the return to origin. Indeed, as Suzette Henke has asserted, this new language is akin to "a mother tongue ritually released . . . from a primitive, instinctual memory obscured by centuries of Anglocentric domination— by the white man's colonial burden and the black man's enforced subservience" (33).

However, on the threshold of becoming "pure and unsullied," the residents of Puamahara are carried away and all remnants of them are removed, an occurrence that would again appear to undermine any avowal or belief in a "mythic past" or a "lost origin." Yet, although Frame's text acknowledges the inability of those who have been colonized to return to a pure "lost origin," *The Carpathians* nevertheless represents the possibility of such a return in the figure of a noncolonizable settler woman, Decima

James. Those "natives" of Puamahara who have been colonized, who have been known—for, in this novel, "knowing people" is an ethnographic exercise and being "known" is shorthand for being the subject of such an ethnography—are exterminated because they represent the impossibility of the subaltern ever to be articulate or articulated outside of his or her colonization. Decima, however, who, more than any other Puamaharian resident, approximates the silent positionality of the subaltern because she has never been and can never be "known," because she has been placed outside the "container of knowledge" (14), who has been labeled autistic and has been shut away in the Manuka Home, and whose presence is marked in Frame's novel by what can be seen to be an "inaccessible blankness," survives.[14] The cataclysm of the Gravity Star, therefore, can be seen to enable the rewriting of the blank left by the epistemic violence of imperialism, and into this blank is written the possibility of the recovery of an autochthonous culture for the settler in the figure of the unknowable, hence uncolonizable, white indigene, Decima James.

Although Decima usually receives little or no attention in critics' readings of *The Carpathians*, a close examination of the character of Decima can enable a reading of the issue of the white appropriation of native voice and culture hitherto unexamined in postcolonial criticism.[15] Decima, who has always lived in a world without language, is the key to Puamahara's survival, for, as Fanon reminds us: "To speak is to exist absolutely for the other." Dinny's foreshadowing of events has in effect prepared us for the instrumental role that Decima will play, predicting even before the onslaught of the midnight rain: "It's a world without words until we have suffered or experienced the transition" (123). Decima, unlike the others, is not known: as her mother says, "Nobody knows her. She's new" (106). Decima's linguistic isolation, her "new"-ness, makes her, just as their own does for a moment to the altered residents of Kowhai Street, entirely uncolonizable: "'Her language,' Gloria said, 'is all her own. She's one person alone in her own country, ruling it and ruled by it, and her own country has its own landscape and other features, and none of us can ever visit it'" (107). Such sovereignty occurs because Decima has her own language, she has resisted in Fanon's terms the "language of the civilizing nation." This sovereign language, I would argue, is precisely the type of language that the settler requires in order to manufacture his or her indigenous relationship to the landscape and hence to origin. As J. M. Coetzee explains vis-à-vis the South African situation:

> This landscape remains alien, impenetrable, until a language is found in which to win it, speak it, represent it . . . a language to fit Africa, a language that will be authentically African. Of course there exist plenty of authentically African languages, languages indigenous to the subcontinent. But their authenticity is not necessarily the right authenticity. . . . Is there a language in which people of European identity, or if not of European identity then of a highly problematical South African-colonial identity, can speak to Africa and be spoken to by Africa? (7–8)

A language created by a "settler-indigene" would presumably never be subject to colonization, it could never be inscribed. And just like the now-vanished residents of Kowhai Street who have no "words of any recognisable language . . . *like the first cries of those who had never known or spoken words*" (126; emphasis added), Decima resists inscription. She is "brand-new." But, unlike the others, she has never been known, and her unsignifiability is what ensures her survival.

> "And she has no words. No word from her, not a word." . . .
>
> "But she has no words to give," Joseph said to Mattina. "She has no spoken language except for a few cries, chortles, laughter, other sounds in her throat." . . .
>
> "She is teenaged now, and she has never spoken to us, no-one knows what's in her mind, she's as new to us and others as the day she was born. Nobody knows her. She's *new* and look at us, being used up faster and faster each day with all our words coming out and being spoken again and again. And look at her. Brand new." (106)

Decima is "new," because she has never been colonized; she cannot be known. Thus, though Spivak asserts that "[f]or the 'true' subaltern group, whose identity is its difference, there is no unrepresentable subaltern subject that can know and speak itself" (CSS 285), Frame has created one in the white settler Decima James.

In *The Carpathians*, then, Decima holds the promise of the silent, hence authentic, subaltern/indigene. According to Jake, "People such as Decima . . . would always be like special touchstones, gauges set with diamonds, to measure human possibilities and impossibilities, fountain-sources where the supposed strong could replenish their strength of being" (185). Up until now Puamahara's fountain-source has been a Maori myth: the legend of the Memory Flower. The legend tells the story of the Maori Girl storyteller: "a young woman, chosen by the gods as col-lector of the memory of her land" who one day mysteriously "vanished and in her place a tree grew" (11). Thus, up until the moment of decolo-nization, the occasion of the midnight rain, just as in Spivak's theory, the "authentic" Maori subaltern is silent, the story gone, with only a trace/tree remaining to mark her silence; the Maori Girl's self or consciousness, her "presence," had been an "inaccessible blankness circumscribed by [the] interpretable text" (CSS 294) of her legend. Here, as Decima becomes the fountain-source, the one who, in Jake's words "will never be *spoken for*" (185), it can be argued (contrary to Jeanne Delbaere, who, though perhaps correctly identifying the Maori legend as a version of the Daphne myth, reads Mattina and not Decima "as a twentieth-century ver-sion of the Maori Girl in the legend of the Memory Flower" [204]) that Decima replaces the Maori Girl by inscribing the Maori subaltern's blank-ness with her own equally unsignifiable text, and thus becomes herself the authentic Puamaharian indigene.

Frame's text, therefore, removes the original silent subaltern pres-ence, a presence that, according to Spivak's analysis, destabilizes and threatens the discursive power of the imperialist, and indeed colonialist, narrative because it cannot be textualized. The space of "inaccessible blankness," which has rendered an "original," "authentic," indigenous presence resistant to incorporation into a settler/imperial fantasy of belonging, is thus inscribed, in this postcolonial text, by precisely that fantasy.

Rey Chow cautions that "by 'resurrecting' the victimized voice/self of the native with our readings . . . we step, far too quickly, into the other-wise silent and invisible place of the native and turn ourselves into living agents/witnesses for her. This process, in which *we* become visible, also neutralizes the untranslatability of the native's experience and the history of that untranslatability" (37–38).[16] In the case of Frame's *The Carpathians*, however, the white settler desires not to bear witness for the native in order to make the settler visible—though this occurs, of course, in the act of ascribing a fullness of presence to that which can only be signified as absence—nor even, it would seem, to make the subaltern speak; rather, the settler desires to be invisible and untranslatable like the native because this untranslatability, this "inaccessible blankness," has become the desirable subject position—an indeterminate, "authentic" marker of alterity that has come to signify origin for the settler. Decima does not "neutralize" the native's untranslatability, then, she appropriates it; she does not aim to *speak for* the untranslatable native, but rather strives to speak (to not speak) *as* the untranslatable native. For the settler, silence does not signify a lack of voice; rather, it signifies an inability to be "spoken for," to be inscribed. Silence or uninscribability thus represents to the settler the possibility of existing outside of all representation, of being the mark of the wholly Other—authentic, autochthonous.

Decima, however, is already unsignifiable, as we have seen. Prior to the midnight rain, though, her blankness or silence did not, as indeed it had done for the Maori Girl, symbolize her displacement from/as origin. Decima was merely unsignifiable; she did not represent the kind of unsignifiability that bears the trace, in silence, of presence. Thus, whereas the Maori Girl's absence had stood in place of an unrecoverable, "authentic" presence, Decima's absence, her silence, which saw her relegated to the Manuka Home, was an absolute void. Before the midnight rain, her silence signified nothing. Now, through an eradication of an original presence marked by an absent trace, the Maori and their legends, Frame enables Decima's silence to appropriate the absent referent of indigenous presence. Just as the Maori Girl "released the memory of the land when she picked and tasted the ripe fruit" and "tasted yesterday within the tomorrow" (11), so too does Decima, having reinscribed the blank left by the silence of the subaltern, establish a "yesterday within the tomorrow" for the white settler who is desperate for his or her own memory of the land, his or her own origin. Thus, in a novel of fantastical substitutions of near and far, and past and future, the "land memory" that the Hanueres have lost and Mattina seeks is found through Decima, whose resistance to both signification and colonization creates the possibility of settler autochthony.

Decima's nonlanguage is offered, then, as the new language, indigenous to a place and a people that will be uncolonizable. Frame attempts through Decima, so often referred to as the Jameses' "burden" (73), to manufacture that "weight of centuries of knowing" that has been "carried out of our reach" (14). The knowledge of a settler's originary belonging to the land.

What my reading of Frame's *The Carpathians* finally demonstrates is that even when no attempt is made to appropriate the native voice, to "speak for" or "speak as" the Other, there is still a risk that, when the silence of the subaltern is acknowledged, that very silence itself might be appropriated. It would appear that, in their efforts to respect the untouchable, and indeed untextualizable, space of subaltern silence, postcolonial writers and critics may be tempted to reinscribe that "inaccessible blankness" with their own history of origin, their own autochthony. In a world where "woman," "Third World Woman," "native," and "indigene" have become the signifiers par excellence of a First World discourse seeking legitimization through that which it perceives as the only incontestable means for obtaining it, Otherness, it is hardly surprising—indeed, unfortunately, perhaps all too predictable—that the project of First (or, in this case, "Second") World legitimization should continue even when that Otherness has become, in the case of the subaltern's silence, mere blankness.

NOTES

This essay is excerpted from my doctoral dissertation, "Becoming-Woman: 'Difference Feminism' and the Race for the Other" (University of New South Wales, 1998). I would like to thank Deep Bisla for reading and commenting on drafts of this essay.

1. Although the Subaltern Studies Group borrows the term *subaltern* from Gramsci and uses it specifically to connote the nonelite native, this specificity, as the ensuing discussion will demonstrate, is often blurred or effaced when it is adopted by other critics. I use the term *subaltern* in the initial part of this essay in order to acknowledge the fact that the debate around silence and the recovery of "lost origins" is one that initially arose vis-à-vis the subaltern qua subaltern, but at the same time, by discussing this debate in relation to the problematics of establishing/recovering an origin or voice for the settler, I am also deliberately misusing the term, in order to problematize its use in the discourse of those who endeavor to theorize a specific national, cultural identity and voice for the settler.

2. There are of course postcolonial theorists who reject altogether the notion of a "lost origin," recoverable or otherwise. For theorists such as Stuart Hall, Paul Gilroy, and Édouard Glissant, postcolonial subjects can be seen to be concerned less with the recovery of a phantom authenticity than with negotiating and articulating a hybrid identity and/or an identity in process. Although such theorists have clearly moved beyond the restrictions of a rigid self/other colonial paradigm, as my reading of Frame will demonstrate, this binary is still very much in evidence in settler–indigene relations.

3. See also Margery Fee, "Why C. K. Stead Didn't Like Keri Hulme's *The Bone People*: Who Can Write as Other?"

4. See Lenore Keeshig-Tobias, "The Magic of Others"; Marlene Nourbese Philip, "The Disappearing Debate: Racism and Censorship"; and Lee Maracle, "Native Myths: Trickster Alive and Crowing."

5. When a person of color "passes" as white she or he is not engaging in a form of "play" but rather in a serious, even dangerous, endeavor usually fraught with the constant fear of disclosure.

6. Subsequent references to "Can the Subaltern Speak?" are taken from the 1988 version and will be abbreviated in the text as CSS.

7. See Spivak, "Subaltern Studies: Deconstructing Historiography" (203), hereafter abbreviated in the text as DH.

8. See Jean-François Lyotard, *The Differend: Phrases in Dispute.*

9. I make the comparison between the white settler and the white Creole here and throughout not because I consider them to be the same thing, but because—as the Rochester character's perception of the ambiguous position of the white Creole in *Wide Sargasso Sea* attests: "Creole of pure English descent she may be, but they are not English or European either" (67)—the white settler and the white Creole occupy a similar place of privilege and estrangement vis-à-vis their relation to the natives and the empire.

10. Subsequent references to "Three Women's Texts" will be abbreviated in the text as TWT.

11. This Spivak departs significantly from the Spivak of "Can the Subaltern Speak?" who recognizes that the subaltern "is itself defined as a difference from the elite" (CSS 285). It should be noted that Spivak does not actually use the term *subaltern* in "Three Women's Texts." She does, however, employ the same phrases that she has used to describe the subaltern in "Can the Subaltern Speak?" to describe both Bertha in *Jane Eyre* and Antoinette in *Wide Sargasso Sea*. In the case of Bertha, she is characterized as "a figure produced by the axiomatics of imperialism" (TWT 266), and in Spivak's reading of her as Caliban Bertha functions as "an inaccessible blank circumscribed by an interpretable text" (TWT 264). Antoinette is the subject of "an allegory of the general epistemic violence of imperialism" (TWT 270) and is described as a "self-immolating colonial subject [constructed] for the glorification of the social mission of the colonizer" (ibid.).

12. An example of this type of white becoming-indigene occurs also in the work of some postcolonial critics. Diana Brydon, for example, in her provocatively titled essay "The White Inuit Speaks," asserts that much literary production in Canada is marked by "the particular circumstances of a Canadian post-coloniality that is not indigenous *but in the process of becoming so*" (198; emphasis added).

13. Although Dinny is just one narrator in this structurally complex book, she consistently reasserts her role as narrator in others' narratives through a "seizing of the point of view." Through this deliberate problematization of the authorial center it becomes difficult to determine who is writing about whom in this novel.

14. It should be noted that both Mattina, a resident of New York, and Connie Grant, a former resident of England, also survive the disaster that befalls the "natives" of Kowhai Street. However, it would appear that their reprieve is only temporary. Mattina eventually succumbs to the malignant tumor invading her body and dies at home in New York. Although Connie initially escapes, it would appear that she too will eventually "disappear," for according to the real-estate agent Albion Cook, "Connie Grant will have to be put away" (184). Connie, unlike Decima, speaks the language of the colonizers, and now that she has "settled" in Puamahara, it would appear that she has become subject to colonial control. Because Connie not only remembers what happened, but can also voice it—"I'm the only one now who remembers, the only one left. And it's a real memory. And

I'm keeping it, I'm keeping it" (184)—she needs to be "put away," contained. Connie's position represents a marked contrast to that of Decima, who is believed by one of the nurses at the Manuka Home to be unable to remember her family, and thus acknowledge their disappearance, simply because she can never say the words "I remember" (190). Unlike Connie Grant, then, Decima remains uncolonizable because she is unrepresentable in the colonizer's language.

15. Those critics who do mention Decima tend to see her merely as a victim. For example, Marc Delrez, in obvious contrast to my reading of Decima as sole survivor, asserts that "Decima and people of her kind are committed to oblivion and thus, in a sense, decimated" (99). Nicholas Birns asserts that "The fate of the disappeared Puamaharans, who are deprived of physical existence, is no more traumatic than the fate of Decima James, who is deprived of verbal and spiritual existence by her institutional-mandated muteness" (24). Suzette Henke, however, recognizes Decima's ambiguous positionality: "A true *infans*, Decima has no words to bind her, no language to communicate—only an idiolect of grunts and gestures that may be either autistic or prophetic. When her family is later decimated, only Decima survives, a speechless witness to what she cannot, empirically, know" (32). Henke does not, however, elaborate on the significance of Decima's survival.

16. Some might suggest that my reading of *The Carpathians* attempts to "neutralize" Decima's "untranslatability" in the way Chow cautions against. However, to see Decima as the "native" here with a "victimized voice/self" to be "resurrected" would be to see Decima as the silent subaltern, in the role of native Caliban, and thus would be to discount her privilege as the white settler Ariel. In other words, it would be to repeat exactly the conflation of creole and native that Spivak performs in her reading of *Jane Eyre* and *Wide Sargasso Sea* in "Three Women's Texts."

WORKS CITED

Ahmad, Aijaz. "The Politics of Literary Postcoloniality." *Race and Class* 36:3 (1995): 1–20.

Alcoff, Linda. "The Problem of Speaking for Others." *Cultural Critique* 20 (winter 1991–92): 5–31.

Appiah, Kwame Anthony. "Is the Post- in Postmodernism the Post- in Postcolonial?" *Critical Inquiry* 17:2 (1991): 336–57.

Ashcroft, Bill, Gareth Griffiths, and Helen Tiffin. *The Empire Writes Back: Theory and Practice in Post-Colonial Literatures.* New York: Routledge, 1989.

Atwood, Margaret. "The Grey Owl Syndrome." In *Strange Things: The Malevolent North in Canadian Literature.* Oxford: Clarendon, 1995. 35–61.

Benterrak, Krim, Stephen Muecke and Paddy Roe. *Reading the Country: Introduction to Nomadology.* Fremantle, Australia: Fremantle Arts Centre Press, 1984.

Birns, Nicholas. "Gravity Star and Memory Flower: Space, Time and Language in *The Carpathians*." *Australian and New Zealand Studies in Canada* 5 (spring 1991): 16–28.

Brydon, Diana. "The White Inuit Speaks: Contamination as Literary Strategy." In
  Past the Last Post: Theorizing Post-Colonialism and Post-Modernism, ed. Ian Adam
  and Helen Tiffin. Hertfordshire: Harvester Wheatsheaf, 1991. 191–203.
Chow, Rey. "Where Have All the Natives Gone?" In *Writing Diaspora: Tactics of
  Intervention in Contemporary Cultural Studies.* Bloomington and Indianapolis:
  Indiana University Press, 1993. 27–54.
Coetzee, J. M. *White Writing: On the Culture of Letters in South Africa.* New Haven and
  London: Yale University Press, 1988.
Delbaere, Jeanne. "*The Carpathians*: Memory and Survival in the Global Village."
  In *The Ring of Fire: Essays on Janet Frame,* ed. Jeanne Delbaere. Mundelstrup,
  Denmark: Dangaroo, 1992. 199–208.
Delrez, Marc. "'Boundaries and Beyond': Memory as Quest in Janet Frame's *The
  Carpathians.*" *Commonwealth Essays and Studies* 13:1 (1990): 95–105.
During, Simon. "Postmodernism or Post-Colonialism Today." In *Postmodern
  Conditions,* ed. Andrew Milner et al. Victoria, Australia: Centre for General
  and Comparative Literature, Monash University, 1988. 111–29.
Fanon, Frantz. *Black Skin, White Masks.* Trans. Charles Lam Markmann. London:
  Paladin, 1970.
Fee, Margery. "Why C. K. Stead Didn't Like Keri Hulme's *The Bone People*: Who
  Can Write as Other?" *Australia and New Zealand Studies in Canada* 1 (1989):
  11–32.
Frame, Janet. *The Carpathians.* New York: George Braziller, 1988.
Goldie, Terry. *Fear and Temptation: The Image of the Indigene in Canadian, Australian,
  and New Zealand Literatures.* Montreal: McGill-Queen's University Press, 1989.
Hall, Stuart. "Cultural Identity and Diaspora." In *Contemporary Postcolonial Theory: A
  Reader,* ed. Padmini Mongia. London: Arnold, 1996. 110–21.
Henke, Suzette. "The Postmodern Frame: Metalepsis and Discursive
  Fragmentation in Janet Frame's *The Carpathians.*" *Australia and New Zealand
  Studies in Canada* 5 (spring 1991): 29–38.
Keeshig-Tobias, Lenore. "The Magic of Others." In *Language in Her Eye: Views on
  Writing and Gender by Canadian Women Writing in English,* ed. Libby Scheier,
  Sarah Sheard, and Eleanor Wachtel. Toronto: Coach House Press, 1990.
  173–77.
Lawson, Alan. "A Cultural Paradigm for the Second World." *Australian-Canadian
  Studies* 9:1–2 (1991).
Lyotard, Jean-François. *The Differend: Phrases in Dispute.* Trans. Georges Van Den
  Abbeele. Minneapolis: University of Minnesota Press, 1988.
Maracle, Lee. "Native Myths: Trickster Alive and Crowing." In *Language in Her Eye:
  Views on Writing and Gender by Canadian Women Writing in English,* ed. Libby
  Scheier, Sarah Sheard, and Eleanor Wachtel. Toronto: Coach House Press,
  1990. 182–87.
Mongia, Padmini, ed. *Contemporary Postcolonial Theory: A Reader.* London: Arnold,
  1996.
Parry, Benita. "Problems in Current Theories of Colonial Discourse." *Oxford
  Literary Review* 9:1–2 (1987): 27–58.

Philip, Marlene Nourbese. "The Disappearing Debate: Racism and Censorship."
    In *Language in Her Eye: Views on Writing and Gender by Canadian Women Writing
    in English*, ed. Libby Scheier, Sarah Sheard, and Eleanor Wachtel. Toronto:
    Coach House Press, 1990. 209–19.
Rhys, Jean. *Wide Sargasso Sea.* New York: W. W. Norton, 1966.
Sharpe, Jenny. "Figures of Colonial Resistance." *Modern Fiction Studies* 35:1 (1989):
    137–55.
Spivak, Gayatri Chakravorty. "Three Women's Texts and a Critique of
    Imperialism." In *"Race," Writing, and Difference*, ed. Henry Louis Gates Jr.
    Chicago: University of Chicago Press, 1986. 262–80.
———. "Subaltern Studies: Deconstructing Historiography." In *In Other Worlds:
    Essays in Cultural Politics.* London and New York: Methuen, 1987. 197–221.
———. "Can the Subaltern Speak? Speculations on Widow-Sacrifice." *Wedge* 7–8
    (1985); rpt. as "Can the Subaltern Speak?" in *Marxism and the Interpretation of
    Culture*, ed. Cary Nelson and Lawrence Grossberg. Urbana: University of
    Illinois Press, 1988. 271–313.

"Ladies," "Gentlemen," and "Colored": "The Agency of (Lacan's Black) Letter" in the Outhouse

Maia Boswell

In "The Site of Memory," Toni Morrison begins to explore some links between her own writing and slave narratives by explaining that "In this country the print origins of black literature (as distinguished from the oral origins) were slave narratives" (299). This is an interesting statement because it highlights a connection between print—the material dimension(s) of our sign system—slave narratives, and the phenomenon we call "black literature." Morrison tells us that the narratives "were written to say principally two things. One: 'This is my historical life—my singular, special example that is personal, but also represents the race.' Two: 'I write this text to persuade other people—you, the reader, who is probably not black—that we are human beings worthy of God's grace and the immediate abandonment of slavery'" (299). In other words, the literary is employed "for one purpose: to change things" (300). And it will do this by using written language (denied by law to the slaves) to tell a story of the transition from being identified as an object to being identified as a person. Slave narratives give a voice to those institutionalized as objects, as voiceless material for labor; they remind us that "literacy was a way of assuming and proving the 'humanity' that the constitution denied them" (ibid.).[1] These are stories about identity and how language creates and positions people, how it organizes their world. Indeed, all of these—the material dimension(s) of the sign system, slave narratives, and "black literature"—engage the question of identity politics. But this emerges as a question not of some monolithic notion of race, of abject or essentialized identities that seek representation, or of a signified that supposedly grounds words in a tangible world, but of something at once more elusive and more material, something that requires us to rethink the ways "historical" events, the "event" of subjectivity, and literary (or textual) events participate in dramas that become part of cultural memory—and cultural change.

Morrison reminds us that texts take place through conventions; in the case of slave narratives, "the milieu (often drawn from the sentimental novel popular at the time) dictated the purpose and style" (301). In other words, "popular taste discouraged the writer from dwelling too long or too carefully on the more sordid details of the experience." In addition to bringing attention to the workings of the reigning system of representation by calling attention to the way identity construction takes place through language, slave narratives (as all texts) are subject to the limiting effects of linguistic and literary convention. Morrison tells us that "whenever there was an unusually violent incident or a scatological one, or something excessive, one finds the writer taking refuge in the literary conventions of the day." In pointing to ways in which the literary (oral or printed) participates in forging identities, Morrison suggests that textual events can intervene in processes of (re)thinking the reigning system of representation. But, in discussing slave narrative, Morrison highlights another link between those stories and her own, suggesting how human institutions—in this case, literary conventions and the politics of publishing—may complicate that process, requiring continuing efforts to probe the limits of the textual as it operates in real-world situations. Playing on the "cultural memory" of slave narratives and the way they give the lie to constructions of identity posited as given or "natural," Morrison sees her practice as a writer to be about doing what the slave narratives could not do; it "rips the veil drawn over proceedings too terrible to relate," and invites us to observe the "violent," the "scatological," and the "excessive." I will be drawing a connection here between that grouping—the violent, the scatological, and the excessive—and the "material" dimensions of language. And I will be addressing how these impact the process that slave narratives concern themselves with (which we might call identity formation) and participate in various practices of intervention into the social and historical domains.

A promising entry, then, might be to consider another text that asks us to reconsider the construction of identity, and that, like Morrison's, does this through attention to the material dimensions of language, attention to the violent, the scatological, and the excessive. In Jacques Lacan's "The Agency of the Letter in the Unconscious or Reason since Freud," as in Morrison's texts, questions of identity lead to another zone, one that involves the "violent," the "scatological," and the "excessive," and is ultimately conflated with the black other of the Western epistemological order. Rather than inscribing the figurative and cultural powers of blackness (what Henry Louis Gates Jr. used to call the "blackness of blackness") in a binary structure, as the concept of "signifyin(g)" was charted in relation to a received white or originally "master's" discourse, blackness in Lacan, as in Morrison, operates in a semiotic and epistemological field of excess accessed through attention to the material dimensions of language. I will begin by tracing one way in which such an other field of blackness operates in one of the key (psychoanalytic) texts of poststructuralist theory—Lacan's "The Agency of the Letter"—to see where an unnoticed politics of race can be said to inflect his text. At the same time, I will ask where, precisely, the figurative chain that passes through (racial) blackness may be connected to the prerepresentational force and excess of a largely unread pair of markers: the (black, material, printed) letter, on the one hand, and the "excessive" and "scatological" (or the excremental) on the other. Two passages from Morrison's *Sula* will participate in exploring how figures of racial otherness, the other of the reigning order, get conflated with blackness, the scatological, excess, and ultimately with the materiality of language itself—the agency of the (black) letter that is denied power (or voice) by the classic (or pre-Saussurean) system of representation. The passages from *Sula*—one in which Helene and Nel travel south by train, the other in which Shadrack confronts the reflection of his face in a toilet—also connect with those from Lacan in that these two sites figure prominently in addressing how identity constructions must be rethought through the materialist, or linguistic dimension, dimensions addressed in *Sula* and Lacan through figures of trains (conflated with the underground railroad) and figures of the outhouse or bathroom. Ultimately, it is my aim to point to a site where the figures of the train (linked to transport across boundaries, including boundaries of identity where one may pass as an other and thus show the constructed nature of identity) and of the outhouse (of what is outside an "official," inherited economy of representation) illuminate the relation between material language and identity politics. Rereading Lacan's text through *Sula*, and *Sula* through Lacan's "Letter," brings vast implications for cultural studies, gender studies, postcolonial studies, and other trajectories touching on identity and identity politics. But if we continue to ignore the interventionist capacity of language put forth in central psychoanalytic texts and in contemporary literature, this materialist dimension will con-tinue to be marginalized, and we will lose the interventionist potential of those stories. Observing this scene allows for a complex but responsible agency to move beyond limiting narratives and inherited structures that inform current impasses in both academic and popular culture.

I

Lacan's "The Agency of the Letter in the Unconscious or Reason since Freud" remains important, not only because it is his "first real interven-tion . . . in the University," but also because it is this lecture in which gen-der, identity, the idea of the unconscious, and pre- and post-Saussurean language models all come together in a powerful commentary still central to many issues in today's debates (Gallop 1985, 114).[2] This text, translat-ed variably as being about the "agency," the "instance," or the "insistence" of the letter, is seen to "lie at the heart of [Lacan's] theory"; redescribing the "entire Freudian enterprise," it "brings into focus [the] inveterately linguistic character" of that enterprise (Benvenuto and Kennedy 103; Bowie 79).[3] Focusing on the letter, or "the material support that concrete discourse borrows from language," it is this lecture in which Lacan dis-cusses how the "unconscious" is the "discourse of the other," how the psy-choanalytic experience "discovers in the unconscious the whole structure of language."[4] In his *Lacan*, Bowie claims that "If *Écrits* can be said to have anywhere a core—a place where Lacan's main teachings are to be found in their most emphatic and exacting form—then that core is perhaps in 'The Letter,'" where it can be seen that "the signifier has a 'constitutive role' in the unconscious realm'" (68). Indeed, it is here that Lacan sug-gests that "the unconscious . . . has no existence outside language and no structure other than the one that language affords" (71). There is, in other words, "no veiled signified-in-waiting that will eventually call the crazy procession of signifiers to order" (72–73). According to Bowie, "'The signifier' and its cognates not only cover the entire field that had previous-ly been designated 'mental' but redramatize the crucial conscious-uncon-scious relations between the speaking subject and the social order" (77).

In "Psychoanalysis and Feminism," Gallop sees the piece to be "one of the major essays in which Lacan exposes his theory of the signifier" (9). She claims that through his "emphasis on the intersubjective dialogue of

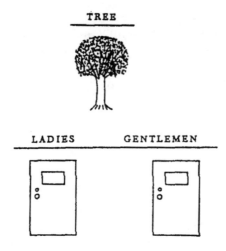

Figure 1

the analytic experience," as well as his "discovery that the ego itself is constituted in an intersubjective relation, Lacan has shifted the object of psychoanalysis from the individual person taken as separate monad to the
intersubjective dialectic" (1985, 117).[5] Malcolm Bowie places the project
more firmly as a nodal point for all post-Saussurean (or Postmodern) theories, calling "The Agency" the "first reformulation of Saussure," the
place where "the keynote of Lacan's entire approach to linguistics is
sounded," the place where "the potency of the signifier" is "symbolized in
a single capital letter" (64).[6]

   In the essay, Lacan uses two pictures to lay out alternate models for
language function. (See figure 1.) The first picture, of a tree with the
word *tree* written over it, appears in the position of the "classic"—or pre-
Saussurean—manner of seeing language as a one-to-one correspondence;
according to this model, reality, which is out there, "given," or material, is
described by a language that is transparent and secondary.[7] The other
picture—of two identical doors marked "Ladies" and "Gentlemen"—
Lacan relates to Saussurean and post-Saussurean model(s); it is used to
explode "the illusion that the signifier answers to the function of representing the signified" (150). In discussing his use of the pictures of the
tree and of the bathroom doors, Lacan notes the "faultiness" of the first
illustration, pointing to how it leads to "error"; Gallop suggests that the
"total inadequa[cy]" of the first image brings about the second image,

which Lacan "produces . . . to underline the inadequacy" (ibid.; Gallop 1982, 9, 10). Lacan supplies a story to accompany the second picture, which situates the doors in the context of two children seeing the bathrooms from the window of the train they inhabit:

> A train arrives at a station. A little boy and a little girl, brother and sister, are seated in a compartment face-to-face next to the window through which the buildings along the station platform can be seen passing as the train pulls to a stop. (152)

"Look," says the brother, "we're at Ladies!"; "Idiot!" replies the sister, "Can't you see we're at Gentlemen." Lacan goes on to comment on what this means for the two:

> For these children, Ladies and Gentlemen will be henceforth two countries towards which each of their souls will strive on divergent wings, and between which a truce will be the more impossible since they are actually the same country and neither can compromise on its own superiority without detracting from the glory of the other. (Ibid.)

But why bathrooms—private sites of defecation, places of excrement— and why from a train that works invisibly as a trope for sheer metonymy or figuration? What has the letter to do with identity, identity with materiality, and materiality with human waste?

Lacan's picture of the bathroom doors presents two identical doors, but with different signifiers, thereby challenging assumptions about a one-to-one correspondence between word and thing. Most readers, paying attention to the gendered markers, see the lecture as having to do primarily with gendered identity. While interrogating a host of misconceptions about language use, the lecture focuses most fully on language and its impact on identity. Gallop, for example, in "Psychoanalysis and Feminism," sees Lacan's "Letter" as "a moment important for its presentation of the inextricable relation between the influence of language and sexual differentiation" (9). Although Lacan's picture raises questions about the assumption that the doors and their meaning are bound up with the veiled activity behind the doors that is the unveiling of the "private parts," and so bound up with the "anatomical difference" between "the sexes," the pictures, for Lacan (I will argue here), dispel these assumptions, at the same time engaging other trajectories at work on the front of and behind the closed doors—namely, the relation between the doors, language, and the excremental function, the categorizing of what is seen as the most material, as "waste." Although Lacan's "Letter" plays a key role in discussions about (gendered) identity formation, it remains apparently silent about other identity categories—for example, race.[8] This impression corresponds with the received notion that psychoanalysis can be seen as an "a-historical," "bourgeois," and "Eurocentric" model that fails to recognize the reality of racial injustice in specific historical horizons, a model that itself needs to be correspondingly "historicized."[9] A closer reading, today, reveals another possibility, which acknowledges racial markers in the text, while at the same time recognizing how those markers might be seen to participate in a wider process that moves beyond the framework assumed by identity politics, a model that may be seen to involve limiting assumptions. Lacan's focus on the material "agency of the letter" manifests those linguistic tendencies that some movements within the broad rubric of "cultural studies" have viewed with political suspicion in "poststructuralism" generally; yet, it is here that the interface with race occurs, and here that we can begin to rethink notions of "history," "identity," and "textuality" in ways that bring increased aware-ness of the operation of various agencies. As I will argue here, Toni Morrison accesses fresh possibilities in each of these categories in her daz-zling relays of "cultural memory." Together, Morrison's and Lacan's fore-grounding of figures of materiality, excess, and scatology reclaims the agency of the black letter.

Passages in Toni Morrison's *Sula* surrounding Helene and Nel's train ride from Ohio down South to pay homage to the material remains of Helene's prostitute mother illustrate one aspect of the connection I wish to make. The passage occurs just after Helene and Nel, missing the "whites only" sign, board the "wrong" train, and are hailed by a white con-ductor who, seeing them hurrying to the "colored" train, tells Helene to "git your butt on in there" (21).[10] The passage that interests me most involves Helene seeing doors marked "Ladies" and "Gentlemen," almost as in Lacan's example; but, knowing that she and Nel could not assume the privacy afforded by those doors, Helene searches in vain for bath-rooms marked "Colored." The marking of the "colored" doors suggest how Lacan's comments on (gendered) identity formation open onto a double or parodic version of gender difference in the possibility of racial difference. The passage raises the issue of the influence of language on racial identity—an issue already present, but largely unread, in Lacan's "Letter."

More important, figures of racial otherness that are conflated with blackness, and with the materiality of language itself (the agency of which is also denied power by the "classic" system of semantics and representation), participate in events surrounding private activity that takes place behind the doors; they link up on the level of what I will call a semiotics of excess, materiality, the letter itself, or excrement. The black other is connected both to the toilet motif of the cited passage from Lacan (present, if unmarked, in the urgency of Helene's need to find a room that would house her "relief") and to the overwhelming excremental motifs of *Sula*. It is also central to troping or "signifyin(g) on" (to use a phrase from Henry Louis Gates Jr.) official language as well as on assumptions surrounding the "classic" manner of language use. As Gates suggests in several references to "signifyin(g)," and as Morrison suggests in "The Site of Memory," this dark figure comes out of the status of the slave and is always linked, through cultural memory, through the (racial) histories of colonialism and postcolonialism and through the imprint of psychic, political, and economic trauma, to various figures on the margins of contemporary power dynamics.[11] Linked to Lacan's unconscious and to the "agency of the (black) letter," this figure subverts and dislocates semantics, or the belief in the imposed protocol of (white) meaning production, itself ultimately linked to the excremental functions at the center of Lacan's lecture.

One can argue that the silence about race in "The Agency of the Letter" is only apparent. To begin with, the presence of the train (as a figure of metonymy) warns us that the example itself is steeped in figuration.[12] Moreover, the racial other—which becomes conflated with figures of blackness, with the unconscious, and with that which is left over or exceeds the semantic order (that is, the materiality of language, the letter itself)—participates in Lacan's "Letter" on several levels. It does so in two primary ways: first by occupying a position outside the gender-segregated bathrooms and the train, and thus on the margins of the sanctioned signifying system, and second, by interrogating the functioning of this order itself. The link between the privileged position and the racial "other" of the West—historically binarized into "light" and "darkness," "white" and "black," the "conscious" and the "unconscious," or the "ideal" and the "material" order itself—is clarified by Lacan in several statements from this essay. Putting into question the integrity of the boundaries themselves, Lacan states: "what the psychoanalytic experience discovers in the unconscious is the whole structure of language" (147). He proceeds to clarify what this means: "Thus from the outset I have alerted informed minds to the extent to which the notion that the unconscious is merely the seat of the instincts will have to be rethought" (ibid.).[13] Dispelling the illusion of a binarized interior/exterior, Lacan suggests the constructedness of the fiction of interiority and thus of the structures that keep the reigning system of representation in place (the notion that the sign for tree represents the thing). This is not to say that one can get outside the signifying system, but rather that Lacan concerns himself here with a focus on something at once on the margins and at its center, something alluded to in terms of a racial other denied identity by that legitimizing system, and yet occupying a position from which one may interrogate assumptions that keep that system in place. And this something, ultimately, is linked to the (black) material letter itself. Lacan states: "By 'letter' I designate the material support that concrete discourse borrows from language . . . language and its structure exist prior to the moment at which each subject at a certain point in his mental development makes its entry into it" (147–48). This something, therefore, bears links with a reality that precedes the subject, and thus precedes figuration. Lacan's statement that we must dispel the "illusion that the signifier . . . has to answer for its existence in the name of any signification whatsoever" is highly relevant here (150).

Other passages from *Sula* relevant here surround Shadrack's return from the horror of having seen the headless body of a comrade running across a frozen field in the war-torn France of 1917; these passages have to do with the unusual pretense of marking and dislocating Shadrack's "mirror stage" as he "returns" from the disruption, madness, and "headlessness" of the war.[14] In a jail cell, where he has been placed for his "disorderliness," Shadrack searches in vain for a mirror (to still his feeling that all is becoming broken into "bits and pieces") until the toilet is found to serve the purpose. If the "mirror stage" inaugurates the fiction of mimetic identity (linked to "classic," pre-Saussurean notions of language use), the scene associates Shadrack with the prefigural Letter, as well as with the status of the priest/artist as "waste," or in excess of society.[15] By opening up Lacan's "Letter" to sites that involve racial segregation and the binaries black/white and dark/light—topoi that already occupy a key position in Lacan's text—we can reread the text for its implications for cultural studies, gender studies, postcolonial studies, and other trajectories touching on identity politics. But this materialist dimension of psychoanalysis itself will become marginalized if we continue to ignore the interventionist capacity of language put forth in central psychoanalytic texts.

It is useful here to take a detour through some feminist commentators, to review how gender gets marked in Lacan and to revisit a scene in
which what begins as an issue of identity politics may migrate, through
the agency of the letter, beyond that zone.[16] In "Psychoanalysis and
Feminism," Jane Gallop suggests that "the relationship between the words
and the doors they indicate is stunningly more complex than any one-to-
one correlation that might be assumed to operate in the first drawing"
(10). The two signifiers in the second illustration refer to "two identical
doors." Thus, according to Gallop, they must "be understood 1) in relation to each other (each is 'not the other') and 2) in what Lacan calls a
'signifying chain.'" Gallop points out that, in the story, "each child is able
to see only one of the rest rooms; thus, each one sees an image which is
more like the first drawing than the second" (ibid.). She helps explain
part of the reason for the persistence of assumptions linked to the model
of language use that claims that "reality" and identity are given, and that
language merely describes, represents, or expresses that reality in a
mimetic relationship. Gallop's claim that this first picture "leads one to be
confident that words have delimitable 'things' which they 'mean'" brings
her to argue that the "'psychical consequences of the anatomical distinction between the sexes' have a structure similar to that of the situation in
this anecdote" (ibid.). She continues: "Through the biological given of sitting on one side of the compartment or the other, each sex is placed in a
structure, and as such is unable to see the structure" (ibid.). Thus, "the
biological differences are only of import" here "in so far as they institute
the subject into the play of the signifier, a play unknown as long as one
accepts the first model of language, the model of one-to-one correspondence" (ibid.).

   Gallop notes how Juliet Mitchell's early attempt to import Freudian
and, by extension, Lacanian ideas into an "Anglo-American" context has
resulted in problems, given the resistance to the implications of the attention to language in the texts. Gallop states: "Mitchell's project follows
Lacan's direction in its emphasis on fidelity to the originality of Freud's
text and in its denial of Freud's biologism. Yet oddly, her relation to
Lacan's theory is never made explicit. For a reader acquainted with
Lacan, he functions as a very present absence" (6). Noting the dangers of
refusing to deal with the language issue, and suggesting the problems
of failing to cap the interventionist potential of the theories, Gallop again
reminds readers that it is not the "biological given of male or female that
is in question . . . but the subject as constituted by the pre-existing signifying

chain, that is, by culture" (11). Her comments serve as a reminder to those who balk at the implications of Lacan's ego-explosive commentaries because they fear losing what they see as their political or real-world power base or because they fear the erasure of boundaries whose softening would be threatening for other reasons.[17] Gallop suggests that even as Mitchell corrects misconceptions about Freudian theory, she fails to deal with Lacanian issues and language events in Freud's texts. Accordingly, she suggests that this "relegation of language to the margins . . . perhaps . . . stems from Mitchell's having trapped herself into a conversation . . . with feminists who reflect the way American psychoanalysis ignores the ego-subverting significance of language" (8).

Ignoring the implications of the language events of psychoanalysis (and "high theory" in general) brings us to align ourselves with the very structures that continue to delegitimate the "others" of Western hegemonic orders. But in what way is there a deeper blindness here? In attempting to clarify the issues, Gallop notes other impasses that have arisen with attempts to allow Lacan's comments to play out. She reminds us that "an understanding of the signifying chain does not mean that the subject can remove himself from his blind situation merely by knowing that the second rest room exists somewhere outside his field of vision" (11). In other words, any "mythical prehistory cannot erase the situation of desire which is the result of the perversion of the need by the signifier's presence." What happens is that the "demand is made within language's imaginary register, where the first model of one-to-one correspondence is presumed to operate," so the demand's "signified . . . is assumed to be delimitable" (ibid.). Considering how this relates to theoretical and experiential approaches to change, Gallop suggests that many feminists would have the subject "consider as illusory the entire structure which makes the realms of Gentlemen and Ladies appear as defined and absolute as they do in the one-to-one correlation" (12). One element Gallop takes issue with in Mitchell, therefore, is her assumption that there are "women"—a category framed as self-evident or given—who "have to organize themselves as a group to effect change in the basic ideology of human society" (13).

That which must be struggled against is not just something occurring within the cultural, legal, and social arenas; that which must be struggled against is also the perpetuation of assumptions about language, meaning, and identity that continue to operate and to delegitimate certain positions and voices aligned with a self seen to be constituted in patriarchal culture (which already assumes biological reductionism). According to Gallop, the "self," rather than being constituted only within patriarchal culture, is constituted in the symbolic realm—a signifying system—which operates differently than an "imaginary" register based on what we might call image or "sight," and which also, significantly, operates differently than the hegemonic system in which biology, anatomy, skin tone, identity, or "concrete reality" are assumed to be events that are "given" and not open to interpretation.

Although critics agree that there is no place to be human outside of signification, Lacan's choice of bathrooms segregated by gender reminds us that bathrooms segregated by race are prominent figures in various textual and experiential histories; and such segregation practices have situated some people in a realm of nonsignification and nonsignificance. In a variety of situations and places, many have found themselves shut out from the doors labeled "Ladies" and "Gentlemen"; many have occupied spaces, if not outside of, at least on the margins of the official signifying system. Lacan's apparent omission of a reference to racial segregation and/or racial differentiation in this context raises a series of questions. Is Lacan simply not concerned with racial difference? Is he suggesting that gender subsumes race, that identity construction along racial lines works in a way parallel to gendered identity construction? Or do a series of cryptic references in the text to blackness and segregated bathrooms mean that it, and potentially psychoanalysis as a whole, comments specifically on the (black) other of Western culture? That Lacan explicitly mentions blackness and segregation at several points in his lecture suggests that race participates in the events.

Lacan first names the institution of segregation in considering the function of the separate rooms (he talks of "urinary segregation") (151). Then, suggesting how history might be inflected by historical materialism that rethinks a monolithic story told by the "Masters," he moves beyond segregation to slavery instituted in various assumptions of identity "politics." Indeed, he uses images of slavery at three points in his lecture: the subject is a "slave of a discourse"; a "negress"—"black but comely"—is "adorned" for her wedding; and a "poor but honest woman" is made "ready for the auction block." The first statement comes as Lacan expounds upon his claim that "language and its structure exist prior to the moment at which each subject at a certain point in his mental development makes his entry into it" (148). Lacan uses "slavery" in a generalized way that makes no explicit reference to race. "Thus, the subject, too, if he can appear to be the slave of language is all the more so of a discourse in the universal movement in which his place is already inscribed at birth, if only by virtue of his proper name" (ibid.). Tangentially invoking the idea of race in the allusion to slavery, Lacan here suggests that the position of the slave can be seen to participate in a variety of contexts involving language and identity.

The second reference comes at a point in which Lacan discusses the "letter," "namely the essentially localized structure of the signifier." Lacan offers an image of "the signifying chain" as "rings of a necklace that is a ring in another necklace made of rings" (153). He continues: "it is easy to see that only the correlations between signifier and signifier provide the standard for all research into signification." But, he warns that it "would be an error" to think that "signification reigns supreme" beyond the limits in which grammar and lexicology are "exhausted." Why? Because "the signifier, by its very nature always anticipates meaning by unfolding its dimensions before it." He gives several examples to demonstrate this phenomenon, "as is seen at the level of the sentence when it is interrupted before the significant term: 'I shall never . . . ,' 'All the same it is . . . ,' 'And yet there may be. . . .'" Claiming that "such sentences are not without meaning, a meaning all the more oppressive in that it is content to make us wait for it," Lacan moves on to the two other clauses I have located as engaging race, gender, blackness, and the eschatological:

> But the phenomenon is no different which by the mere recoil of a "but" brings to light, comely as the Shulamite, honest as the dew, the negress adorned for the wedding and the poor woman ready for the auction block. . . . From which we can say that it is in the chain of the signifier that the meaning "insists" but that none of its elements "consists" in the signification of which it is at the moment capable. (Ibid.)

Lacan frames the examples of the "negress" and the "poor woman" merely as ways of speaking of grammatical constructions centered on the word *but* functioning as a coordinating conjunction; the anticipatory function carries over, however, in these contexts, so that Lacan thus arrives at the conclusion that "we are forced, then, to accept the notion of an incessant sliding of the signified under the signifier."

Exploring the "anticipatory" function and the incessant sliding, Lacan notes that Saussure "illustrates" this with an image denoting linearity (154). Claiming that "all our experience runs counter to this linearity,"

Lacan proposes "something more like 'anchoring points' as a schema for taking into account the dominance of the letter in the dramatic transformation that dialogue can effect in the subject."[18] For Lacan, the "linearity that Saussure holds to be constitutive of the chain of discourse," if it is necessary, is "not sufficient." Jane Gallop, noting that in "The Agency of the Letter," "'anticipation' occurs in the context of incomplete sentences, . . . when [the sentence] is interrupted before the significative term," links this to Lacan's revision of Saussure, of putting the signifier always on top (120). This construction gives the signifier (linked to the [black] letter) "preeminence, or 'instance,' agency" (121). Mary Ann Doane suggests that "the signifier with no signified, indicates the perpetual deferral of meaning, its failure to coagulate" (128). Her claim that "There is no doubt that Lacan attempts to disrupt the spatialization of the classical philosophical dialectic between surface and depth, appearance and being," that "the 'beyond' is a function of desire and hence deessentialized but not entirely negated," is more to the point, given that her phrase "deferral of meaning" allows many readers to assume that Lacan's project disallows the occurrence of "meaning" on any level.

Citing the limitation of applying the idea of the "chain of discourse only in the direction in which it is oriented in time," Lacan notes that poetry (and I would add, fiction, and potentially all language events) provides a counterexample. This brings him to suggest that there is "no signifying chain that does not have . . . a whole articulation of relevant contexts suspended 'vertically.'" And "what this structure of the signifying chain discloses is the possibility . . . of us[ing] it in order to signify something quite other than what it says" (155). The examples of the "negress" and the "poor woman" have to do on a rhetorical level with the very issues at stake when we consider not only the historical scenes of slavery and the subjectified, colonized subject but also the systems that continue to deny various forms of agency that participate in and around scenes in which various subjects continue to be "slaves of a discourse" or slaves of a particular (phallogocentric, patriarchal, white) discourse. Lacan's text thus gestures toward a situation that instigates the position of being "off the train" as being interpellated into the system, not as people, but as things (slaves), animals, creatures of darkness in the "outhouse." Yet, like the Hegelian master/slave dialectic, Lacan observes that all depends on the abject element here, on the position of the *but* at the center of the grammatical scene—a *but* that becomes the link between the grammatical and the more fluid rhetorical scene that opens onto the agency of the others.

It is significant that both "women" and "blacks" are included in this emphasis on the word *but*, which functions grammatically as a means of showing opposition. Rhetorically, the word occupies another space. It is used to show relationships between, and to emphasize an assumed innate depravity; the poor woman is "poor" and a woman, but in spite of one's expectations she is "honest," and the "negress" is "black," but in spite of this she is "comely."[19] Significantly, the two figures introduced at this point are not a "Lady" and a "Gentleman," as might be expected from the earlier diagram, but a woman being sold on the auction block and a negress being prepared for marriage. Both of these positions, tellingly, have been read as positions of nonsubjectivity; the slave for obvious reasons, and the woman, according to Luce Irigaray, because in the Western symbolic system, which she calls a "homosexual" system, there is only one sex: "this sex which is not one" does not occupy the position of a "subject."[20] Significantly, it is at this point that Lacan goes on to say that "the subject . . . if he can appear to be the slave of language is all the more so of a discourse in the universal movement in which his place is already inscribed at birth" (148).

The point I am making is that since identity construction within culture, segregation, blackness, and slavery all surround the bathroom picture, racially segregated bathrooms and the idea of blackness open onto an other scene at the center of this choreography. It is this scene and its implications that continue to get ignored, and that feed the division in psychoanalytic trajectories between the "ego psychologists" and those who argue that language function must be prioritized. Reading this scene clarifies why accusations of ahistoricism, abstraction, and an unwillingness to grapple with the lived experience of living individuals continue to threaten various reading practices and interventionist attempts grounded in the implications of Lacan's theories;[21] it suggests that such accusations may be linked to a desire not to let go of that which has meant power—but a power bought at the price of regressive claims that diminish that power in the name of victimhood or inequality and in the name of an "us"-against-"them" mentality rather than a win-win vision that sees that all stand to lose by clinging to worn-out, normalizing frameworks that pit "men" against "women" and "whites" against "the others." This impasse touches on the entire realm of reading, that is, not only humanities departments, literature programs, communication, cultural, and media studies, but also a range of social and theoretical events currently in jeopardy of being misunderstood and so dismissed. For a vision of power for all to be manifested, each side must forfeit fears of giving over limiting narratives and structures.

II

The two passages from Toni Morrison's *Sula*—Helene and Nel's train ride, and Shadrack's toilet-mirror scene—provide ways of reading how these signifying problems get situated in social sites, and how theoretical and literary texts can be seen to participate in joint interventionist practices (for, certainly, that is what any "Agency" of the Letter implies). The first passage—involving Helene and Nel on the train—is clearly relevant in discussing implications of Lacan's focus on bathrooms and trains.[22] Once Helene and Nel make their way onto the "colored" train, Helene asks of another woman seated next to her: "Is there somewhere we can go to use the restroom?" (23). "The woman," we are told, "looked up at her and seemed not to understand." The text continues: "'Ma'am?' Her eyes fastened on the thick velvet collar, the fair skin, the high-toned voice. 'The restroom,' Helene repeated. Then, in a whisper, 'the toilet.' The woman pointed out the window and said, 'Yes, ma'am. Yonder.'" This gesture of pointing out the window, to a space occupied not by "Ladies" and "Gentlemen," nor even by "Colored Ladies" and "Colored Gentlemen," but rather to the supposed space of "Nature" is what interests me here. "Helene," we are told, "looked out of the window halfway expecting to see a comfort station in the distance; instead she saw gray green trees leaning over tangled grass." "Where?" she asks of the woman. When they arrive at Meridian,[23] Helene, "still not comprehending, looked about the tiny stationhouse for a door that says 'colored women,'" while the other woman "stalked off to a field of high grass on the far side of the track." Nel recognizes only a head rag bobbing in the sea of grass.[24]

  What I want to open up is the way in which the racial other can appear set outside of the signifying chain. Designated to a space "yonder," among the grass, the leaves, and the animals, Helene and Nel are not defined as either "Ladies" or "Gentlemen," "white" or "colored," but as figures of elsewhere. They are placed outside "place," without privacy, perhaps in a space of the nonhuman.[25] Beyond "public" and "private" and beyond the gender division, the black figure in some ways occupies a privileged position, a position outside—like materiality or the letter itself—or constitutively "beyond" the margins of the official system of meaning. The letter, by itself, cannot be reassimilated into the system of meaning; without meaning of itself, it thus becomes associated with excess. The train suggests a chain of signifiers or metonymy as a trope for narrative consciousness and identity. Certain branches of psychoanalysis in some ways still seem halted at the gender labyrinth of this train station; even as they gesture toward interrogating limiting assumptions, they still unwittingly hold the binary order together (including racial differentiation), along with the extended implications of that order. This entire system remains situated in a Western anthropology, which is the station at which the train arrives.

But Lacan's picture from a train, surrounding images in "The Letter," and the train episode in *Sula* mark sites where that system can be seen to involve rifts. In Lacan, those rifts are manifest in a series of unexpected allusions: to segregation, to racial difference, to the condition of slavery and its many corollaries in which subjectivity is unequally distributed, and to sites where the binary order is exposed; in *Sula*, those rifts have to do with being cast "yonder," to the place of the beyond. *Yonder* is a key term here; it represents a prepositional space, nonfigural and outside the economy of metaphors. And it reminds us of how the material legacy of slavery participates in other sites of institutionalized "dis-equality" of power through identity. Calling our attention to the illusory nature of binaries founded on mimeticism, the concept of "yonder" also raises the issue of excrement itself to an exponentially empowered position.[26] The agency of the letter emerges here; a formal principle, it seems, appears figuratively associable with the signifying chain of "race," blackness, and the excremental.

In addition to troping on Lacan's "Letter," the train scene in *Sula* recalls a figure from *Frederick Douglass's Autobiography*, which is useful in opening up implications of the memory of slavery and of the persistence of damaging effects of allowing inherited assumptions about language use to go unquestioned. For Douglass, the central event of slave narratives occurs on the train ride from South to North; here one witnesses the "leitmotif of the journey North and the concomitant evolution of consciousness within the slave—from an identity as property and object to a sublime identity as human being and subject" (quoted in Gates, "Binary," 85). Helene and Nel's journey—involving the trip not from South to North, as in Douglass's narrative, but from North to South, that is, from the head of an idealist community (seen in Helene's self-importance, as Morrison describes it) to the material or "Bottom" (feet) of the signifying order (expressed in Rochelle's position, as Helene's mother [origin]) in Louisiana, as prostitute—reverses Douglass's central trope.[27] The scene in *Sula* thus revisits the scene of transition from slavery, from nonsubjectivity, that slave narratives explore, only in a different way.[28] Acknowledging the presence of this figure and its logic suggests not only that the trauma of slavery underlies the repeated traumas of *Sula*, but that it marks language awareness as central to the project of continuing the fight to overcome traumas based on race or other identity categories (that is, the trajectory of Sula herself). Sula's movement up to her death in Part II, in keeping with this reading, is organized around the experience of leaving behind received, social definitions of identity according to gendered and racial categories. She gets "annihilated" and "emerges" as some sort of power comparable to the material forces of fire, earth (or loam), air, and water.

Gates, commenting on Douglass's narrative, notes that the writer's "rhetorical strategy directly reflects his sentiment through the use of what . . . the structuralists have come to call the binary opposition" ("Binary," 87). The way this works, according to Gates, is that

> we see an ordering of the world based on a profoundly relational type of thinking, in which the strict barrier of difference or opposition forms the bases of a class, rather than, as in other classification schemas, an ordering based on resemblances or the identity of two or more elements. These binary oppositions produce through separation the most inflexible of barriers: that of meaning. (89)

What Douglass's narrative does, according to Gates, is expose how the system functions through linguistic operations. His narrative "brings together two terms" by showing how they share some quality; then, "by opposing two seemingly unrelated elements such as the sheep, cattle, or horses on the plantation and the specimen of life known as the slave," Douglass uses language to show how language "is made to signify the presence and absence of some quality—in this case, humanity" (ibid.).

Gates points out that Douglass explores the difference between the slave who does not use language in the same way the master does and so does not know his birth date, and the master, in order to explicate the slave's understanding of himself and his identity "through the system of the perceptions that defined the world the planters made" (ibid.). In this regard, the slave becomes the correlative of a trace without origin, comparable to Helene moving toward the encounter in the South where her "origin" is sacrileged—by having the mother exposed as a prostitute and so having "mother" and "origin" demystified. Yet, in the process, the slave is (always) also translated outside the generative order of property and meaning. What happens in Douglass's text, an event re-membered in *Sula*, is that "the deprivation of the means to tell time [in *Sula*, the means to have privacy] has created a gap in the slave's imagination between self and other, between lord and bondsman, between black and white"; and this deprivation creates an "apparent likeness between the slave and the plantation animals" (90).

Morrison's *Sula*, in continually referring not to what the reigning culture calls "black" and "white" people but to people who are "salmon-colored," "custard-colored," "chocolate-colored," or even "shit-colored," breaks with fictive and abstract designations operative within many familiar binaries (21, 22, 39). Similarly, Gates, in considering Douglass's narrative, focuses on how the "deprivation of the hallmarks of identity can affect the slave but also on how the slaveowners' world negates and even perverts those very values on which it is built" ("Binary," 9). According to Gates, Douglass's text becomes a "complex mediator between the world as the master would have it and the world as the slave knows it really is. It shows that the oppositions, all along, were only arbitrary, not fixed." At the "structural center" of his narrative, as he moves North, Douglass says, "you have seen how a man was made a slave. Now you shall see how a slave was made a man." In evoking and reversing this, Morrison's train episode does more than position the black other as marked somehow outside the system. It returns the "economy" of the master's house to the politics of naming, and to the politics of the lower bodily order (Bakhtin), or the outhouse, what seems exterior to (yet constitutively composes) the *oikos* or house itself. Moving from Gates's Douglass to *Sula* entails moving from shaking binaries in the name of reversing power and identity ("becomes a man") to exceeding this structure of the house, or identity, itself. It reminds us that Lacan's pictures continue to be seen as functioning side by side (see figure 2). The "colored" figure, in other words, has always been present, like a shadow, squatting out there somewhere beside the tree.[29] Reading the context surrounding Lacan's pictures exposes how traces of the first or mimetic model of language use are perpetuated, not only within damaging social configurations of identity that occupy lived experiences in the past, but also within various forms of identity politics participating in today's intellectual debates. Before moving on, it is important to investigate more fully Morrison's own articulation of the connection between her work and slave narratives. In "The

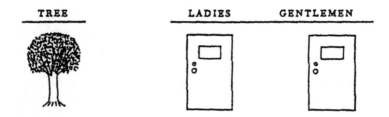

Figure 2

Site of Memory," Morrison notes of slave narratives: "whenever there was an unusually violent incident or a scatological one, or something excessive, one finds the writer taking refuge in the literary conventions of the day" (32). The writers "pull the narrative up short with a phrase such as 'But let us drop a veil over these proceedings too terrible to relate.'" Morrison's task becomes "how to rip that veil drawn over 'proceedings too terrible to relate.'" Her focus on the "scatological and the excessive"—both of which concern me here—is apparent in her repeated focus on outhouse images. Nel's discovery of "yonder" without the convenience or privacy of a door provides an ironic consideration of the process of how the veil gets "ripped" from the surface to expose proceedings usually considered "too terrible [or too private] to relate."

Although Lacan's lecture does not include a picture of a "colored" bathroom or a picture of "yonder" outside the station house, the black figure is, in many ways, at the center of his essay. Positioned "yonder," or out of the house, the black figure nonetheless inhabits the material (dedefined) center of this system. Gates probes this site, asking: "What did/do black people signify in a society in which they were intentionally introduced as the subjugated, as the enslaved cipher?" ("Signifying," 47). Yet, as we have seen, blackness is not just the "enslaved cipher" of a binary but the other of the binary system as such—the runaway slave, the passing figure, the play of the outhouse, the exteriority of the body as excrement or excess—giving the lie to the entire metaphorics of the interior. Before exploring this nonsite more fully, it is necessary to ask again—why bathrooms? It is necessary to take a last detour into the segregated rooms and their activities.

Significantly, Lacan, like Morrison, describes his textual endeavor as involving how one might "rip the veil" that has been drawn—by conventions, institutionalized forms of language use—over the dominant system of representation. He comments on his choice of bathroom pictures as follows: "It is not only with the idea of silencing the nominalists debate with a *low blow* that I use this example, but rather to show how in fact the signifier enters the signified, namely, in a form which *not being immaterial,* raises the question of its place in reality" (151; emphasis added). "Not being immaterial" raises the issue of a materiality that is not part of the normally conceived signifying chain. Lacan goes on to characterize this signifier as one whose "signified would in this call receive its final honors from the double and solemn procession from the upper nave" (151). The joke here is the linking of the signified with the signifier and the signifier with excrement; the signified, like the holiest of holies hidden from view, is here exposed as involving not the transcendent but the most material— the excremental function and its product—another so-called figure of a darkness that is not the other of light or whiteness but precedes and total-ly ruptures the prior's construction. Lacan plays on this when he com-ments on how the pictures allow us to "see from what radiating centre the signifier sends forth its light" (152). We must not ignore, here, an implied critique of the entire metaphorics, invariably binarized into light (or whiteness) and blackness; one might speak, rather, of a black light of the "material" in a situation where light is exploded as an organizing metaphor of knowledge. The center, rather than being a transcendental other, or an innate, private selfhood, is linked to an elusive material order: that, we may say, of inscription before any perception.

Thus, in addition to linking the signified and semantics to "shit," Lacan plays on the excremental motif in another way. Noting that this "allegory . . . reveals only the structure of a signifier in this transfer," Lacan links the signifier, the material trace it all comes down to, with (human) waste. The "not immaterial," the triple negatived waste product, is thus bound to the "letter," to the material trace that cannot be reassimi-lated by the semantic or symbolic order. Visually, at the center of the pic-ture is excrement, blackness, a void, the silence of the mark itself. Yet, it is material, and it generates visibility, or reading itself; and, rhetorically, just as the "Agency of the (Black) Letter" is the subject of the lecture, materi-ality is central to Lacan's project of redefining the unconscious as lan-guage, as the "discourse of the other," participating in social space. Blackness and excrement are linked, and both are linked to the "letter," to the material thing. Like excrement, which occupies a position within and yet outside the boundaries of the body, the black other (in this context), and the blackness of the material signifying system (seen as secondary, descriptive, nonsignificant), occupy positions outside the house, in the outhouse.

This point can be tied with the idea of passing (for example, passing *for* another—as Helene's "fair skin," rich clothes, and haughty demeanor momentarily confuse the other woman on the "colored" train and give the lie to the institutionalization of the binary order as one based on "Nature"—or passing *toward* another identity position, as in Douglass's narrative), crossing the borderlines of identity, which is significant in that it reveals the constructedness of the borderline, thus exposing the arbitrariness of racial or gendered signs of identity.[30] Here materiality (connected still to the train) and excrement have to do with the spacing of linguistic memory, with anteriority. They can be marked as sites of inscription, preceding representation. Like the head rag floating in a sea of grass,[31] which cannot be seen or named outright, the material other draws aside the door, the veil, and exposes the secret event, "stirs up shit," by pointing out that the signifier as excrement is at once ground of the material order and a by-product of human activity.[32] Blackness here asserts the priority and "agency" of the signifier. It puts us in touch with the formerly delegitimized, the silenced, the process that brings us into relation with sheer anteriority. This is not to pronounce an absence of meaning, but rather to announce alternative models for its production, management, and transmission. The suppression of the "racial other" is clearly identified with that of the materiality of signification—and here, at odds with any "identity politics" that thinks it can address "politics" without revolutionizing conceptions of "identity" by altering the economy of signification.

The other scene from *Sula* enters the picture here. The episode, from the "1919" section, involves Shadrack in a jail cell, unable to find a mirror to confirm his identity that has become shattered through seeing a war-torn soldier's body in bits and pieces. In lieu of a mirror, Shadrack finds a toilet: "There in the toilet water he saw a grave black face. A black so definite, so unequivocal, it astonished him. He had been harboring a skittish apprehension that he was not real, that he didn't exist at all. But when the blackness greeted him with its indisputable Presence, he wanted nothing more" (13). Looking in the toilet, like a Narcissus, but beyond that image and the mirror stage, Shadrack sees a blackness like excrement that simulates the face; it is a blackness that, preceding the face, or figuration, exceeds the binary system and identity itself.

But here there appears another inversion. The blackness is, simply something with an "indisputable Presence," and thus something occupying, for those who care to look, the space in which some expect to find (white, light) presence, or full meaning—the signified (in the passage, the "meaning" behind Shadrack's physical, material self). As in Lacan's passage, the figures (signifier/signified) are not only reversed; both are seen to come down to the issue not of invisible, "given" meaning, but of the pure trace of a materiality before any thought or perception. Lacan furthers this reading with his claim that "one cannot go further in this line of thought than to demonstrate that no signification can be sustained other than by reference to another signification" (150). A further statement of this comes with Lacan's image of the "closed order" that is our language, an order that remains within the realm of signification. This is the point at which he notes an image of "the signifying chain" as a necklace; it is "rings of a necklace that is a ring in another necklace made of rings" (153). Linked to what has been called the "chora," this "blackness" occupies a presignifying space.[33]

It is not at all insignificant that *Sula* features not only a protagonist who "stirs up shit," but excrement as a dominant image that appears and reappears, sometimes in the most unexpected places, and frequently as a marker of especially significant episodes. And it is not unimportant in this context that *Sula* repeatedly draws connections between Shadrack, Sula, and excrement, and repeatedly reminds readers—as in the episode on the train, with its haunting memory of how slavery deprived slaves of an identity as human subjects—of how the binary order of the West continues to divide the masters from those who are figures of "excess." In addition, readers will recall Eva's difficulty with the baby Plum (whose name functions ironically in that it is the name of a laxative fruit) resulting in an episode in the frozen outhouse, of struggling to "stir up the shit," with the aid of a "piece of beet" and the "remnants of a lard can." The barrage of references to excrement—from the soldiers' "shit-colored uniforms," to the bird droppings that literally pelt the Bottom on Sula's return from her ten-year absence,[34] to Eva's comment that "Pearl was shittin' worms and I was supposed to play rang-around the rosie?" to Nel's comment to the dying Sula that "you ride the pony and we shovel the shit"—suggests that the novel reaches beyond the social code of blackness (or even anality) in some sheer juncture of excess and abjection (21, 89, 69, 149). Sula, too, will exceed the binary formulations of man or woman, black or white, in forging a new identity experience. Ultimately, this identity exceeds the boundaries of the living and the dead, as Nel encounters what can only be called "Sula" years after Sula's death. "'Sula?' she whispered, gazing at the tops of trees. 'Sula?'" (174). As Nel whispers her friend's name, "Leaves stirred; mud shifted; there was the smell of overripe green things. A soft ball of fur broke and scattered like dandelion spores in the breeze." Nel senses the shifting of something that had been previously clogged, as she realizes "all that time, all that time, I thought I was missing Jude."

Gates suggests that black "Signifyin(g)," aligned with rhetoric—and with poetry, art, and other endeavors juxtaposed against what one might call "right uses of language"—critiques white "signification" or semantics and the order of fixed meaning. He notes that tales of the Signifying Monkey "had their origins in slavery" and that they frequently involve excrement ("Signifying," 51). These mark another direct link with *Sula*. Here is a typical example:

> Deep down in the jungle so they say
> There's a signifying monkey down the way
> There hadn't been no disturbin' in the jungle
> > for quite a bit,
> For up jumped the monkey in the tree one day and
> > laughed,
> "I guess I'll start some shit." (Gates, "Blackness," 239)

This Signifyin(g) has to do with a trickster figure who dwells at the margins of discourse. Ever punning, ever troping, it "primarily mediates, but its mediations are tricks" (Gates, "Binary," 93). Gates suggests that (black) Signifyin(g), while it involves reinscribing silenced identities, moves beyond an order in which binaries are assumed and are seen to have to do primarily with identity categories. Sula's cryptic speech on her deathbed, that she will be loved "After all the old women have lain with the teen-agers; . . . when all the white women kiss all the black ones; . . . after all the dogs have fucked all the cats and every weathervane on every barn flies off the roof to mount the hogs" performs a similar "stirring up" of shit—to the extent that categories are mixed and jumbled and torn apart in a violence that resolves itself in the words *love* and *always* (145). "Signifyin(g)" moves beyond the binary "signifier/signified" and the privileging of one; it "turns on the play and chain of signifiers and not on some supposedly transcendent signified" (ibid.).

Thus, Lacan's picture of segregated bathrooms raises the issue of racial segregation in addition to sexual segregation and the functioning of language in the constitution of a self within a particular symbolic system. But his pictures occur in an unexpected way that do not return to simple "identity politics." As Lacan's "Letter" foregrounds that which had been deemed "waste" (the materiality of language, seen as secondary and "dispensable" according to the "classic" pre-Saussurean model of language use), it links the black "other" (the letter, the slave, the subject seen as material and expendable, not worthy of a private room) and excrement, seeing these as modalities outside the borders of the official, inherited system (or "house"); that is, as linked to the material function of language and to the language of the unconscious, the "discourse of the other," the "agency of the (black) letter." A psychoanalytic field that both engages the subject in culture and speculates on the possibility of thinking outside that subject position seems here actively to comment on the racial "other" of the Western hegemonic system—with vast implications if we think of problems linked to constructions of postcolonialism, immigration, educational, media, economic, and legal attitudinal and policy decisions. Becoming aware of the vast networks of interacting signifying orders provides an opportunity for transforming from within possibilities for interrogating received trajectories of meaning and identity. This project, noted in Lacan's title "The Agency of the [Black] Letter," has to do with the agency or materiality of signification itself. It and its counterparts—supposedly hidden excremental gestures, and shit itself—all function as corollaries for a postsymbolic figure, a sort of thing-function that threatens the order of metonymy and the law itself. It also marks the site where what we now call "high theory," in a retrospective gesture, returns to join cultural critique in passing out of impasses that have kept the textual, the rhetorical, the "material," and the "fictive" exiled from assuming power.

NOTES

1. Morrison reminds us that "A literate slave was supposed to be a contradiction in terms" (300).

2. Jane Gallop points out, referring back to comments by Philippe Lacoue-Labarthe and Jean-Luc Nancy, that "Lacan is thus intervening in the reigning order of knowledge, not only in the university as a place but in the university as a symbolic structure" (114). Perhaps even more important for my essay is the reminder that, given its position as the "first of the *Écrits* to be published in English, this text is seen to be "Lacan's first real intervention into the American

academy." The "Letter," arising from a meeting with "literary specialists" (a term widely discussed by scholars of this essay), has to do with what Bowie calls "the formation of analysts," which is seen to require "a knowledge of literature"; it is thus appropriate to read this text in coordination with literary works (see Bowie 104; Gallop 1985, 114).

3. Gallop notes that it appeared in 1966 in the *Yale French Studies* issue on structuralism, under the title "The Insistence of the Letter in the Unconscious" (1985, 114).

4. Gallop points out that "at the beginning of the lecture, [Lacan] poses the question of how to take the 'letter' in his title. He answers, 'quite simply, *à la lettre.*'" Gallop's response is "*À la lettre*: that is, literally, 'to the letter'; figuratively, 'literally'" (1985, 115). Claiming that the problem of translation "marks with an efflorescence of bad jokes the point where a conflict between the spirit and the letter becomes telling," Gallop sets up for some of my own remarks (to come in this essay) about other "bad jokes" touching on the "conflict between the spirit and the letter."

5. Commenting on the "difficulty" and "violence" of Lacan's style, Gallop notes that it has the "capacity to make the reader feel nonidentical with herself as reader . . . to make the reader feel inadequate" to her role as the purveyor of Lacan's style. The ego-subverting influence of the text, and its experiential and disruptive mode of intervention, are suggested by Gallop as she looks at Lacan's comments in the essay on Freud comparing a dream to a rebus. Gallop argues for reading the text on the "agency of the letter" as a "rebus, a picture-puzzle in which the elements do not belong together, have no representational unity" (1985, 118). Suggesting that part of the need to do so involves the text's subversion of the "signified" as it is understood within phallogocentric practice, Gallop notes that "the only way to understand a rebus, to interpret it, is to consider the elements one at a time." She suggests that we interpret Lacan's "Letter" in this way "rather than feeling responsible for understanding the totality" of the lecture. The text thus participates in forcing readers out of the "habit of discursive reading, our assumption that each sentence flows out of the preceding one"; it disrupts at the level of reading. Keeping this in mind allows me to focus more exclusively on a few brief episodes in the lecture, episodes that do, in the end, link up to the overall project of the piece. Similarly, Lacoue-Labarthe and Nancy, in *Le Titre de la Lettre* (a text "highly recommended by Lacan"), suggest that they decipher Lacan's text through a certain "metaphorical interplay," seen to "constitute both the issue and style of the paper" (quoted in Benvenuto and Kennedy 146). Malcolm Bowie, also making note of the difficulty of this text, points out that it "seeks to be at once an emancipatory 'way out' from the structure of the unconscious and a constricted 'way in' to that same structure" (3).

6. Bowie also notes that sentences such as "the unconscious is structured like a language," "the unconscious is the discourse of the Other," and "A letter always arrives at its destination," which he calls "memorably simple," are "glimpses of what a fully intelligible and transmissible psychoanalytic theory might be like" (3).

7. This story may be linked with the "official" interpretation of the biblical story of the Tower of Babel, that there is one language, one reality that is and

serves as the measure of meaning. This would be parallel to Bakhtin's "monolog-ic" language, which exists only as a concept, not in lived reality; Bakhtin dubs this "Adam's language" (1981, 279).

8. Gallop notes, in "Psychoanalysis and Feminism," that "Lacan has found his principal American audience among literary academics, and so this text addressed to those in Letters rather than to psychoanalysts, is particularly appro-priate for American readers of Lacan" (116). Considering the veiled allusions to race, slavery, or blackness, I will argue that this text is "particularly appropriate for American readers of Lacan" for another reason.

9. Introducing the "Psychoanalysis and Race" forum at the 1996 Modern Language Association convention in Washington, D.C., Claire Kahane, of the State University of New York, Buffalo, noted these representations of psychoanaly-sis and argued that it offers unique resources, and is the most penetrating model for intervening in issues of representation, the body, and race, especially given the centrality of the body in the politics of race.

10. This focus on the "butt," on scatological things, begins in *Sula* with the relegation of Sula's people to the "Bottom," and extends throughout the novel. It migrates from a trope useful in exploring the community of the Bottom as it exists alongside the "others" on "top," to something wholly other.

11. See Henry Louis Gates Jr., "Binary Oppositions," "Introduction" to *The Signifying Monkey,* "The Signifying Monkey and the Language of Signifyin(g)," and "The Blackness of Blackness."

12. The figure of the train, in an American context, assumes links with segre-gation and the compartmentalization of people according to "race," as well as links with a structure subversive of the institution of slavery—the underground railroad. Also the train becomes the site where people cross boundaries—political boundaries, and boundaries of identity.

13. "Seat" will connect with "bottom" and other figures of abjection as this argument proceeds.

14. It is perhaps no accident that Shadrack as a "waste of war" is a figure of excess no longer assimilable into society after his post-traumatic stress; he is por-trayed as having been sacrificed for a system that would offer him little in return, because, as Ajax succinctly pus it: "Nothing good—white man running it" (Morrison 1973, 102).

15. Vashti Criutcher Lewis, in "African Tradition in Toni Morrison's *Sula,*" argues that Sula and Shadrack are both linked to the priest or priestess who is sometimes scapegoated or ousted from the community; she points out that it is these figures who are most needed for the community to maintain vitality and health.

16. Kwame Anthony Appiah's mode of "wondering aloud" whether or not "a structuralist poetics is inapplicable in Africa because Structuralism is European" reminds us that such importations must be carried out with caution, so that we are not falling into the trap of "substituting one form of neocolonialism for another" (quoted in Gates 1986, 15).

17. Valerie Smith, in "Black Feminist Theory and the Representation of the 'Other,'" points to the debate in *Diacritics* between Nancy K. Miller and Peggy

Kamuf on this issue. She suggests that "Miller's reassertion of the significance of women as historical, material subjects" suggests that the "destabilization of all categories of identity, including the category of 'woman,' may well serve the interests of a male hegemony whose own power is under siege" (41). Other "feminist" thinkers, including Hélène Cixous and Julia Kristeva, suggest that all people stand to lose by failing to interrogate inherited categories of identity.

18. Lacan's allusion in a note at this point to "the savage dramas of Shakespeare" (by which he might be seen to refer to *The Tempest*, given his allusion at this point in the essay to the tempestuous scene of a "tossing off by a highbrow critic," and his allusion in the passage to waves and "streaks of rain") suggests another possible allusion to race here, in the figure of Caliban.

19. Valerie Smith notes that "the move to include black women as historical presences . . . in critical discourse" is often used "as a defense against charges of racial hegemony on the part of white women and sexist hegemony on the part of black males" (45). She cites Gates in this context repeatedly. What Smith takes issue with is her observation that "at the moment when Anglo-American feminists and male Afro-Americanists begin to consider the material ground of their enterprise, they demonstrate a return to earth, as it were, by invoking the specific experiences of black women" (45). For her, this "resembles . . . the associations, in classic Western philosophy and in 19th century cultural constructions of womanhood, of women of color with the body and therefore with animal passions and slave labor." In invoking the phrase "I am black, but comely . . . ," from the "Song of Solomon," and "the nineteenth-century cliché of a 'poor, but honest' woman," Lacan foregrounds the use of the black woman (and the white woman) in biblical and colonialist discourse, seemingly as a way of confronting (by excavating and interrogating) the very issue Smith addresses.

20. Irigaray's conception of "the sex which is not one" also refers to the presence not of one erogenous zone, but of "several" (*This Sex Which Is Not One*).

21. Valerie Smith notes of Houston A. Baker and Henry Louis Gates Jr. that "such a theory of language, literature, and culture suggests that 'literary' meanings are conceived in a non-social, non-institutional manner" and are "maintained and transmitted, without an agent, within a closed circle of 'intertextuality'" (43). She suggests that such language-based approaches "extract black writers from their relationship to their audience and from the circumstances in which they wrote and were read."

22. It is no less significant that this mass-transit system, associated with the nineteenth century, with the great age of colonialism, involves class and race. In Hitchcock, the train functions as a partial trope of metonymy, the machinal, the symbolic; the term *transport* can be seen in its association with "meta-phor."

23. Significant in its marking of a boundary, "Meridian" becomes the place of passage between the North (segregated, but with facilities for all) and the South (designating the travelers to "yonder" for the carrying out of their "private" functions).

24. This figure of the head bobbing in the sea of grass may be compared to the head of Pip in *Moby Dick*, fallen overboard, and gone too deep for retrieval. The image suggests Morrison's position within an American literary tradition,

reminding us of the presence of race, but also of the participation of figures within and on the margins of the binary order. Pip, gone too deep, also bears links with Shadrack.

25. In "Binary Oppositions," Gates notes of the world that Frederick Douglass inhabits: "The deprivation of the means to tell time [functioning like the deprivation of privacy in the train scene] is the very structural center of this initial paragraph, in which [Douglass] defines what it means to become aware of one's own enslavement. . . . Slaves, he concludes, are those who cannot plot their course by and who *stand outside of* the linear progression of the calendar." Gates continues: "And precisely here Douglass summarizes the symbolic code of this world, which makes the slave's closest blood relations the horses . . . (also without the means to tell time, and so outside the signifying system) (90–91; emphasis added).

26. See Mikhail Bakhtin's discussion of excrement and the lower bodily functions in "Images of the Material Bodily Lower Stratum" and "The Grotesque Image of the Bodily and Its Sources" from *Rabelais and His World*.

27. Here "materialism" is contrasted to "idealism"; the feet are contrasted to the head; and the top is contrasted with the bottom ("The Bottom"). It is not unimportant that the trip down South also involves a trip to the lower orders, a trip to the space belonging to Rochelle (now pure materiality), the prostitute-mother whose identity position Helene seeks to deny at every step.

28. Designated to a space "yonder," among the grass, the leaves, and the animals, the "colored" subject occupies a position beyond the binary Ladies/Gentlemen, and beyond the distinction between public and private, a position occupying the symbolic realm, but also not occupying that realm, because, within the symbolic, this figure is not subject but object.

29. In "Marginality as Site of Resistance," bell hooks mentions a similar "shadow," and links it to a specifically identity-based position. She notes, in the context of discussing her voice as one coming from the margins, speaking "in resistance, I open a book. There are words on the back cover 'never on the shadows again.'" Asking "who stands in the shadows?" she responds that "it is the space where black women are represented voiceless" (343). I want to concede hooks's point, while also arguing that gaining a voice sometimes involves reinscribing how meaning and identities get positioned within structures.

30. It is significant that the idea of passing spans projects as disparate as the work of Douglass in the 1840s and the work of Judith Butler (*Gender Trouble*), Jenny Livingston (*Paris Is Burning*), and some of Barbara Johnson's recent work on "Passing and Impasse."

31. The connection between the black heads bobbing in the sea of grass and the figure of Pip in *Moby Dick*, having fallen into a swirling sea to become lost in the water that is too deep for his retrieval, acknowledges *Sula's* position, in a tradition not only of African American writers (following Frederick Douglass), but also of Anglo-American writers, including Melville.

32. It is not unimportant that Lacan describes the unconscious in similar terms.

33. For an elaboration of this in Derrida's work, see *On the Name*. In feminist

theory, Kristeva has come to be most visibly associated with the concept of the "chora."

34. The novel states: "You couldn't go anywhere without stepping in their pearly shit" (89).

WORKS CITED

Bakhtin, Mikhail. "Discourse in the Novel." In *The Dialogic Imagination,* ed. Michael Holquist, trans. Caryl Emerson and Michael Holquist. Austin: University of Texas Press, 1981. 259–422.

———. *Rabelais and His World.* Trans. Helene Iswolsky. Bloomington: Indiana University Press, 1984.

Benvenuto, Rice, and Roger Kennedy. *The Works of Jacques Lacan: An Introduction.* London: Free Association, 1986.

Bowie, Malcolm. *Lacan.* Cambridge: Harvard University Press, 1991.

Cixous, Hélène. "Sorties." In *New French Feminisms: An Anthology,* ed. Elaine Marks and Isabelle de Courtivron. New York: Schocken Books, 1980. 90–98.

Derrida, Jacques. *On the Name,* ed. Thomas Dutoit. Stanford, Calif.: Stanford University Press, 1995.

Doane, Mary Ann. "Veiling Over Desire: Close-ups of the Woman." In *Feminism and Psychoanalysis,* ed. Richard Feldstein and Judith Roof. Ithaca, N.Y.: Cornell University Press, 1989. 105–41.

Douglass, Frederick. *Narrative of the Life of Frederick Douglass, an American Slave.* New York: Doubleday, 1845.

Gallop, Jane. "Psychoanalysis and Feminism." In *The Daughter's Seduction: Feminism and Psychoanalysis.* Ithaca, N.Y.: Cornell University Press, 1982. 1–14.

———. "Metaphor and Metonymy." In *Reading Lacan.* Ithaca, N.Y.: Cornell University Press, 1985. 114–32.

Gates, Henry Louis, Jr. "Editor's Introduction: Writing 'Race' and the Difference It Makes." In *Race, Writing, and Difference.* Chicago: University of Chicago Press, 1986. 1–19.

———. "Binary Oppositions in Chapter One of Narrative of the Life of Frederick Douglass an American Slave Written by Himself." In *Figures in Black: Words, Signs, and the "Racial" Self.* New York: Oxford University Press, 1987. 80–97.

———. "The Blackness of Blackness: A Critique on the Sign of the Signifying Monkey." In *Figures in Black: Words, Signs, and the "Racial" Self.* New York: Oxford University Press, 1987. 235–51.

———. "Introduction." In *The Signifying Monkey: A Theory of Afro-American Literary Criticism.* New York: Oxford University Press, 1988. xix–xxviii.

———. "The Signifying Monkey and the Language of Signifyin(g): Rhetorical Difference and the Orders of Meaning." In *The Signifying Monkey: A Theory of Afro-American Literary Criticism.* New York: Oxford University Press, 1988. 44–54.

hooks, bell. "Marginality as Site of Resistance." In *Out There: Marginalization and Contemporary Cultures,* ed. Russell Ferguson, Martha Gever, Trinh T. Minh-ha, and Cornel West. New York: New Museum of Contemporary Art, 1990. 341–45.

Irigaray, Luce. *This Sex Which Is Not One.* Trans. Catherine Porter. Ithaca, N.Y.: Cornell University Press, 1985.

Kahane, Claire. "Introduction to 'Psychoanalysis and Race' Panel." Modern Language Association convention. Washington Sheraton, Washington, D.C., December 29, 1996.

Lacan, Jacques. "The Agency of the Letter in the Unconscious or Reason since Freud." In *Écrits: A Selection.* Trans. Alan Sheridan. New York: W. W. Norton, 1977. 146–78.

Lacoue-Labarthe, Philippe and Jean-Luc Nancy. *Le Titre de la Lettre.* Paris: Éditions Galilée, 1973.

Lewis, Vashti Criutcher. "African Tradition in Toni Morrison's *Sula.*" *Atlanta University Review of Race and Culture* 48 (1987): 91–97.

Morrison, Toni. *Sula.* New York: Plume (Penguin), 1973.

———. "The Site of Memory." In *Out There: Marginalization and Contemporary Cultures,* ed. Russell Ferguson, Martha Gever, Trinh T. Minh-ha, and Cornel West. New York: New Museum of Contemporary Art, 1990. 299–347.

Smith, Valerie. "Black Feminist Theory and the Representation of the 'Other.'" In *Changing Our Own Words: Essays on Criticism, Theory and Writings by Black Women,* ed. Cheryl A. Wall. New Brunswick, N.J.: Rutgers University Press, 1989. 38–57.

"Karmic Realignment": Transnationalism and Trauma in *The Simpsons*

Eva Cherniavsky

> Capitalism today quickens the pace at which significance diminishes away from text and moves toward things themselves.
>
> — BEN AGGER, *Fast Capitalism*

> HOMER: You're selling what, now?
> APU: Only the concept of karmic realignment.
> HOMER: You can't sell that. Karma can only be portioned out by the cosmos.
> APU: He's got me there.
>
> — *The Simpsons*

In an age when cultural studies has moved well beyond the Frankfurt school disdain for popular culture, to assume instead the irreducible political polyvalence of popular cultural texts, I propose to revisit that hoary line of inquiry concerning the possibilities and limits of counter-hegemonic representation within the commodified forms of popular culture. It is not my intention to sound a retreat, as though Adorno and Horkheimer were right all along about the intellectual bankruptcy of culture for profit. I say this despite the fact that for a week now and counting the screen in my living room has been possessed by the images of a photogenic British aristocrat and a "world in mourning" for her finishing-school polish, for the imperial vision of gracious white womanhood made (video) flesh. Whatever currency this most recent, dismal mediation of "our" human commonality as dehistoricized affect might impart to such a nostalgic reconsecration of Frankfurt school avant-gardism, my inquiry presumes precisely the impossibility of such a return—presumes, with

Laura Kipnis, the erosion of contexts for critique outside the commodity form (Kipnis 14). Certainly, the versatility and mobility of late-capitalist production methods have made "narrowcasting" and niche marketing increasingly viable, so that cultures of resistance are now promptly repro- duced and disseminated as fresh new styles sold under corporate labels to carefully targeted consumer populations, as David Harvey has noted (Harvey 156, 303). Yet, precisely insofar as capitalist enterprise has learned to incorporate the local and ephemeral forms that once appeared as the proper domain of oppositional culture, it becomes newly urgent to consid- er how a critical perspective on the policies of multi- and transnational capital might be sustained within the scenes of commodity culture. My motive in re-posing an old question is the evident demise of the old answer.

Among the many cultural products I might propose to read, and certainly of anything I might select from the bill of contemporary televi- sion fare, the Fox Television Network's long-running animated series *The Simpsons* heralds itself with unusual vigor and consistency as a critically self-reflexive commodity.[1] To borrow Ben Agger's useful distinction, the series *as a text* is centrally concerned with the forms, pleasures, and mind- zapping effects of the late-twentieth-century commodity culture in which the series *as a thing* is so thoroughly implicated. For Agger, admittedly, it is the failure of text and thing to remain distinct that characterizes the accelerated, or "fast," capitalism, of the present moment. Under fast capi- talism, "textuality, [understood as] a possible medium of critical resis- tance, fails to stand apart," so that texts become things, "provoking their thoughtlessly ready readings," just as things become the bearers of an already prescribed text for the world (Agger 5). If *The Simpsons* as image- commodity are paradigmatic of Agger's thing-texts, things through which circulate an increasingly circumscribed repertoire of cultural meanings, then I would argue that it is the aspiration of *The Simpsons* to make of its very conscription a critical resource. In its continuous, satiric represen- tation of corporate ethics and advertising, of the franchised suburban landscape, and of television, its representation, in short, of the "degrada- tion of significance" in which the series itself participates (Agger 6), *The Simpsons* appears committed to assuming the intellectual's function, prof- fering a noniterative version (text) of its own conditions of possibility.[2]

In addressing *The Simpsons*'s critical ambitions, I am drawn to an episode from the 1994–95 season titled "Homer and Apu," which thematizes the deterritorialized operations of multi- and transnational capital, and thus resonates directly with the circumstances of *The Simpsons*'s overseas production. The episode centers on the otherwise marginal figure of the South Asian convenience store clerk, Apu, who is fired from the Kwik-E-Mart after selling tainted food products to Homer. Desperate to be reinstated, Apu undertakes a pilgrimage to Kwik-E-Mart corporate headquarters, which are located, it turns out, on a remote mountaintop in India.[3] This representation of transnational enterprise thus furnishes a potentially retextualized frame in which the series might reflect on its own producer's practice of outsourcing animation, though only the most dedicated viewer is likely to have gleaned from the series's accelerated closing credits the notable fact of its transpacific origins. The speed at which the production credits flash by degrades the meaning of this textualized thing in the most material sense, of course, rendering nearly illegible the inscription of the commodity's relation to embodied labor. As industry sources divulge, however, Film Roman subcontracts the labor-intensive aspects of production on the series, including the drawing and coloring of cels, to one of six "animation houses" in South Korea.[4] According to studio owner Phil Roman, underpriced Asian labor has become indispensable to the animation industry in the United States: "If we had to do animation here," Roman notes, "it would cost a million dollars instead of $100,000 to $150,000 to produce a half-hour, and nobody could afford to do it except for Disney" (quoted in Edelstein 38).

Inderpal Grewal and Caren Kaplan have proposed understanding transnationalism as marking both the emergent organization of capitalist accumulation and a field of potential resistance to the new modalities of neocolonial domination that sustain this emerging order. The advantage of transnationalism as a model for globalization under late capitalism, they argue, lies in its capacity to query the geopolitical binaries that stand as the apparent legacy of colonialist world-making: "We use the term 'transnational,'" they write, "to problematize a purely locational politics of global-local or center-periphery in favor of what [Armand] Mattelart sees as the lines cutting across them" (Grewal and Kaplan 11). Imagined in this way, transnationalism formulates a decisive challenge to the reductive concept of "a homogenizing West" that saturates the globe with capital and commodities, remaking its historical others in its image.[5] Certain-ly, one contribution of postcolonial scholarship, and particularly, I would emphasize, of subaltern studies, has been to understand how the "periphery" marks the "center," as well as the "center" the "periphery."[6] Thus, as Grewal and Kaplan remind us, the West itself must be addressed, presently and historically, as no less a hybrid zone than its (former) dependencies. Building on the proposition that cultural flows are not unidirectional, Grewal and Kaplan invite a more nuanced interrogation of global commodity culture, one in which we ask, for example: "What aspect of a commodity gets utilized in what way and where? Can we see these commodities as artifacts? How do we trace the cultural baggage of commodities from their point of origin (if this can be ascertained)?" (ibid.).

Tellingly, as this essay goes on to explore, "Homer and Apu" splits itself in relation to what we might call the two faces of Grewal and Kaplan's critical project. Although the series as a whole routinely acknowledges and occasionally investigates the diasporic presence of the formerly colonized in the metropolis, in "Homer and Apu" this hybrid look of the multicultural West finds its mirror image in the Westernized look of the postmodern East, so that hybridity is transformed from an index of multidirectional flows across historical divides to the paradoxical sign of global homogeneity.[7] Homer and Apu's transglobal journey to Kwik-E-Mart headquarters reveals everywhere the same hybridity, in other words, divested of its regional/historical specificity. More particularly, in representing India, "Homer and Apu" effects its own "karmic realignment" of historical forces, conflating transnational corporatism with cosmic awareness and the hyperreality of commodity culture with the fabled Orient's monumental time. In this sanitized vision of India as the quaintly syncretic fusion of premodern holism and postmodern simulation, the question of this nation's access to the benefits of modernity is conveniently elided. Yet, this degraded (if ironic) textualization of transnational capital as the newest (and the oldest) of cosmic dispensations falls under scrutiny at precisely those moments where the episode attends to the forms and practices of consumption in the West. If Marx's famous dancing table fails to divulge the social relations that animate it, commodities on this episode of *The Simpsons* seem very nearly disposed to reveal their origins and mark their destinations, to disclose their "cultural baggage" to the baffled and traumatized shopper. Furthermore, moving against the conventional association of consumerism with middle-class women, "Homer and Apu" situates white men as the paradigmatic Western consumers. Here it is specifically the white male body that is touched and refigured by its encounter with the fruits of global capital.

WHO NEEDS THE KWIK-E-MART?

The answer to this question, sung by Apu in a toe-tapping musical sequence, is Apu himself, whose allegiance to the Kwik-E-Mart corporation turns out to be no less defining of his identity than Apu's stereotyped Indian ethnicity. After Homer's avid consumption of Kwik-E-Mart snacks lands him in the emergency room for the third time, Apu sits disconsolately on the Simpson's roof, gazing across the suburban treetops to the neon Kwik-E-Mart sign, and croons the final line to his melody: "Who needs the Kwik-E-Mart? I dooo . . ." At stake for Apu is not the underpaid service position that his neighbors view as a job of last resort, but the corporate membership it confers. Kwik-E-Mart personnel flown in to handle the public relations crisis generated by Homer's salmonella poisoning ritually divest Apu of his corporate insignia, including his "Try Our Fried Pickles" badge, and solemnly insist that he hand over his pricing guns, one of which Apu attempts to conceal in an ankle holster. This satiric staging of Apu's dismissal as a kind of dishonorable military discharge implicitly redefines the economic unit of the corporation as a quasi-political unit, whose employees' connection to local and national community has been supplanted by their corporate citizenship. That Apu's relation to his neighborhood clientele is subsumed by the corporate profit motive is made laughably apparent in the episode's opening sequence, in which Apu gleefully markets 29-cent stamps for $1.85 and charges $4.20 for "two dollars' worth of gas."[8] We learn that Apu is not blind but simply indifferent to the damaging effects of corporate greed on the community he supposedly serves after his dismissal, when he attempts to take his own life by ingesting a Kwik-E-Mart hot dog. His menial functions notwithstanding, Apu thus becomes representative of what Masao Miyoshi defines as an emergent transnational managerial class, culled from various nationalities and ethnicities, whose corporate loyalties displace both local and national affiliations (Miyoshi 741).

In an initial attempt to redeem his disgrace by rededicating himself to Homer's well-being, Apu briefly labors in the Simpson household as cook, gardener, manservant, and purveyor of an enlivening and exoticized ethnicity, offered up in the form of yoga, spicy food, and the sounds of the shenai. Yet, as the melancholy Apu quickly deciphers, this overtly colonial arrangement is a poor substitute for what the episode represents by contrast as the ecstatic shopping mall multiculturalism of the transnational corporation. Apu thus resolves to petition in person for his reinstatement and purchases a pair of plane tickets for himself and Homer, who has grown attached to his domestic and insists on sharing his pilgrimage to the distant corporate offices. Briefly harassed by chanting evangelists at the airport ("Oh great, Christians!" grumbles a saffron-clad Hare Krishna with shaved head and topknot, as he pushes past them), Homer and Apu tread their way through several filmic clichés, including the train scene from *Gandhi* (the passengers ride on the outside of the car) and a desert caravan sequence, complete with romantic orchestral score, lifted straight from *Lawrence of Arabia.*

This brief transit through Hollywood's "big" pictures concluded, the duo enters the zone of generic citations: the travelogue, the mountain-climbing epic, the "lost world" romance. Standing at the base of a snow-covered mountain, Apu gestures skyward toward a modest wooden temple perched near the summit, and announces with evident pride: "There she is, the world's first convenience store!" Homer demurs ("This isn't very convenient"), and the pilgrims make their way up the mountain trail, through the automatic glass doors, and across a large, empty hall where Muzak sounds obnoxiously. As they approach the dais at the far end, Apu alerts Homer that the aim of their quest is at hand: "Here's the benevolent and enlightened president and CEO of Kwik-E-Mart and in Ohio Stop-O-Mart. He's the one I must ask for my job back." At this point, sitting in the lotus position beneath a giant poster that cautions "The Master knows all except combination to the safe," we notice a beatific old man, in a plain white tunic, noisily slurping a Kwik-E-Mart "squishy" through a straw. Having slaked his thirst (or completed his meditation ritual), he advises the visitors that they may ask three questions. "That's great, because all I need is one," Apu replies, but before he can continue, Homer intercedes:

"Are you really the head of Kwik-E-Mart?"

"Yes."

"*Really?*"

"Yes."

"*You?*"

"I hope this has been enlightening for you," the sage concludes the interview, cutting off Apu's several attempted appeals with a chirpy "thank you, come again." As the doors close behind them, Homer is moved to observe: "Well that was a big bust! Is he *really* the head of Kwik-E-Mart?"

The joke, of course, is that the Indian postmodern looks exactly like a Disneyland installation of India, where holy places beckon beyond automatic doors and "thank you, come again" is repackaged as the stuff of transcendental consciousness. If the (literalized) figure of the corporate guru seems to trigger Homer's suspicions about a loss of authenticity, moreover, this ungrounding of appearances is detached from historical experience to become instead the timeless message of enlightenment that the wise man would impart to Homer. But the joke is also, in its fashion, quite pernicious. At Kwik-E-Mart headquarters, the simultaneity of electronic transfer and satellite communication, and the decentralization of production that it enables, is thematized through an Orientalist construction of India's indelible antiquity. In this way, what David Harvey terms the "time-space compression" endemic to capitalist expansion figures as a return to a phantasmic land that time forgot, rather than as a timely phenomenon linked to the formation of chronically underdeveloped zones and their differential incorporation within capital's social regime. With respect to its representation of transnational corporatism, in short, the episode draws from the colonialist archive on India in order precisely to erase the history of colonialism and its legacies. Insofar as India's colonial past reduces to decontextualized cinematic allusions, "Homer and Apu" would seem to exemplify Fredric Jameson's famous dictum that we have emerged into "a new and original historical situation in which we are condemned to seek History by way of our own pop images and simulacra of that history, which itself remains forever out of reach" (Jameson 25).

IT'S GONNA GET YOU, SUCKA

As Masao Miyoshi has observed, multi- and transnational corporations capitalize on the cheap labor, minimal environmental regulation, and underdeveloped unionism, feminism, and civil rights consciousness that are often the colonizing nation's bequest to its former territories, in a renewal and extension of (neo)colonial practice that this episode of *The Simpsons* effaces (Miyoshi 740). At the same time, in its representation of consumerism, "Homer and Apu" registers the force (if not precisely the content) of the present and historical conditions it participates in derealizing, as though the relations of production so meticulously purged from its vision of transnational enterprise might yet somehow be grasped at the site of the commodity's consumption. In an inversion of a normative Marxist critique, which rejoins the commodity to the material scene of its production and the extraction of surplus value from the laboring body,

The Simpsons seeks to unpack this portion of the commodity's baggage on the consumer body and the consumer psyche. Such a privileging of consumption as the site of critical possibility, I suspect, may well be the hallmark and the extraordinarily vexed imperative of critique in the commodity form. At its worst, such a critique reclaims the consumer from his depthless state, elevating him (anew) from subject-effect (a node through which capital circuits) into authorial subject. The consumer classes (professional, administrative, and service personnel with a disposable income) are recast as the guarantors of a subaltern history that they participate, through consumption, in erasing. Yet, at its best, I will argue, such a critique recalls Walter Benjamin and Ernst Bloch in its insistence on a utopian potentiality that simultaneously inhabits, and surpasses the existing state of things. In this view, the consumer is made repository of an encrypted history—of unassimilated knowledge that overloads his "own" discursive resources and speaks *him*.[9]

"Homer and Apu" is notably self-conscious about the consolationist ruses of commodity culture, which reckons history as loss and loss as something it can compensate. In a brief scene bearing little relation to the ostensible plot, we witness Homer watching an African American comedian on TV parody the driving habits of "black guys" and "white guys." Pointedly depicting the white male subject as anxious, defensive, and lacking in style, the comedian impersonates a white male driver by hunching over the dashboard, nervously scanning the terrain ahead, while his black male counterpart eases back into the seat, casually holding the wheel in one hand. Homer laughs delightedly at this display and affirms the comic's insight: "It's true, it's true," he chortles, "we're so lame." Homer's pleasure in the recognition of white men's inadequacy is here sustained by the television's commodification of black masculinity as style, which thus becomes available to the intrepid white consumer, such as Homer. White guys may be lame, but Homer is not, exactly insofar as he can appreciate this bold racial wit, in an act of what bell hooks would call "courageous consumption." That this sketch is neither bold nor especially witty is precisely hook's point: "the commodification of difference," hooks remarks, "promotes paradigms of consumption wherein whatever difference the Other inhabits is eradicated, via exchange, by a consumer cannibalism that . . . denies the significance of that other's history through a process of decontextualization. . . . [I]t is by eating the other that one asserts power and privilege" (hooks 31, 36).

The inclusion of this sketch, and Homer's response, seems to register

Figure 1. *"I like to keep a lollipop there."*

the critical impasse of the series itself, which similarly construes Apu's narrative as a palatable set of "ready readings." But "Homer and Apu" also affirms the potential failure of such consumption paradigms to divest the commodity (and the image-commodity) of the alternative significations that adhere to it, or so the episode suggests, in the form of an un- or underarticulated remainder.[10] In two sequential scenes, placed just before Apu and Homer's departure, we witness commodities inscribe the white masculine consumer with this unassimilated "baggage." In the first of these, Homer emerges from the shower into the waiting embrace of Apu, who (in an apparent escalation of his role as house servant) is standing at the ready with a towel. When Homer shrieks and recoils, Apu smoothly reassures him: "Relax, you don't have anything I haven't seen before." Now it is Apu's turn to be startled, however, and we see him jerk forward, gasping in confusion "What?" The next frame discloses the cause of Apu's trouble, as Homer, looking down at the lollipop embedded in his chest hair, professes with some embarrassment, "Uh . . . I like to keep a lollipop there" (figure 1). Homer is thus marked and claimed by a commodity that he has either forgotten or is no longer able to ingest.

Although Apu's comic discovery of Homer's sucker invokes the

Figure 2. *Homer discovers a Japanese detergent that uses his face as a trademark.*

myriad mobilizations of nonwhite masculinity in the colonial imaginary
(as serviceable/feminized body; as homoerotic object), it also reopens the
question of who, to put it bluntly, the sucker is. It is precisely not the colonial subject who sucks in this scene, but the white male subject himself,
reimagined as the sign and symptom of his fantastic appetites, of his
propensity to incorporate others and/as objects. Apu's initial, slyly dou-
ble-edged reassurance that Homer possesses nothing he has not already
seen references a sexualized economy of meaning, in which one either
has or is the phallus, either authorizes the meaning of things or circulates
as a significant thing for others. Hinting at the banality of white bourgeois
masculinity, whose eroded capacity for authorship in the already pre-
scripted landscape of fast capitalism leaves him manifestly underwhelmed,
Apu demotes the emblem of white male privilege to a thing like any other;
and, of course, the monstrous duplication of "things" on the avid consumer body only confirms the propriety of Apu's condescension. The
cause of Apu's surprise is not that he was wrong about Homer's condition,
but rather that he could not know how right he was. Partially concealed
beneath this glancing bit of Freudian humor, however, lies another possibility: that Homer is not simply dispossessed (castrated), but possessed—

and possessed *not* by an other (by an embodied or symbolic master), but by the terrifying world of animate (de-objectified; de-fetishized) *objects*. At a minimum, we can say that white masculinity's historical claim to embody a universal corporeal norm dissolves, as Homer's consumer body assumes its comic specificity. But, more suggestively, this scene primes us for *The Simpsons*'s reimagination of mass consumption as trauma.

In a discussion of trauma that represents both a synthesis of classic Freudian thought on the subject and a somewhat polemical amplification of those aspects most responsive to the conditions of postmodernity, Cathy Caruth defines the traumatic event, not by virtue of its content, but by its belated temporality, its failure to signify, or signify fully, at the moment of its occurrence:

> [T]he pathology cannot be defined either by the event itself—which may or may not be catastrophic, and may not traumatize everyone equally—nor can it be defined in terms of a distortion of the event, achieving its haunting power as a result of distorting personal signifi-cances attached to it. The pathology consists, rather, solely in the structure of experience or reception: the event is not assimilated or experienced fully at the time, but only belatedly, in its repeated pos-session of the one who experiences it. To be traumatized is to be pos-sessed by an image or event. (Caruth 4)

From this vantage, Homer's possession by the unincorporated lollipop constitutes a visual invocation of the structure of trauma, without the actual experience. Homer seems curiously unassailed by the presence of this extra appendage, which he treats as only a minor deformation of the normative masculine body, and by no means his most potent source of corporeal shaming. But the comparison of this scene to a sequence in another episode, from 1997, is instructive, in terms of what it suggests about Homer's susceptibility to his belated seizure by the world of objects.

The episode "In Marge We Trust" begins when a trip to the city dump yields a disturbing find: a box of detergent, imprinted with Japanese text and Homer's beaming face, or something that looks remarkably like it (figure 2). Rather than the jubilant assumption of the image theorized by Lacan as the mirror stage, Homer undergoes a palpa-ble unmaking, in an almost literal demonstration of Hal Foster's claim that possession by an image entails the breakdown of the visual codes that screen us from the real, or, in more strictly Lacanian terms, from the "devouring" gaze of the object world. In Foster's paradigm, this traumatic incursion of the gaze constitutes the other face of Baudrillard's ecstatic postmodernity, of the disappearance of the scene and our immersion in the space of informational flows. Although this hyperreality is often associated with the obliteration of the world beyond the image, Foster tellingly suggests that our impossible proximity to the image/screen erodes its capacity to insulate us from the world's consuming gaze:

> The breaching of the body, the gaze devouring the subject, the subject becoming space, the state of mere similarity: these are conditions evoked in much art today. But to understand this convulsive possession in its contemporary guise it must be split into its constituent parts: on the one hand an ecstasy in the imagined breakdown of the image-screen and/or the symbolic order; on the other hand horror at this breakdown followed by a despair about it. (Foster 121)

If *The Simpsons* is sometimes prone to revel in what the series represents as our collective dissolution in the simulated world of the image-screen, the detergent box manifests as the horrifying breach in the screen that Foster describes. It is not the paranoid delusion of being watched that the discovery of the box effects in Homer, but a belated *recognition* that he is being watched, that he is nothing but a function of this subjectless surveillance, this unseeing gaze. Ultimately, the episode opts for a narrative (a narratable) resolution: Homer will learn that this image is a corporate logo for the detergent company, a joint venture of a fishery and a heavy manufacturing firm, which have fused their respective fish and lightbulb logos into the bulb-headed, fish-eyed icon that so resembles and traumatizes him. The restored possibility of comparison, of a signifiable relation, however grotesque (similarity to this or that specific thing), revokes the abject "state of mere similarity" that characterizes Homer's possession by the object-gaze. Needless to say, Homer marks his release and restoration to the differential order of meaning with a snack.

WHEN SHOPPING IS A BAFFLING ORDEAL

Significantly, Homer's trauma in this episode seems connected to history only in the most general, epochal sense; hence, its fit with Foster's analysis, which usefully insists on the relation of trauma to the hypermediation of postmodern existence, yet dispels Caruth's emphasis on history. Indeed, for Caruth, "the surprising *literality* and nonsymbolic nature of traumatic dreams and flashbacks" renders post-traumatic stress disorder "not so much a symptom of the unconscious, but a symptom of history. The traumatized, we might say, carry an impossible history within them, or they become themselves the symptom of a history they cannot entirely possess" (Caruth 5). As the stress on literality alerts us, this historicity is associated with the moments, or the places, where mediation (figuration) is suspended. It is "the overwhelming immediacy" of the traumatic event, Caruth suggests, that produces its belatedness. Turning at last to the second of the two scenes I invoked a while ago, I want to suggest how Barney's shopping ordeal joins Caruth's emphasis on trauma as a pathology of unmediated history to Foster's implied proposition that trauma is the effect and the remainder of the hypermediation of events.

Following the revelation of Homer's prosthetic pseudophallus, Marge and Apu undertake an expedition to the Monstromart ("where," as the store's marquee stalwartly proclaims, "shopping is a baffling ordeal"). Boasting "great selection at rock-bottom prices," as Apu observes, the Monstromart features oversized commodities that dwarf these daring shoppers. Marge wrestles with a twelve-pound box of nutmeg almost as tall as she and our attention is soon diverted to Barney, the town drunk, wheeling a (literally) man-sized keg of Duff beer, and an equally ample container of antacid. Approaching a cluster of giant Mrs. Butterworth containers (filled, just as their more diminutive counterparts, with pancake syrup), Barney politely inquires: "Excuse me, ma'am, where are the lamb shanks?" (figure 3). When the figure fails to reply, he persists in drawing her attention, eventually nudging her arm and overturning the bottle, which spills its syrupy contents into the aisle. Appalled, Barney confesses "I've killed her! It's all happening again," careens wildly into a cranberry juice display, which topples, breaks, and sweeps the shoppers away in a "cramtastic" crimson tide.

The message of love and consumer consolation that the corporate managers dispense ("Attention shoppers," the loudspeaker blares, "just a reminder that we love each and every one of you") cannot appease the passive aggression of these commodities that yearn, or so it seems, to disclose their "cultural baggage" on the (white male) consumer. Barney's encounter with a life-sized Mrs. Butterworth, whom he mistakenly addresses as a person, leads to his belated experience of homicide, though it remains somewhat ambiguous what specific murderous history has possessed him here. Has he "killed" the African American woman, whose stereotyped image is further appropriated as corporate logo? Or has he

Figure 3. *"Excuse me, ma'am, where are the lamb shanks?"*

"killed" a laborer earning below-subsistence wages in the foreign location where, we might plausibly speculate, these racist plastic icons are manufactured? Either way, Barney's trauma registers not (like Homer's) the collapse of symbolic order, but the decrypting of an abjected history, sealed in the commodity-artifact. In this respect, the figure of Mrs. Butterworth imposes on Foster's paradigm precisely the critique that Judith Butler has made of Slavoj Zizek's similarly orthodox Lacanian treatment of the real: that the real of the object world does not lack historical content, but rather marks the place where historical experience has been subjected to its forced desymbolization (Butler 187–222). Whereas the inexplicable appearance of the detergent box displaces Homer from the register of meaning (and thus history) altogether, Mrs. Butterworth deposits her cryptic significance on Barney, who is thereby violently and involuntarily (re)inserted into a field of historically constituted social relations. If the belated structure of trauma ensures that our access to the scene of an actual killing is always barred, it is nonetheless worth stressing that the "breakdown of the image-screen" at the Monstromart triggers a resurgence of unspoken histories, rather than the further seepage of historiographical resources.

From this perspective, Barney's trauma seems less susceptible than Homer's to what Foster shrewdly identifies as the prospect of trauma's reauthentication of the subject:

> [I]n therapy culture, talks shows, and memory mongering, trauma is treated as an event that guarantees the subject, and in this *psychologistic* register the subject, however disturbed, rushes back as survivor, witness, testifier. Here a traumatic subject does indeed exist, and it has absolute authority, for one cannot challenge the trauma of another: one can only believe it, even identify with it, or not. *In trauma discourse, then, the subject is evacuated and elevated at once.* (Foster 124)

Although the traumatic image or event seizes the subject and drains him, the subject revives in the act of claiming this trauma as his own—so that the subject's disappearance becomes, in Foster's critique, his own most unimpeachable experience. Insofar as Barney has been resignified, rather than designified, overinvested rather than drained, the burden of Foster's suspicions is shifted and we are left to ask instead how acceptable a bearer of the murdered woman's history the murderer might be. To what extent does the inscription of the laborer's trauma on the consumer render it, simply, the consumer's traumatic history, in other words? In this context, the underarticulation of Barney's confession becomes something less final, and more hopeful, than a failing. Barney's barely formed acknowledgment—he can not express exactly whom he has killed, or how, or why—warrants this death-dealing history without assigning it to Barney's discursive control. Like the intimations of utopia in Benjamin's account of German tragedy, the woman's trauma speaks in and through Barney's breached, or ruined, form.[11] And thus, like Benjamin's anticipatory utopia, Barney's consumer trauma decrypts, however faintly, a prospect of transnational class struggle: script and animation both insist that the compulsion to kill is not Barney's own, but a structurally mandated violence, a violence liable to seize any hapless shopper cruising the aisles of the world's monstromarts.

In the end, what seems most telling about Mrs. Butterworth's agitation is its obvious kinship to the series's own. Profoundly implicated in a system of global capital that requires and perpetuates the existence of a casual, chronically impoverished labor force—for example, at Akom, the largest of the South Korean animation houses, where *The Simpsons* is produced, 1,100 of 1,200 employees are temporary workers, paid around

$1.50 per cel for the tedious job of inking and painting—*The Simpsons* cannot reflect on its own transpacific origins (Edelstein 38).[12] Rather, in its representation of Barney's trauma, "Homer and Apu" seems to refer, or refract, its own critical impulse to us, as consumers. Less predictably, it is possible to read this commodity as addressed to the intellectual consumer, in particular. Lest we prefer to imagine that the decryption abilities of the academic shopper are superior to Barney's, I would emphasize that the intellectual elite may not have the edge on the town drunk in commanding the history with which the commodity is freighted. Up and down the information highway, the data on transnational corporate production, on the origins and circuits of commodities, remains remarkably unavailable, reminding us, if we need a reminder, that strategic knowledges are less democratically accessible than ever. For example, barring a stroke of good fortune (local labor unrest, union activism, a journalist's exposé), the most assiduous Web search is unlikely to reveal where and by whom Mrs. Butterworth containers are actually manufactured, under what conditions, and for what pay.[13]

There are, of course, important stylistic differences between Barney and most intellectuals, distinctions tied in obvious ways to class. Yet, structurally speaking, our position as consumers of commodity culture is less removed from Barney's than we might wish to believe and thus invites alternatives to the affirmation of an increasingly illusory privilege: the privilege of our ownership (real or imagined) of the means of inquiry; the privilege to assimilate our objects, even as we critique capital's assimilationist practices more generally. What might it mean, instead, for the historiographer to pattern herself after Barney, as traumatized consumer— assailed and overinscribed by a subaltern history that abjects her, insofar as it exceeds her discursive repertoire? I suggest that to respond to Barney's hail is to address the other side of interdisciplinary scholarship: to understand ourselves, not just as implicated in the reproduction of the social relations of power, but as having no *necessarily* privileged purchase on our implication. This is not to advocate acquiescence in our condition, or to downplay the urgency of investigating commodities with the very best methods we can devise. My point is that, under the conditions of transnational capitalism, the project of reading commodities (or image-commodities) demands that we remain accountable to the blank part of their text. In imagining ourselves exclusively as the agents of knowledge, we risk muting once again, and ever more violently, the questions that ruin us. To what do we, as viewers of *The Simpsons*, need to confess?

NOTES

   This essay was originally written for a panel on transnationalism. My thanks to my copanelists Purnima Bose and Tom Foster for their careful reading of earlier drafts and their insightful comments.

   1. Other examples include *Married with Children, Dream On, Seinfeld,* and *Cybil.*

   2. This perspective on *The Simpsons* owes much to the conversation on dissent within media criticism, although I find that the series raises a somewhat different question about the mediation of counterhegemonic thought than the critics themselves have generally tended to pose. Television scholars who read the mode of production as determining have emphasized both the limits and the possibilities of the televisual product and its reception. Rather than reducing television to a univocal instrument of corporate interests, these critics have stressed its function in the ongoing work of creating and maintaining the hegemony of the ruling bloc. Thus, as Douglas Kellner contends, television necessarily reflects the *differences* among a political and corporate elite (9). In a similar vein, others have argued that the televisual text is positioned vis-à-vis both a television "archive" (Deming) and an "intertext" (Spiegel), or set of ambient popular and institutional discourses, that opens it to multiple (though not unrestricted) interpretations. Within this body of scholarly work, there are, of course, important polemical variations and shadings. For some critics, consumer agency in the form of "choice" constitutes a significant variable, which drives the culture industry toward some degree of innovation (Fiske 4; Spiegel and Curtin 5). For others, the consumers are subordinate to the medium's ideologically saturated forms and conventions (Rabinovitz), or themselves transformed into a commodity sold by the networks to the advertisers (Dallas W. Smythe, quoted in Rabinovitz).

   Across the field, however, the point of resistance, such as it is, remains extrinsic to the operation of the medium itself and finds a limited reflection within it—a reflection more likely to serve than to imperil the imposition of hegemony. What interests me about *The Simpsons* is the extent to which the critical impulse seems to inhere in the series—not as a reflection of surrounding pressures, in other words, but (in Agger's terms) as a will-to-its-retextualization intrinsic to the thing itself.

   3. In recent years, the Indian government has pursued a programmatic effort to attract transnational capital.

   4. Headquartered in and linked to its country of origin, Film Roman is not a transnational or even a clearly multinational corporation (for example, it does not appear to have acquired any of the South Korean animation houses, such as Akom, with whom it contracts). Nevertheless, outsourcing represents one of the defining strategies of multi- and transnational corporations.

   5. See also Ella Shohat and Robert Stam, "From the Imperial Family to the Transnational Imaginary," which emphasizes local variations in the consumption of image-commodities.

   6. Subaltern studies tends to frame itself as intervening in the project of nationalist historiography. Nonetheless, as Gayatri Spivak suggests, this method also serves to make visible the mark of the colonial subaltern on Western epistemes, which function only on condition of effacing the subaltern subject. See

Spivak, "Can the Subaltern Speak?" and *In Other Worlds*, chapter 12.

7. *The Simpsons* attends to the presence of two notably underrepresented groups: Indians (in the figure of Apu) and Arabs (in the figure of "Mo"—or Mohammed—the bartender).

8. I am grateful to Purnima Bose for alerting me that "420" refers to a section of the Indian penal code governing theft, and particularly theft by duplicity, or deceit. Inasmuch as Apu is here engaged in thievery under cover of service, one must assume the scriptwriters' rather extensive command of South Asian cultural referents. This suggests that the representation of India via Hollywood is a function of what the producers perceive as the series's generic constraints, rather than lack of knowledge of contemporary India.

9. Indeed, for both Benjamin and Bloch, this utopian prospect opens onto the alterity of history—history as it escapes the imperative to author(ize) the present, the necessity of the way things are.

10. I take the concept of the image-commodity from Mitsuhiro Yoshimoto, who argues that images have "emerged as ideal commodities, which can be consumed and disappear instantaneously" (115). This arguably renders their "baggage" equally ephemeral, and proportionately harder to trace.

11. There is a further harmonization of the two texts insofar as we read Barney's trials at the Monstromart as an allegory of commodity culture; for Benjamin, allegory stands in a privileged relation to utopian meaning, as a discursive edifice that evokes its own decomposition.

12. In addition to India, other episodes have featured representations of France and Australia. However, East Asian nations, and the economy of the Pacific Rim, have never, to my knowledge, been visualized in the series.

13. It is undoubtedly on account of these real methodological difficulties that the essays in Grewal and Kaplan's collection address the representation of transnationalism, rather than engage directly in the "unpacking" of transnational commodities that the editors advocate in their introduction. In a forthcoming essay, Purnima Bose meticulously models such a practice, and argues for the value of constructing and circulating the commodity's archive. See Bose, "The Scent of a Conflict."

WORKS CITED

Adorno, Theodor, and Max Horkheimer. *Dialectic of Enlightenment*. Trans. John Cumming. New York: Continuum, 1972.

Agger, Ben. *Fast Capitalism: A Critical Theory of Significance*. Champaign: University of Illinois Press, 1989.

Baudrillard, Jean. *The Ecstasy of Communication*. Trans. Bernard Schutze and Caroline Schutze. New York: Semiotext(e), 1987.

Benjamin, Walter. *The Origin of German Tragic Drama*. Trans. John Osborne. New York: Verso, 1985.

Bloch, Ernst. *The Utopian Function of Art and Literature*. Trans. Jack Zipes and Frank Mecklenburg. Cambridge: MIT Press, 1988.

Bose, Purnima. "The Scent of a Conflict: Kashmir, Transnationalism, and the National Imaginary." *Passages* (forthcoming).

Butler, Judith. *Bodies That Matter: On the Discursive Limits of Sex.* New York: Routledge, 1993.

Caruth, Cathy. "Introduction." In *Trauma: Explorations in Memory,* ed. Cathy Caruth. Baltimore: Johns Hopkins University Press, 1995. 1–12.

Deming, Robert H. "*Kate and Allie:* 'New Women' and the Audience's Television Archive." *Camera Obscura* 16 (January 1988): 155–66.

Edelstein, Bill. "People Still Draw." *Variety* (June 19, 1995): 38.

Fiske, John. *Reading the Popular.* Boston: Unwin Hyman, 1989.

Foster, Hal. "Obscene, Abject, Traumatic." *October* 78 (Fall 1996): 106–24.

Grewal, Inderpal, and Caren Kaplan. "Introduction: Transnational Feminist Practices and Questions of Postmodernity." In *Scattered Hegemonies: Postmodernity and Transnational Feminist Practices,* ed. Inderpal Grewal and Caren Kaplan. Minneapolis: University of Minnesota Press, 1994. 1–33.

Harvey, David. *The Condition of Postmodernity: An Enquiry into the Origins of Cultural Change.* Cambridge, Mass.: Blackwell Publishers, 1990.

hooks, bell. *Black Looks: Race and Representation.* Boston: South End Press, 1992.

Jameson, Fredric. *Postmodernism, or the Cultural Logic of Late Capitalism.* Durham, N.C.: Duke University Press, 1991.

Kellner, Douglas. *Television and the Crisis of Democracy.* Boulder, Colo.: Westview Press, 1990.

Kipnis, Laura. *Ecstasy Unlimited: On Sex, Capital, Gender, and Aesthetics.* Minneapolis: University of Minnesota Press, 1993.

Miyoshi, Masao. "A Borderless World? From Colonialism to Transnationalism and the Decline of the Nation-State." *Critical Inquiry* 19 (summer 1993): 721–51.

Rabinovitz, Lauren. "Sitcoms and Single Moms: Representations of Feminism on American TV." *Cinema Journal* 29: 1 (fall 1989): 3–19.

Shohat, Ella, and Robert Stam. "From the Imperial Family to the Transnational Imaginary: Media Spectatorship in the Age of Globalization." In *Global/Local,* ed. Rob Wilson and Wimal Dissanayake. Durham, N.C.: Duke University Press, 1996. 145–70.

The Simpsons. "Homer and Apu." Original broadcast, October 8, 1994.

———. "In Marge We Trust." Original broadcast, April 27, 1997.

Spiegel, Lynn. "White Flight." In *The Revolution Wasn't Televised: Sixties Television and Social Conflict,* ed. Lynn Spiegel and Michael Curtin. New York: Routledge, 1987. 46–72.

Spiegel, Lynn, and Michael Curtin. "Introduction." In *The Revolution Wasn't Televised: Sixties Television and Social Conflict,* ed. Lynn Spiegel and Michael Curtin. New York: Routledge, 1987. 1–18.

Spivak, Gayatri Chakravorty. "Can the Subaltern Speak?" In *Marxism and the Interpretation of Culture,* ed. Cary Nelson and Lawrence Grossberg. Urbana: Illinois University Press, 1988. 271–313.

———. *In Other Worlds.* London: Routledge, 1988.

Yoshimoto, Mitsuhiro. "Real Virtuality." In *Global/Local,* ed. Rob Wilson and Wimal Dissanayake. Durham, N.C.: Duke University Press, 1996. 107–18.

Race, Land, Nation: A(t)-Tribute to Raymond Williams

Donald M. Nonini

> Williams spoke for the speechless, and found in other voices, who had
> not always been heard on such terms, a prior speech.
>
> —FRED INGLIS, *Raymond Williams*

NATION, RACE, LANGUAGE, STATE

It is interesting to note that in Raymond Williams's *Keywords*, the term *race* has no separate entry of its own, and instead is discussed only in connection with the concept "nationalist," which *does* have an entry, but which is, in its turn, in a important way, defined *by* "race." Williams writes:

> *Nation* (from fw [immediate forerunner of word] *nation,* F [French], *nationem,* L [Latin]—breed, race) has been in common use in English from lC13 [later thirteenth century], originally with a primary sense of a racial group rather than a politically organized grouping. Since there is obvious overlap between these senses, it is not easy to date the emergence of the predominant modern sense of a political forma-tion. . . . The persistent overlap between racial grouping and political formation has been important, since claims to be a *nation,* and to have *national* rights, often envisaged the formation of a *nation* in the political sense, even against the will of an existing political *nation* which included and claimed the loyalty of this [racial] grouping. It could be and is still often said, by opponents of *nationalism,* that the basis of the group's claim is *racial. (Race,* of uncertain origin, had been used in the sense of a common stock from C16 [sixteenth centu-

ry]. *Racial* is a C19 [nineteenth-century] formation. In most C19 uses
racial was positive and favourable, but discriminating and arbitrary
theories of *race* were becoming more explicit in the same period, gen-
eralizing national distinctions in supposedly radical *scientific* differences . . .). In practice, given the extent of conquest and domination,
nationalist movements have been as often based on an existing but
subordinate political grouping as upon a group distinguished by a
specific language or by a supposed *racial* community. (R. Williams
1976, 178–79)

Thus does Williams deflect the "nation" away from "race." This long
passage from *Keywords* is pivotal and exemplifies an ambivalence toward
"race"—an ambivalence that has come to haunt Williams postmortem,
as his accomplishments have been assessed by his postmodernist
critics, especially those from black cultural studies. Paul Gilroy's charge
that Williams incautiously acceded to a "new racism" propounded by
Thatcherites but implicitly approved of by many socialists, including
Williams, has merit.[1] Therefore, Williams's ambivalence toward "race"
needs to be taken seriously. This ambivalence arose from the tensions
(and resentments) he confronted within his identity first as Welsh-
become-British, and later as "Welsh European," an identity he claimed
explicitly only late in his intellectual career to distance himself from the
national consumerist culture and from what in *The Year 2000* he derisively
referred to as the "Yookay." The tensions he mediated in being simultaneously Welsh, British, and European "British" are discernible in his masterpiece, *The Country and the City*, and in *Politics and Letters*, his interviews with
the editors of *New Left Review:* recurrently he makes recourse to the position that it is the "city" that does violence to the "country," and to the
"actual," "lived identities" that country life generates. For Williams, as the
passage quoted suggests, "race" was more often than not removed "in
practice" from the "nation," but, I would argue, he implicitly but forcibly
resituated "race" in the "city"—the source not only of capitalist exploitation but also of self-generating heterogeneity, constituted not only by the
"English" industrial proletariat, but also by (those most often referred to
in Britain as) "blacks" or people of color from throughout the empire
and Commonwealth. When, for Williams, the "city" became the focus of
the oppressions of capitalism—not only the exploitation of labor but also
colonialism and empire overseas—so too it came to connote the hostile
otherness and human difference composed by race.

Williams's failure to problematize race within the modern nation

and its state is here an important point of entry into the challenge that
certain poststructuralist and discursive theorizations of the construction
of the subject have come to pose to the British cultural Marxism that
Williams, E. P. Thompson, and others in the British New Left did so
much to articulate from the 1950s onward. These theorizations provide a
challenge in at least two ways. First, those poststructuralists who do not
deny outright the existence of the subject tend to point to the centrality
of discourse in the construction of subjects—or, put in more congenial
terms—of multiple "subject positions." Foucault, despite his explicit
denial of being a "poststructuralist," appears to hold such a position.[2]
Although it sounds distinctly odd to hold that Williams might be insensi-
tive to discourse and language—indeed, on the whole, far from it—in *The
Country and the City* and in other works, he does largely oppose them to
"experience," that is, the centuries-long experience by the rural peoples
of the "British" Isles—not only their experience of the period of agrarian
capitalist exploitation of the last three to four centuries, but also of the
oppressions of the feudal order and mode of production preceding it,
and indeed, of the Roman period of conquest of the Celtic peoples of
these isles. This historically varying but nonetheless geographically specific "experience" for Williams dated back to originary "Neolithic shepherds" and their "primitive communal" society in Wales, Scotland, and
Ireland. Language, particularly the pastoral poetry that articulates those
historically specific "structures of sentiment" centered on the English
country house, Williams viewed for the most part as the property and pre-
rogative of the poets and other organic intellectuals of the upper and
middle classes, that is, the gentry and nobility of the "city." "Poets,"
Williams wrote, "have often lent their tongues to princes, who are in a
position to pay or to reply. What has been lent to shepherds, and at what
rates of interest, is much more in question" (1973, 22).

In contrast, poststructuralist and discursive theories would problematize and deconstruct the concept of "experience," viewing the term
itself as a rhetorical construct founded on the modernist assumption of a
unitary subject, whereas "experience," if it can be said to exist at all, must
be viewed as always partitioned by discourse and so implicated in those
configurations of knowledge and power characteristic of modernity and
its disciplines.[3] The ways in which discourse constructs experience (and
what it is in experience that lies beyond discourse) is here a relevant and
vital question. The project of vindication by British cultural Marxists of
the "popular" in the radical history "from below" (in the works of

Thompson, Christopher Hill, and others), insofar as it rests on the truth claims of popular or subaltern "experience," then also is called into question.[4] This challenge applies with as much force to Williams's historical sanctioning of "country" experience.

A second way in which certain poststructuralist theories confront Williams's cultural Marxism is their focus on the state, and on its place in the making of modern subjectivities. Again, I find this challenge most forcibly, if problematically, put in the historico-philosophic analyses of Foucault, in works such as *Discipline and Punish* and *The History of Sexuality*. Foucault employs a diction that, although consistent with his argument for the historicity of the modern subject and for the impersonality of "knowledges/powers" and their multiplex "microtechnologies," is ambiguous as to agency—who does what to whom, under what determinate conditions. Nonetheless, it is clear from the historical examples he provides—armies, schools, clinics, asylums, prisons, and so on—that there is a proliferation of agents within that complex that his analyses presuppose—the modern state, whose functionaries engage in surveillance, control, and the deployment of its institutionalized language and practices. In works that have selectively appropriated Foucault's insights, such as that of Corrigan and Sayer on British state formation, this question of the agencies of the state is more directly and forthrightly confronted. Such approaches would suggest the inadequate problematization in Williams's *The Country and the City* and in his other works of the various subterfuges and strategies by which the "popular" is co-opted, and non-"popular" others marginalized or silenced through the project of constructing hegemony undertaken by the capitalist state, its functionaries, allied political parties, and their organic intellectuals. Thus, for example, the "authoritarian populism" of Thatcherist rule studied by Stuart Hall (1980) depended on just such language of inclusion ("we, the British people") and of exclusion ("they"—"the enemy within"—striking coal miners and West Indian immigrants), and the enemy without ("the Argies"—Argentinians during the Falkland/Malvinas war).

As this example suggests, such practices and the language in which they are imbricated have been no more consequential and vicious than in the making of race. As Omi and Winant demonstrate in their discussion of "racial formation" and the (United States) American "racial state," and as Brackette Williams has trenchantly stated, "state making" and "race" making have historically been intimately interconnected. The empirical work of Raymond Williams shows a selective blindness to both of these issues—the role of hegemonic language in organizing experience, and the place of agencies of the state—in the making of "race" and race relations, both historically and in contemporary (Thatcherist and post-Thatcherist) Britain.

Recent work in critical studies on whiteness in the United States and in European colonial empires, much but not all of it informed by post-structuralist and discursive approaches, has at last opened precisely this terrain of racial formation and of blindness by whites to the peculiarly unmarked category of whiteness within it, to careful interrogation. Historians such as David Roediger, Alexander Saxton, and Theodore Allen have produced important reconstructions of the making of a majority white racial identity emerging within the transformations of industrial capitalism, postbellum racial politics, and emergent mass cultural formations of nineteenth- and twentieth-century North America. Anthropologists have examined the contradictory constructions of contemporary white identity as an unmarked social category defining "Americanness," while racial others are positioned as socially different from "us" and only questionably "American."[5] Eric Lott, in his studies of North American blackface, has pointed to white identity as grounded in a mixture of hatred and attraction toward nonwhite cultures, of "love and theft" (in Lott's words), as have others.[6] The crafting of a white identity through contrast with the black "other" in American literature and film has also been examined.[7] Scholars in American cultural studies have focused attention on "white trash" culture, and the deep ambiguities of whiteness when it confronts the class hierarchies of contemporary American society.[8] One conclusion from white trash studies, a transferable insight for this essay, is that although whiteness is spoken of as one pole of a binary, people in daily practice are defined as more or less "white" depending on their class, gender, ethnic, and national positions relative to these hierarchies of privilege. In this sense, to foreshadow an argument in this essay, Raymond Williams, the poor Welsh country boy, was perhaps not quite white and not quite British—at least not quite enough of either— and his peculiar ressentiment and intellectual shortsightedness with respect to the place of nonwhites within Thatcherist racial politics may have had everything to do with his ambivalent striving to become both sufficiently white and sufficiently British within the confines of elite British academic life.

These considerations have been most forcibly brought home to me in my ethnographic research on consciousness and identity among contemporary urban working-class Chinese men in Malaysia. When I began this ethnography in the early 1980s, I set out a research design with a focus on voices "from the bottom," one grounded in a democratic sympathy with the "popular" in Malaysian history, informed by my readings of Williams, E. P. Thompson, and other British Marxist historians. Yet, I foundered on an inability to comprehend, much less interpret, the construction of the identities of my urban Chinese male informants in postcolonial Malaysia.[9] My search for authentic working-class "experience" innocent of the cultural politics of gender and ethnicity proved futile; issues of representation—who spoke for whom, in what contexts—were paramount. The project of Malaysian governing elites in constructing a hegemony centered on the discourse of an indigenist nationalism with which poor Chinese had to contend was omnipresent. In short, the theorizations provided by British cultural Marxism, although at times inspiring, were incomplete and crucially inadequate for the purposes of my ethnography.

In contrast, I found that recent retheorizations of ethnicity, race, and gender within the contexts of state formation, informed by the poststructuralist and discursive approaches alluded to earlier, have proven valuable for this project (see Omi and Winant; Corrigan and Sayer). For instance, I find it promising to consider the constitution of the subjectivities of these men as taking place within the race and ethnic formations of late-colonial and postcolonial Malaysia—a process in which class formation and class-related discourses about "position" or "status" (*pangkat* in Malay; *diwei* in Chinese) are definitely implicated, but which is not reducible to the latter. My reconceptualization of the role of governing elites and the place of their naturalized discourses of "races," or *bangsa*, as they are called, in contemporary Malaysia, has been crucial.[10] Moreover, gender construction and state formation are intimately connected processes in Malaysia as elsewhere.[11] The modal active Malaysian "citizen" is constructed not only as indigenous (thus, most specifically, non-Chinese), but also as male. In my ethnography, I have discovered that working-class Chinese men in Malaysia have both played with and played off of these stigmatizing discourses and the forms of domination connected to them, in a strategic bricolage that asserts the privileges of their own male-based mobility vis-à-vis working-class Chinese women (Nonini 1997). All this ranges far from the concerns with "class struggle," agency "from the bottom," and "experience" put forth by E. P. Thompson and other British Marxist historians, although it is profoundly relevant to these concerns.

The considerations in this essay about the aporia and elisions in the work of Raymond Williams, as they bear on race and race relations in both contemporary Britain and to a lesser extent the United States, arise out of this rethinking. And, in alluding to the contributions of poststructuralist and discursive theorizations to this rethinking, I do not mean to celebrate them uncritically. I would also insist on certain of their limitations, such as the shortcomings of discourse (i.e., language-driven) theories for the study of embodied subjectivities, a topic beyond the scope of this essay.[12]

WILLIAMS AND "THE MOST RECENT IMMIGRATIONS OF MORE VISIBLY DIFFERENT PEOPLES"

In his 1983 book *The Year 2000*, Williams set forth his vision of the British nation, as an alternative to Thatcherist "national statism" expressed in an ersatz patriotism that ensured the exploitative operation of the transnational capitalist market, while at times protecting citizens from its worst excesses, in the form of the residual Labor welfare state. In contrast, writes Williams, "what is from time to time projected as an 'island race' is in reality a long process of successive conquests and repressions, but also of successive supercessions and relative integrations (1983, 193–94). The centuries-long process of struggle and co-optation between the "varied peoples who have lived on this island" and their conquerors and exploiters cannot be reduced to the simplistic symbolism of a "recent and originally alien monarchy and a flag" that index conquest and political integration, much less to the vulgarities of jokes about the Irish, or of English upper-class "public" schoolboys' identification with Roman imperial invaders against "the 'native tribes'" (ibid.).

It is against the failure by the reactionary, antihistorical, "narrow orthodox perspective" associated with Thatcherism and transnational capitalism to acknowledge these "misrepresented and obscured pasts" that Williams poses the question of "the most recent immigrations of more visibly different peoples" (ibid.). When these immigrants—from the Caribbean, from South Asia and West Asia—interact with the "more recent selective forms of identity" (the "'true-born Englishman' and "the imperial 'British'"), "angry confusions and prejudices" are evident (194–95).

What then occurs? According to Williams, there is a characteristic hostility on the part of "formerly diverse," now integrated "peoples" toward the immigrating "more visibly different peoples" of the postwar years. However, neither party is blameless, for both resort to "ideology":

> This is the phenomenon now crudely interpreted as "racism." It is not that there is no actual racism. . . . But it is a profound misunderstanding to refer all the social and cultural tensions of the arrival of new peoples to these ideological forms. The real working of ideology, both ways, can be seen in that most significant of current exchanges, when an English working man (English in terms of the sustained modern integration) protests at the arrival or presence of "foreigners" or "aliens," and now goes on to specify them as "blacks," to be met by *the standard liberal reply that "they are as British as you are."* Many people notice the ideological components of the protest: the rapid movement, where no other terms are available, from resentment of unfamiliar neighbours to the ideological specifications of "race" and "superiority."
>
>   But what of the ideology of the reply? It is employing, very plainly, a merely legal definition of what it is to be "British." . . . it is a serious misunderstanding, when *full social relations* are in question, to suppose that the problems of *social identity* are resolved by formal definitions. For unevenly and at times precariously, but always through long experience substantially, an effective awareness of social identity *depends on actual and sustained social relationships.* To reduce social identity to *formal legal definitions,* at the level of the state, is to collude with *the alienated superficialities of "the nation"* which are the limited functional terms of the modern ruling class. (P. 195; emphasis added)

Williams then proceeds to set out his own "socialist position on social identity" as one favoring "*lived and formed identities,*" preferably those of "a settled kind," for "practical formation of social identity" has to be "lived." "Real social identities" are formed "by working and living together, with some real place and common interest to identify with" (196; emphasis added).

Some problems with Williams's position here should be obvious; he is trolling in deep and troubled waters with this discourse on "real" and "lived" social identities. To begin with, bluntly, what of black British citizens—whose heritage is Caribbean or South Asian and West Asian, and many of whom are of one generation or more in residence in England? Without long historical association with the land and forcible "integration" upon it, are they assured a "social identity" sufficient to certify "real" citizenship for Williams? What of immigrant British "subjects"—the peoples of color of empire and Commonwealth—is their lack of "lived and formed social identities" of a "settled kind" the sign of an inauthenticity sufficient to deny them citizenship, or render their claims to it suspect? And what of Williams's argument in light of Stuart Hall's affirmation when, reflecting both on his own colonial heritage and on the lives of countless other persons of color, he writes: "I am the sugar at the bottom of the English cup of tea. I am the sweet tooth, the sugar plantations that rotted generations of English children's teeth. There are thousands of others beside me that are, you know, the cup of tea itself. Because they don't grow it in Lancashire, you know. Not a single tea plantation exists within the United Kingdom"? What could Williams say to this—this "outside history that is inside the history of the English"? (Hall 1991, 48–49).

The comments cited above by Williams in *The Year 2000* have been the object of cogent and forceful attack by critics—by those in black cultural studies and by others.[13] In connection with peoples of color residing in or immigrating to England, Gilroy has pointedly asked, in considering Williams's criteria for "lived and formed identities": "how long is long enough to become a genuine Brit?" (Gilroy 1987, 49). Indeed, Gilroy argues, Williams's pronouncements here, like those of others on the socialist left, have come to converge intellectually with the rhetoric of vulgar racists such as Enoch Powell, who have favored the exclusion of immigrating peoples of color from the "sceptred isles," and even the repatriation of those already in residence. There is, Gilroy points out, a "new racism" grounded in a discourse of "nation," "the enemy within" and without, and "race." The new racism rejects, at least at the superficial level, biological determination, claiming instead that it is the perduring *cultural* traits of minorities that show them to be essentially undeserving of citizenship and equal treatment before the law (see Barker). It is precisely at the point of parsing what Gilroy calls "authentic and inauthentic types of national belonging" (1987, 49) that the claims from the established left, including Williams, join with those from the right.

If Gilroy's critique has substance (and I do think it has merit), then the implications for the antiracist struggle in Great Britain of such co-optation are serious enough; but there are also consequences of his critique for the emergent field of British cultural studies, and indeed cultural studies elsewhere. Gilroy states these baldly:

> I have grown gradually more and more weary of having to deal with
> the effects of striving to analyze culture within neat, homogeneous

national units reflecting the "lived relations" involved; with the invisibility of "race" within the field and, most importantly, with the forms of nationalism endorsed by a discipline [i.e., cultural studies] which, in spite of itself, tends towards a morbid celebration of England and Englishness from which blacks are systematically excluded. (12)

Gilroy refers to the "strategic silences" about blacks in English culture as historically "symptomatic" (ibid.), and in *The Black Atlantic* he develops this theme further. These silences, and the practices of bracketing "race" and both blackness and whiteness that underwrite them in British cultural studies, are as long-standing as the field itself. For instance, the neglect of the work of the (Caribbean Trotskyist) historian C. L. R. James, writing from the 1930s through the 1980s about resistance to imperialism and cultural formation in the Caribbean, has been almost complete. New works on the roles of race and of racial whiteness in British history and cultural formation have only in recent years begun to redress this shortcoming, particularly as they are related to gender.[14] Similar elisions prevail on the other side of the Atlantic. For example, Harrison and Nonini note the long-standing negligence and silence by the majority regarding the gifts of W. E. B. Du Bois to the discipline of American cultural anthropology.

RAYMOND WILLIAMS AS "COLONIAL" AND AS "WELSH EUROPEAN"

Many may feel ambivalent toward the critique by Gilroy of Williams's position—on one hand, assenting to it in some large part, but on the other, judging it as somewhat unfair as well. I agree. It is unfair for several reasons, the principal one being Williams's clear and public dedication over several decades not only to socialism, but to emancipation in all its dimensions—to freedom from class exploitation, racial discrimination, militarism and the threat of nuclear cataclysm, national chauvinism, and gender violence. He was consistently, in this sense, always a radical and public intellectual rather than a mere academic or scholar, as the biography by Fred Inglis demonstrates. There are, as well, theoretically redemptive features to Williams's work for the study of race and race relations that have perhaps not been sufficiently appreciated by Gilroy and others, in particular his brilliant mappings of the linguistic terrain of domination in *Keywords, The Country and the City,* and several other works, and his sympathies for those who are silenced by it—sympathies manifested not only in his literary writings, but also in his interventions on the left in British public life over two postwar decades (see Inglis, chapters 9–10).

Nonetheless, the silences and misconstructions about "race" present in Williams's work do bear explaining. I suggested earlier that these are connected to Williams's provisional and ambiguous status within British public life as colonial and Welsh, but also as British. Williams was born and raised to adulthood on the Welsh "border country" but then "educated" elsewhere—"educated" in that distinct and refined sense in which "education" can only be the acquisition of the highest form of cultural capital[15] attainable in Great Britain: he was educated at Cambridge, in the heart of the metropole. I propose that Williams's provisional status—like that of so many others on the British New Left—led him to a certain ambivalence toward the "city" and thus toward its foil, the "country," particularly as these relate to "experience." It was "experience" for Williams that constituted the "actual and sustained social relationships" of genuine national belonging, and these he identified as primarily situated in "the country" over and against "the city." In short, despite his historical and historicist bent, Williams adopted an elective affinity for "the country" as a way of mediating his own complex identities as Welsh and colonial and also as—British. This is evident in his masterpiece on English country-house poetry, *The Country and the City*, and in the interviews published as *Politics and Letters*. I can only sketch out the argument briefly here.

The Country and the City begins by invoking "experience" and its ties to both "country" and "city," but primarily to the former, in particular how the city—its wealth, power, and cultural influence—is *experienced* in the country:

> "Country" and "city" are very powerful words, and this is not surprising when we remember how much they seem to stand for in the experience of human communities. In English, "country" is both a nation and a part of a land; the "country" can be the whole society or its rural area. In the long history of human settlements, this connection between the land from which directly or indirectly we all get our living and the achievements of human society has been deeply known. And one of these achievements has been the city. (1)

The theme of association between "experience" and country is then instituted in the first chapter by Williams's lyrical memories, physical in their striking singularity, of his own experiences in the country: "I was born in a village, and I still live in a village" (3). "This country life then has many meanings: in feeling and activity; in region and in time" (4).

Nevertheless, for Williams, the "experience" of the vast majority of people in the English countryside—irrespective of the epoch (feudal, capitalist, etc.) and of its associated "structures of sentiment"—was largely one of terror and *silence*: terror and exploitation because of the depredations of the city (dispossession, engrossment, enclosures, etc.) visited on the country and its subaltern residents; silence because the literary men who commanded language did so largely at the behest of those members of the citied upper and middle classes engaged in depredation. Those who wrote were, with very few exceptions such as John Clare,[16] not the small farmers, cotters, shepherds, and poor others residing in the "country," although Williams observes that there were almost always "spokesmen" for the rural "intermediate" classes.

Hence, for example, in chapter 2 of *The Country and the City*, Williams discusses the receding "escalator" of perspectives on which ride the successive generations of pastoral poetry, with each generation, whatever its distinctive style, positing an earlier period in which there existed an "organic community" in a bucolic and peaceful rural setting—a countryside without exploitation, complication, or unhappiness—which had disappeared by the time of its being written of. That the escalator existed at all, while such unoppressive relations were nowhere to be found in the historical evidence, suggested an inevitable chasm between language and experience: the writers—the poetasters of the country-house pastorals and their ilk—were not those who *experienced* the traumatic changes so lamented by their literary inheritors in the genre.

For Williams, the experiences of the rural lower classes—particularly, although not noted as such, of their men—were *real* in contrast to their literary representations, and one's political sympathies had to be with those who were thus silenced, whose voices were preempted:

> There is only one real question. Where do we stand, with whom do we identify, as we read the complaints of disturbance, as this [feudal] order in its turn broke up? Is it with the serfs, the bordars and cotters, the villeins; or with the abstracted order to which, through successive generations, many hundreds of thousands of men were never more than instrumental? And supposing we could make that choice rightly—though the historian who really places himself with the majority of men, and tries to see the world as they were experiencing it, is always improbable. (38–39)

The literary "structures of sentiment" that Williams sought to ana-
lyze, then, always came up against the silent, hostile alterity of the subaltern of the country who could not speak or write, but it was out of just
such endurance—such experience—of the rural subaltern that genuine,
"lived" social identity was created.

That, for Williams, "experience" and "actual social identity" were
not articulated in language, but rather had a different reality, being constructed by the endurance of living under exploitation and silently paying
one's dues in the country over the long term, is evident precisely when we
return to Williams's unfortunate intervention regarding "race" in *The Year
2000*. There, to illustrate the possibility of "lived and formed identities"
on which a socialist position is to be based, in contrast to the "alienated
superficialities of 'the nation'" that predicate a "formal legal" relation of
citizenship, he invokes the Welsh countryside of his youth:

> It happens that I grew up in an old frontier area, the Welsh border
> country, where for centuries there was bitter fighting and raiding and
> repression and discrimination. . . . It is with this history in mind that I
> believe in the practical formation of social identity . . . and know that
> necessarily it has to be lived. Not far away there are the Welsh mining
> valleys . . . in which, after two generations, there were some of the
> most remarkably solid and mutually loyal communities of which we
> have record. These are the real grounds of hope. (1983, 196)

MAKING THE (INTERNALLY) COLONIZED SUBJECT

The process that Williams wrote about and spoke to in *The Country and the
City, The Year 2000,* and *Politics and Letters* is the process of being colonized,
but of a very specific colonization, of being colonized *internally*. By this I
mean a colonization of the body, and even more of the intellect and spirit,
but also a process that occludes itself by dint of taking place within "national" boundaries, rather than across them. Writing about colonization was,
for Williams, a Welshman, necessarily autobiographical and self-referential,
and it was the experience of his "country" being silenced, and transformed
by the language of the metropole, the "city" that was at its core.

Here it is helpful to record a few autobiographical observations that
Williams makes of his entry into the metropole—into Cambridge
University. Coming from the village of his birth in the Welsh border
country, he arrives at Cambridge; then, having found some welcome at

the Socialist Club, and armed with his new and emerging socialist perspective and values, he seeks thereafter to confront his "British" schooling and his schoolers. Coming to Cambridge: "I was wholly unprepared for it. I knew nothing about it" (1979, 39). Contesting with his tutor (E. M. W. Tillyard) over his Marxist interpretations of the English novel: "I was continually found out in ignorance, found out in confusion. . . . I just met a total miscomprehension and sense of put-down" (51–52).

Williams is perhaps more terse than he could have been. The Cambridge arrival can, for the purposes of this essay, be more clearly and candidly construed by the sympathetic portrayal of it by another "colonial"—by Stuart Hall, the "black" or person of color, from Jamaica. Hall writes of Williams's autobiographical reflection on arriving at Cambridge ("I was wholly unprepared for it"):

> Though I myself came from a very different background, to Oxford not Cambridge . . . those stark sentences carried enormous reverberations for me. I still feel a strong sympathy for that way in which the bright young lad from the "periphery," coming to Oxbridge as the idealized pinnacle of an *intellectual* path, first experiences the actual *social* shock of discovering that Oxbridge is not only the apex of official English intellectual culture, but the cultural centre of the class system. I know at once what Williams means by remarking, in his usual understated way, that "the class stamp of Trinity was not difficult to spot." . . . Williams arrived in Cambridge at the end of the 1930s as the bright "scholarship boy" from the valleys. He records with feeling how that brash, radical certainty was constantly broken against the effortless assumption of superiority of the system. . . . I still experience that undefinable sense of being absolutely placed and put down even today, whenever I cross the threshold between Oxford railway station and Broad Street, gateway to the "dreaming spires." In the light of these pages I know what is meant by thinking of this as a "colonial" experience. (Hall 1989, 56–57)

All the same, Williams appeared to have achieved some greater accommodation with this experience of being "colonized," perhaps by virtue of its being—unlike for Hall—*internal* colonization. Williams speaks of changing his name not long after arrival in Cambridge:

> All the people [in Wales] who knew me till I was eighteen called me Jim. I adopted my legal name Raymond at university. The two names in the novel [i.e., *Border Country*], and in my own experience, point up

the problem of being two persons to know, and negotiating between two different worlds. Yet I always find it strange how quickly one adjusts to being called a certain name in a certain place. (Williams 1979, 283)

Moreover, as Inglis's biography makes clear, Williams found refuge in the Cambridge Socialist Club, which, with its exuberant language of solidarity with the working class, allowed him to mediate between his own class background from the "border country" and the conservatism of Cambridge at large, and in the company of other (white) young men, he flourished there (Inglis, chapter 4). One cannot but wonder whether Stuart Hall, an external "colonial" and black (and from a different and more affluent class background), was able with so much ease to make a similar adjustment, in the heart of the metropole, even as one admires Williams's retrospective candor in the passage just cited.

It was only much later in his life, Williams claims, that he was able to recover his colonized "Welsh" identity from the "British" universalizations bestowed on him in the course of his extraordinarily successful trajectory of participation as Cambridge don in the "cultural centre of the class system." I propose that it was precisely his ambivalent recovery of a colonized Welsh identity that chained him so rigidly to the association we find in *The Country and the City* between country life, the land, experience, and "actual and lived identities"—an association that accounts for his partial blindness to the pervasiveness of racial oppression, Thatcher-style. Part of the working through of this recuperation occurred, I would argue, during the period of the overlapping production of *The Country and the City* and his third "Welsh" novel, *The Fight for Manod,* in the late 1960s and early 1970s. It was during these years that Williams claims that he came into contact with Welsh writers and intellectuals, "all highly political in the best tradition of the culture" (1979, 295–96), and began to be deeply influenced by them; and, in the same period, alternating between the writing of *The Fight for Manod* and *The Country and the City,* he came to see "the whole country and city relation . . . as for me the crucial relation in contemporary social analysis" (292).

For Williams, however, the "experience" in the colonized countryside of Wales, from his childhood through his mature years, was never one in which "race" at all figured, unlike the "experience" of innumerable subjects of empire sojourning in the metropole such as Stuart Hall. Williams shifted over his academic life in how he dealt with being incompletely British, but the implicit whiteness of his position within what Hall correctly called "the cultural centre of the class system"—Cambridge— was never open to question, nor did he ever (to my knowledge) appear to question it. Perhaps he saw Cambridge, unlike London, as truly not of "the city," nor therefore in need of his critique of the city. In the chapter "The New Metropolis" in *The Country and the City*, "the city" as such colonizes the "country" even in the case of Britain's overseas empire, as rural life overseas is subsumed by the rhythm and agendas of exploitation and uprooting by the cities of the colonies and postcolonies. "Race" and its workings are even *here* not present for Williams, as when he writes of the novels of Jame Ngugi, *Weep Not, Child* and *A Grain of Wheat in Kenya*, or of Han Suyin's novel *And the Rain My Drink*, set in the anti-insurgency terrors of British Malaya, that they express not anticolonialism, nor protest against the British racial color line, but (Williams writes, almost pathetically) "the resistance movements of the country people against English power" (1973, 286)—not, mind you, even against *British* imperial power. European colonization is, for Williams, no more than a tragic recursion of past "penetration, transformation and subjugation of 'the country' by 'the city'": the colonized peoples of Africa and Asia, with the now forcibly integrated Welsh and other Celtic peoples of the British Isles, share, "a common history," one that can be perceived if we bypass "the alienating screens of foreignness and race" (288). Although Williams's universal humanism on behalf of a common, suffering, and exploited humanity is, in one way, admirable, in another it represents a systematic misreading of those novels and works by Ngugi, Achebe, Han, Lamming: as exemplifying structures of feeling, they are not silent about race; on the contrary, in different ways each author writes devastatingly about European racism and the abuses of late-colonial color lines. Here is where Williams's preconceptions about "experience" and "actual and sustained relationships" of silent, communal suffering among those residing for epochs untold in their place do him least service, for his humanism is one of being Welsh, then British, then being Welsh (European) once more, but always subsumed by a normalizing whiteness, albeit one at times tending toward social prominence or apotheosis, and at other times not. Williams's biography and his views of social difference are linked by this fatal blindness to race, indexed in his use of the axial term *experience*. The misreading extended far beyond the anticolonial novel, and constrained the limits of his vision in *The Year 2000* of his argument about the British reception of "more visibly different peoples" in the postwar years.

The close association between his Welsh identity, countryness, and lived "social identities" in general appeared to have remained with him from the period of *The Country and the City* for the rest of his life. Opposed to it were what he saw as the ongoing antagonisms and condescensions toward rural life on the part of "metropolitan," "city" intellectuals, including socialists who, despairing of country backwardness, invoked Marx's epithet about the "idiocy of rural life." For someone who could write so articulately and yet so understatedly, I find nothing elsewhere in his vast corpus that rivals the sharp vehemence and fine rage of his condemnation in the 1979 interviews in *Politics and Letters* of those "British" intellectuals and their pronouncements on rural Wales:

> In Wales I have friends and neighbors who are being forced out by a whole alliance of forces, from large-scale capital to the left of the Labour Party, because they are "antique"—meaning they are food-producers. Even a Keynesian economist could tell me—ironically from a country pub, since it is part of the ideology that the country is where you go on Sunday—that "the sheep is an uneconomical animal" and that the sooner the sheep farmers of Wales give up or get engrossed the better; leaving those hills, presumably as an empty recreation area, for the discovery of nature. When I hear that kind of final economic universalism, I not only feel anger, because I have neighbors who are raising sheep and who are doing a sight more than most economists to contribute to society, but because within the existing bureaucratic system "advisers" could have more say in the future of hill sheep farming than any hill sheep farmer. (1979, 314)

It was, finally, in such everyday struggles over the land, its value, and the experience of it that Williams in his later years grounded his Welsh identity, while also increasingly referring his cosmopolitanism to his being a "European," rather than to his "Britishness" with its "alienated superficialities of 'the nation,'" as he put it in his flawed reaction to antiracists in *The Year 2000.*

COUNTRY, RACE, PLACE, DISPLACEMENT

How does one simultaneously know the past and come to understand domination? How can one deploy one's critical knowledge of the past and of domination within one's praxis, insofar as that extends beyond one's intellectual work sensu stricto to engage with the practical exigencies of contemporary life in capitalist society, in a project of emancipation? How does one's knowledge of "society" and of its past and one's position in that "society" condition, even at times determine, how (and indeed whether) one can engage in this project? The curious, partial, but compelling blindness of Raymond Williams to the issues of race and the new racism of contemporary Great Britain, and the links between this blindness and his attempts to mediate between his Welsh and British identities, between "the country" and "the city," may have much to instruct us when seeking to answer these questions.

Poststructuralist approaches help us think through some of the aporia and silences in the work of Williams as a prototypical modern radical intellectual, and go to the core of the more general issue of the place of Marxism and class politics in emancipatory projects today. Labor's day is not over, and class politics and the struggles these carry with them will be with us for some time to come. But the labor movement in Britain, in the United States, and elsewhere in the industrialized world is indeed in a sorry state, and not merely—nor, I would add, primarily—because of the "fall" of official socialism. Most important, the labor movements of the United States and Britain have suffered severely from legal and police repression by their capitalist states, whether one thinks of airport traffic controllers in the United States or coal miners in Britain. Yet, they have also in part foundered on their internal contradictions—their racisms, sexisms, their narrow nationalisms and xenophobias—which the employers and states of both countries have taken advantage of. This is demonstrable in the work of labor historians, including those who do not identify themselves as poststructuralists or show sympathies with them. For instance, David Roediger's *The Wages of Whiteness,* following the insights of W. E. B. Du Bois in *Black Reconstruction in America,* shows that the formation of the North American working class was inextricably tied to the racism practiced by the "popular," in this case, the new American industrial proletariat against African American slaves, then freed persons, in the nineteenth century. Mike Davis, in his *Prisoners of the American Dream,* provides more general but nonetheless substantial historical evidence for this claim.

Returning to the theoretical issues, poststructuralist and discursive approaches may have much to offer us in understanding how such a denouement occurred, and the instance before us is well worth examining as an example. Poststructuralist theorists argue two important points of relevance. First, language and power are always associated; domination has to be understood in terms of what language does, perhaps in the form of ideology as a "material force," as Marx put it, perhaps in other ways, in securing class rule and capitalist accumulation. Moreover, there are forms of oppression other than class exploitation—racial oppression, for instance—that contribute to the constitution of domination. The poststructuralist focus on discourse and power has much to say about these alternative forms (and indeed, about class struggle, too), their loci and modes of operation and transformations, as well. Language forms subjectivities and shapes "experience." Yet, this is not all. The dilemma of the radical historian is that, as Walter Benjamin put it in thesis 6 of his *Theses on the Philosophy of History*, "even the dead will not be safe from the enemy if he wins. And this enemy has not ceased to be victorious" (1968, 255); that is, by and large those who command the resources of the upper classes also command the discourse of the everyday, or at least have substantial influence over those intellectuals who do produce it. Although those in the "lower orders" articulate their "experience," often in critical expressive genres (such as, originally, blues or reggae music for North American blacks or Afro-Caribbean groups), much of the time they are constrained to do so by appropriating the authoritative discourse of the more powerful, at times parroting it, or at best—through some forms of irony—turning it against their oppressors in petty forms of "everyday resistance" (Scott). Such challenges to hegemony remain that—petty. In this connection, Williams's work goes part way toward the crucial insight that state and elite terror inflicted on rural people has always, as it were, gone fist in glove with authoritative discourse. For the neoliberal doctrine of a Milton Friedman and every economist's band of "Chicago boys," there is a Pinochet and a military apparatus of violent repression, for each Chile; the former constitute and mold positively what the latter first destroy, reduce, and disarticulate.

Williams saw this in part, I think, fairly clearly early on. The "structures of sentiment" or "structures of feeling" described in *The Country and the City* are in effect *the* language of the country in its broadest sense "of the whole society or its rural area" (1). Williams's sympathy for those peoples of "the country" who were dispossessed, exploited, and violated by the incursions of the upper and middle classes of "the city" is not only obvious and credible, but also laudable, indeed unassailable. But when he views their "experience" as either nonlinguistic or prelinguistic (I think his emphasis varies), as shaped by terror but bounded by silence, then his interpretations need to be questioned. Poststructuralist accounts assure us that domination, in the "country" as in the "city," necessarily involves language, *and* that such language shapes experience—that of the "country's" poor as well as the "city's" wealthy. At the same time, poststructuralist and discursive approaches fail to attend to the terror visited on large numbers of rural (and urban) people by elites in ways that disorganize and displace prior "experience" and its discursive articulation. Williams was, then, exactly right in pointing to the violence visited on the "country" by the "city," which made the modern world; but poststructuralist and discursive theorists are correct in pointing to the constitutive effects of language in making power and securing domination. Yet, going beyond poststructuralist and discursive approaches, I find it necessary to incorporate Williams's insight by arguing that domination and experience of it both involve much more than language: both are embodied and immediate, in the quotidian, and therefore not accessible *au fond* to the hermeneutics of discourse analysis.[18] "You had to be there"—or at least render the "thereness" of experience into an order of language that pushes beyond language, as Wittgenstein's analyses of "language games" within "form of life" strongly intimate.

Even so, much of the time politics centers on discourse, on categories formed by language—"blacks," the "enemy within," "freeborn Englishmen," and so on—that orient and constrain experience on the one hand, and enter into various fields of power and contestation on the other.[19] Such language seizes on, and works largely toward, the construction of "popular" subjectivities: people become black, freeborn English-men, and so on, through the deployment of such labels in political rhetoric. Such rhetoric, in turn, buttresses class and other forms of domination in its major(ity) key, and contests these in its minor(ity) key.

A second poststructuralist insight that Williams's example points us to is the relationship between language and the multiple instrumentalities and agencies of the state. Classical Marxism's notorious underproblematization of the capitalist state, its multiple sites, its discourses, heterogeneous structures, programs, and so on, left a mark on Williams's work as well. In the making of states, so too are citizens, races, nations made, and again, language is a central element of the processes of these makings. *The Country and the City* has little to say about this; instead, Williams's search for authenticity in "the country" and in the experiences of its lower classes anchors identity in the foundation of the mutual interaction between the land and its rural lower-class stewards, and thus brackets out the state and its multiple operations on subjectivities as "alienated superfi-cialities." But the "political integration" that Williams sees as formative to the modern conception of "nation," and as a tragic but historically neces-sary process for "the country" and its peoples to undergo, is not some process that is innocent in the making of subjectivities: to even be in "mutual interaction," the stewards of the land must have at least some provisional (and empirically, usually more assured) status of "citizenship" vis-à-vis the state, and such a status has, historically, as Williams points out in the passage from *Keywords* that began this essay, been anchored in nega-tive and antagonistic definitions of "race" and "nation"—we are all of the "island race" who are not "non-British"—as well as more affirmative organ-ic ones. This is certainly an important implication of Gilroy's critique. Williams's position as Welsh nationalist, organically connected to the land of Wales, makes little allowance for this *actuality*.

In the case of "race," Gilroy's critique is more than merely a negative one. This becomes clearer in his book *The Black Atlantic*, where he propos-es alternative conceptions of community and identity to those that are lit-erally "grounded" in the land and citizenship, as in the work of Williams and others in British white cultural studies: instead, for Gilroy, there is the notion of diaspora—the community in dispersion, in displacement. I find this proposal extraordinarily exhilarating, and not merely for its theoreti-cal contribution. It is a new way of thinking not only about the Afro-American "holocaust" of the Middle Passage and its sequela, but other dispersions as well, say, those of "overseas Chinese" across the Asia Pacific, or—most telling for the themes of this essay—the diaspora of Europeans throughout the non-European world, their connections over space and over time, and the interconnected formations of races (and of "white-ness"), classes, nations, and genders.[20] Here there is the need to attend to the new critical studies of whiteness I alluded to earlier, as these bear on this latter diaspora and the obsessive and recursively oppressive processes of the constitution of whiteness that have historically accompanied it in the spaces of the colonial and postcolonial worlds.[21] For instance, why the contrast in the nineteenth-century between the Irish of Ireland and the Irish diaspora in the New World when it came to matters of "race"? Was this not a pivotal moment in the formation of race in North America? Whereas, according to Roediger, the Irish of Boston and elsewhere in the Northeastern United States in the antebellum and postbellum periods despised and feared black laborers as inferior, as backwardly preindustri-al, as sexually threatening, as simultaneously "lazy" and yet willing to do the most onerous physical labor (which they called "nigger's work"), at the same time, there appeared little, if anything, similar among the Irish still residing in Ireland. Roediger writes of the prominent Irish nationalist and abolitionist addressing an angry crowd in the United States: "'It was not in Ireland,' thundered Daniel O'Connell to proslavery and white supremacist Irish-Americans, [that] 'you learned such cruelty'" (137). On the other hand, European diasporas have also had their potentially redemptive and emancipatory moments, as in the case of the rebellious "many-headed hydra"—a racial polyglot of English sailors and transported radicals, escaped slaves, and other subalterns who formed "dangerous" combinations against British imperial authority in the form of colonists' insurrections, slave rebellions, and pirate maraudings throughout the Caribbean Atlantic.[22]

That diasporic cultural formations are now the subject of new study is exciting, for they point to an alternative conception of identity to the view of Williams that has been the subject of much critique. I am optimistic. When the oppressive histories and cultural practices of the European diaspora that make up whiteness come to be tracked and brought into public view, as well as made subject to critical academic examination, they will, one hopes, begin to be denaturalized, and appear as consciously historical constructions, and, in that sense, as powerful fictions. In consequence, global structures of white privilege and entitlement to/in the modern world may lose yet another buttress for their power.

NOTES

1. Paul Gilroy, *"There Ain't No Black in the Union Jack,"* 49–50, refers to Williams's argument in *The Year 2000*, 195ff. On the "new racism" in Britain associated with the rise of Thatcherism, see Martin Barker, *The New Racism*.

2. See Michel Foucault, *Language, Counter-Memory, Practice, Power/Knowledge*, and *The History of Sexuality*, vol. 1.

3. See Foucault, *The History of Sexuality* and *Discipline and Punish*.

4. See Perry Anderson's critique of Thompson's invocation of "experience" in *Arguments within English Marxism*, 25–39.

5. See Ruth Frankenberg, *White Women, Race Matters* and "Whiteness and Americanness"; Karen Brodkin Sacks, "How Did Jews Become White Folks?"

6. Eric Lott, *Love and Theft* and "White like Me"; Stuart Hall, "What Is This Black in Black Popular Culture?"

7. Richard Dyer, "White"; Walter Benn Michaels, "The Souls of White Folk";

Toni Morrison, *Playing in the Dark*; bell hooks, "Representing Whiteness in the Black Imagination"; Mike Hill, "Can Whiteness Speak?"

8. See Matt Wray and Annalee Newitz, eds. *White Trash*.

9. Donald M. Nonini, *British Colonial Rule and the Resistance of the Malay Peasantry, 1900–1957* and "Popular Sources of Chinese Labor Militance in Colonial Malaya, 1920–1941."

10. See Ariffin Omar, *Bangsa Melayu*.

11. See Geraldine Heng and Janadas Devan, "State Fatherhood"; and C. J. W. L. Wee, "Contending with Primordialism."

12. See Donald M. Nonini, "The Dialectics of 'Disputatiousness' and 'Rice-Eating Money'" and "'Chinese Society,' Coffeeshop Talk, Possessing Gods."

13. See Gilroy, *"There Ain't No Black in the Union Jack,"* and Francis Mulhern, "'Towards 2000.'"

14. See, for example, Catherine Hall, *White, Male and Middle-Class*.

15. See Pierre Bourdieu, "The Forms of Capital."

16. "Clare is in every way a deeply significant figure, for in him there is not only the literary change but directly, in his person and his history, the inwardness of the social transformation" (Williams 1973, 134).

17. See Donald M. Nonini, "Du Bois and Radical Theory and Practice."

18. See Nonini, "'Chinese Society,' Coffeeshop Talk, Possessing Gods"; and "Dialectics of 'Disputatiousness.'"

19. See Ernesto Laclau and Chantal Mouffe, *Hegemony and Socialist Strategy*.

20. See James Clifford, "Diasporas."

21. See Roediger, *Wages of Whiteness*; Frankenberg, *White Women, Race Matters*; Leonard J. Moore, *Citizen Klansmen*.

22. See Peter Linebaugh and Marcus Rediker, "The Many-Headed Hydra."

WORKS CITED

Allen, Theodore W. *The Invention of the White Race,* vol. 1, *Racial Oppression and Social Control.* London: Verso, 1994.

———. *The Invention of the White Race,* vol. 2, *The Origin of Racial Oppression in Anglo-America.* London: Verso, 1997.

Anderson, Perry. *Arguments within English Marxism.* London: Verso, 1980.

Ariffin Omar. *Bangsa Melayu: Malay Concepts of Democracy and Community 1945–1950.* Kuala Lumpur: Oxford University Press, 1993.

Barker, Martin. *The New Racism: Conservatives and the Ideology of the Tribe.* London: Junction Books, 1981.

Benjamin, Walter. *Illuminations: Essays and Reflections.* New York: Schocken Books, 1968.

Bourdieu, Pierre. "The Forms of Capital." In *Handbook of Theory and Research for the Sociology of Education,* ed. John G. Richardson. New York: Greenwood, 1986. 241–58.

Clifford, James. "Diasporas." *Cultural Anthropology* 9:3 (1995): 302–38.

Corrigan, Phillip, and Derek Sayer. *The Great Arch: English State Formation as Cultural Revolution.* Oxford: Basil Blackwell, 1985.

Davis, Mike. *Prisoners of the American Dream.* London: Verso, 1986.

Du Bois, W. E. B. *Black Reconstruction in America: 1860–1880.* New York: Athenaeum, 1935.

Dyer, Richard. "White." *Screen* 29:4 (1988): 44–64.

Foucault, Michel. *Discipline and Punish: The Birth of the Prison.* New York: Vintage Books, [1975] 1977.

———. *The History of Sexuality,* vol. 1, *An Introduction.* New York: Vintage Books, 1980.

———. *Power/Knowledge: Selected Interviews and Other Writings 1972–1977.* Ed. Colin Gordon. New York: Pantheon Books, 1980.

———. *Language, Counter-Memory, Practice.* Ithaca, N.Y.: Cornell University Press, 1997.

Frankenberg, Ruth. *White Women, Race Matters: The Social Construction of Whiteness.* Minneapolis: University of Minnesota Press, 1993.

Gilroy, Paul. *"There Ain't No Black in the Union Jack": The Cultural Politics of Race and Nation.* Chicago: University of Chicago Press, 1987.

———. *The Black Atlantic: Modernity and Double Consciousness.* Cambridge: Harvard University Press, 1993.

Hall, Catherine. *White, Male and Middle-Class: Explorations in Feminism and History.* New York: Routledge, 1992.

Hall, Stuart. *The Hard Road to Renewal: Thatcherism and the Crisis of the Left.* London: Verso, 1980.

———. "Politics and Letters." In *Raymond Williams: Critical Perspectives,* ed. T. Eagleton. Cambridge: Polity Press, 1989. 241–58.

———. "What Is This Black in Black Popular Culture?" *Social Justice* 20 (spring–summer 1993): 104–14.

———. "Old and New Identities, Old and New Ethnicities." In *Culture, Globalization, and The World-System: Contemporary Conditions for the Representation of Identity,* ed. Anthony D. King. Current Debates in Art History 3. Binghamton: Department of Art and Art History, State University of New York, Binghamton, 1991. 48–49.

Harrison, Fave V., and Donald M. Nonini. "Introduction: W. E. B. Du Bois and Anthropology." *Critique of Anthropology* 12:3 (1992): 229–37.

Heng, Geraldine, and Janadas Devan. "State Fatherhood: The Politics of Nationalism, Sexuality, and Race in Singapore." In *Nationalisms and Sexualities,* ed. Andrew Parker, Mary Russo, Doris Summer, and Patricia Yaeger. New York: Routledge, 1992. 343–64.

Hill, Mike. "Can Whiteness Speak?" In *White Trash: Race and Class in America,* ed. Matt Wray and Annalee Newitz. New York: Routledge, 1997. 155–76.

hooks, bell. "Representing Whiteness in the Black Imagination." In *Cultural Studies,* ed. Lawrence Grossberg, Cary Nelson, and Paul A. Treichler. New York: Routledge, 1992. 338–46.

Inglis, Fred. *Raymond Williams.* London: Routledge, 1995.

Laclau, Ernesto, and Chantal Mouffe. *Hegemony and Socialist Strategy: Towards a Radical Democratic Politics.* London: Verso, 1985.

Linebaugh, Peter, and Marcus Rediker. "The Many-Headed Hydra." *Journal of Historical Sociology* 3 (1990): 225–53.

Lott, Eric. *Love and Theft: Blackface Minstrelsy and the American Working Class.* New York: Oxford University Press, 1993.

———. "White like Me: Racial Cross-Dressing and the Construction of American Whiteness." In *Cultures of United States Imperialism,* ed. Amy Kaplan and Donald E. Pease. Durham, N.C.: Duke University Press, 1993. 474–95.

Michaels, Walter Benn. "The Souls of White Folk." In *Literature and the Body: Essays on Populations and Persons,* ed. Elaine Scarry. Baltimore: Johns Hopkins University Press, 1988. 185–209.

Moore, Leonard J. *Citizen Klansmen: The Ku Klux Klan in Indiana, 1921–1928.* Chapel Hill: University of North Carolina Press, 1991.

Morrison, Toni. *Playing in the Dark: Whiteness and the Literary Imagination.* Cambridge: Harvard University Press, 1992.

Mulhern, Francis. "'Towards 2000': News from You Know Where." *New Left Review* 148 (November–December 1984): 5–30.

Nonini, Donald M. *British Colonial Rule and the Resistance of the Malay Peasantry, 1900–1957.* Southeast Asia Monographs 38. New Haven: Yale Southeast Asia Studies, 1992.

———. "Du Bois and Radical Theory and Practice." *Critique of Anthropology* 12:3 (1992): 293–318.

———. "Popular Sources of Chinese Labor Militance in Colonial Malaya, 1920–1941." *The Politics of Immigrant Workers: Essays on Labor Activism and the World Economy since 1830,* ed. Camille Guerin-Gonzales and Carl Strikwerda. New York: Holmes and Meier, 1993. 227–55.

———. "Shifting Identities, Positioned Imaginaries: Transnational Traversals and Reversals by Malaysian Chinese." In *Ungrounded Empires: The Cultural Politics of Modern Chinese Transnationalism,* ed. Aihwa Ong and Donald Nonini. New York: Routledge, 1997. 227–55.

———. "'Chinese Society,' Coffeeshop Talk, Possessing Gods: The Politics of Public Space among Diasporic Chinese in Malaysia." *positions: east asia cultures critique* 6:2 (1998): 439–73.

———. "The Dialectics of 'Disputatiousness' and 'Rice-Eating Money': Class Confrontation and Gendered Imaginaries among Chinese Men in Peninsular Malaysia." *American Ethnologist* 26:1 (1999).

Omi, Howard, and Michael Winant. *Racial Formation in the United States: From the 1960s to the 1990s.* 2d ed. New York: Routledge, 1994.

Roediger, David R. *The Wages of Whiteness: Race and the Making of the American Working Class.* London: Verso, 1991.

Sacks, Karen Brodkin. "How Did Jews Become White Folks?" In *Race,* ed. S. Gregory and R. Sanjek. New Brunswick, N.J.: Rutgers University Press, 1994. 78–102.

Saxton, Alexander. *The Rise and Fall of the White Republic: Class Politics and Mass Culture in Nineteenth-Century America.* London: Verso, 1990.

Scott, James C. *Domination and the Arts of Resistance: Hidden Transcripts.* New Haven: Yale University Press, 1990.

Wee, C. J. W. L. "Contending with Primordialism: The 'Modern' Construction of Postcolonial Singapore." *Positions* 1:3 (winter 1993): 715–44.

Williams, Brackette. "A CLASS ACT: Anthropology and the Race to Nation across Ethnic Terrain." *Annual Review of Anthropology* 18 (1989): 401–44.

Williams, Raymond. *The Country and the City.* New York: Oxford University Press, 1973.

———. *Keywords: A Vocabulary of Culture and Society.* New York: Oxford University Press, 1976.

———. *The Fight for Manod.* London: Hogarth Press, [1979] 1987.

———. *Politics and Letters: Interviews with New Left Review.* London: Verso, 1979.

———. *The Year 2000.* New York: Pantheon Books, 1983.

Wittgenstein, Ludwig. *Philosophical Investigations.* Trans. G. E. M. Anscombe. New York: Macmillan, 1953.

Wray, Matt, and Annalee Newitz, eds. *White Trash: Race and Class in America.* New York: Routledge, 1997.

Deleuze, Monet, and Being Repetitive

Briankle G. Chang

> There are pictures that take refuge in the frame, pictures that
> burst it open and pictures that don't care about it.
>
> —HANS-JOST FREY

> The other is related only to the other: the other repeats.
>
> —MAURICE BLANCHOT

Perhaps to countervail the complexity of what is to unfold, Gilles Deleuze begins *Difference and Repetition* with a simple statement: "Repetition is not generality" (1). In view of the simplicity of the sentence and without the benefit of forthcoming arguments, readers are likely to infer that because repetition is not generality, it most probably has to do with something specific or unique, something that resists universalization as well as abstraction. This hermeneutical tactic, by which the meaning of a statement is decoded momentarily *ex negativo*, yields a reading of the sentence that seems to be confirmed by the passage that ends the first page of *Difference and Repetition*:

> [R]epetition is a necessary and justified conduct only in relation to that which cannot be replaced. Repetition as a conduct and as a point of view concerns non-exchangeable and non-substitutable singularities. . . . [Repetitions] do not add a second time and a third time to the first, but carry the first time to the "nth" power . . . it is not the Federation Day which commemorates or represents the fall of the Bastille, but the fall of the Bastille which celebrates and repeats in

advance all the Federation Days, or Monet's first water lily which repeats all the others. Generality, as generality of the particular, thus stands opposed to repetition as universality of the singular. (Ibid.)[1]

Why should repetition entail singularity? How can repetition, both as a conduct and as a point of view, not presuppose a plurality on the basis of multiple occurrences of the same? When I blink my eyes twice, don't I repeat blinking my eyes? When I observe a man knocking on my neighbor's door three times on end, don't I see him repeat the act of knocking on a door three times? In both instances, one sees a particular conduct being reenacted, one time after the other. The result is that the first occasion of the act, a singular occurrence, as it were, is immediately stretched by its second occasion, by another appearance as a reenactment of a prior instance. Because one act can be performed (or can be seen to be performed) more than once, isn't this "more than once" evidence that the act in question can be viewed as a repetition of the same event? Why, then, does Deleuze invite us to think about repetition as the occurrence of singularity? If it makes sense to speak of repeated or repeatable events, how does one comprehend Deleuze's admonition that repetition be understood as "universality of the singular"?

In this essay, using these questions as a lead, I track some of the moves that Deleuze must have made before turning "repetition" into a proper concept, an operative "invention" that guides his earth mapping (*geo-metry*) of being, a neo-Baroque counterdiscourse capable of reconfiguring philosophies of identity as second-order discourses predicated on dissimulation and retroconstitution. By way of this inventive retracing, I intend to do two things: first, to explicate Deleuze's generalized view of "pure difference" through what might be called difference's "expressive self-abandonment," and second, to demonstrate how and to what extent the self-annulling activity of difference as "expression-in-withdrawal" justifies the link he establishes between "repetition" and "what cannot be replaced." In keeping with my narrowly defined focus, I shall limit my analysis to themes that Deleuze introduces at the opening of *Difference and Repetition*. To guide my inquiry, I select as my starting point two sentences from the passage cited earlier:

1. "[Repetitions] do not add a second time and a third time to the first, but carry the first time to the 'nth' power."
2. "Monet's first water lily . . . repeats all the others."

The first sentence directs me to a discussion on Deleuze's reflection on the concept of origin, an immanence-based critique of the "originality" of origin itself that anchors Deleuze's Nietzschean affirmation of the absolute becomingness of events by deconstructing the punctual purity of origin's putative firstness. The statement regarding Monet's water lilies series will provide me a reference by which to show why a certain *untimeliness*, caused by nonreplaceable and nonoriginary repetition, haunts the very passage of presence: an internal vibration *of* the present undermines the event's proper presence as such. By cross-referencing these ideas and relating them to well-known themes within what is loosely called "poststructuralism," I hope to render in slow motion Deleuze's daunting "mobility of thought" and to shed some light on one important aspect of a truly critical thinking that, by alloying ideas as different from each other as Levant is from Prussia into its own signature, rightly justifies Foucault's vatic appellation of our century as "Deleuzian."

IN THE BEGINNING WAS THREE

Yet we'd have to wait until there were more than two to begin.

—JACQUES DERRIDA

Only in the denial is there a beginning.

—W. J. SCHELLING

The bell tolls. No sooner does the knell start to peter out than the bell tolls again. While the second strike is still chiming, the bell tolls one more time. And so on. The same pattern occurs when, for example, I shop for tomatoes: I reach for one, then another, and another. One, two, three. Three tolls, three selections of tomatoes, each series beginning with the count of "one." Just as there is a first strike that breaks the silence and a first choice of a tomato that begins to fill the empty basket, one can justifiably speak of an event's "first time," its inaugural moment, by virtue of which the clocking of time, the counting of vegetables, and the like can begin. This first event will have to be regarded as the onset of an unfolding series of events: a barely recognizable spark that creates the towering inferno, the first ominous raindrop that presages the opening of the sky. It is the initial of all initials, the first comer to the gathering.

How does one locate the first time temporally? Where does this first time begin and where does it end? When one speaks of the first time, one is speaking of more than simple becoming; for to speak of the first time as the moment of initiation is not only to speak of the mere passing of events but, more importantly, to discriminate among those events such that one can refer to some as being earlier than others. It is, *in nuce*, to speak of a decision making that disrupts the flux of time as the universal container of being, or to speak of the discovery of a hidden rhythm as the timing of things—a turning and re-turning of happenings that punctuate a temporal continuum and mark it into intervals. To speak of the "first time," therefore, implies not only the imagination of time travel but also the capacity of distinguishing among events that would otherwise pass undifferentiated in a continuous flow. Essentially, it is to speak of the possibility of chronology, a formal framing that makes possible the sequential placement of what are indifferent to any framing in their unfettered mode of being-there. The identification of the first time is thus the birth of objective ordering, the moment when everyday happenings become classifiable on the basis of "before" and "after" in relation to one another. This is the moment of our becoming "historical," but more immediately and practically, this is also the moment of numbering, the moment when things—be they tomatoes, bags of dog food, or dollar bills—can be enumerated by being subjected to the universal signifiers of quantification, 1, 2, 3 . . . , irrespective of their varying and variable qualities. And, from that moment on, we can begin counting things by uttering (or thinking) "one," "two," "three," . . .

To count is human. To count is to organize multiplicity; it is to create order on the surface of things, to connect as well as to separate phenomena, to establish relationships as well as to make distinctions among objects within the visible plenitude. The act of counting may well be the cardinal principle (*archē*) in which is seen the work of reason (*logos*) turning disorder (*chaos, physis*) into order (*kosmoi*). Through the act of counting, we organize things that come under reason's purview, and through setting things apart either formally, by assigning symbols to them, or informally, by simply bending our fingers while saying "one," "two," "three," we play and replay the appropriative act of counting.

Behind the obvious utility of this most practical of human activities, however, lingers the skeptic's question, "How does the act of counting begin?" If we agree that numerical ordering articulates the latent principle of universal measurement by which a multiplicity is organized, how does one initiate this act of serial organization? To ask a concrete question, when I put several tomatoes one by one into a basket held by a blind person while informing him of my actions by uttering "one," "two," "three," what is it that sets my speech act of counting in motion and determines the kind of effect my utterances have on my sightless partner? On what basis do I link a particular tomato with the uttering of "one," thus designating it "the first" among the many and enabling me to apply "the second," "the third," and the like to the rest? These seemingly trivial questions tie Deleuze's statement with which I began to his critique of "origin," a critique prerequisite to the mutual articulation between singularity and repetition.

"Origin" signifies a beginning point, a first cause. To designate the sounding of a bell at a particular moment as its "first," to use the earlier example, implies an identifiable break in the flow of one's perceptual experience, a certain rupture in one's consciousness that separates a present sound from prior silence and subsequent hubbub in the environment. At the same time, however, one should not overlook the plain fact that we have all heard a bell ringing before. In fact, we must have known what it sounds like quite well. Were this not the case, how could we recognize it as the sound of a bell rather than some random noise? The first toll and all other so-called first instances are, therefore, not really first, for our recognition of their "firstness" is the result of our prior knowledge of precedents—what Peirce calls the "ampliative inference"—on the basis of which judgment regarding the identity of repeated events (indeed, any judgment of identity at all) anticipates its own grounding (32). In principle and in fact, then, the firstness of a particular event, its alleged position as the beginning of a series of like events, cannot be what it is without even earlier beginnings or firstnesses, ancestors whose history or memories, momentarily held at bay, give that "first event" an anterior witness, a future-perfect reference as its condition of possibility.

Because the firstness of the present depends on that of the past, firstness as new beginning cannot be but an invention. Yet, as just indicated, the invention of a "first time" cannot come to pass without the help of its own shadowy ancestors, its own anterior appearance that vouchsafes to it its standing as a member of the group of which it is said to be first. What emerges here is an apparent paradox of the first time, a conceptual peculiarity that undermines the claim to primacy of any first instance that purports to be original. Ordinarily, what comes first is thought to be nothing if not original, and what is original is always regarded as first. Because firstness and originality imply one another, the "first time" properly characterizes origin, and "originality" denotes the distinguishing feature of what appears first. Can this relationship of mutual implication be maintained without contradiction? If originality always qualifies firstness, and vice versa, is it ever possible to establish an order of priority with regard to recurrent events, one of which necessarily precedes others and thus appears as the first time, the originary moment, of the series?

The answer is not what one would expect. The first time cannot claim an unconditional status of being original because if it were the only first time, if it were to remain the first time all the time, it would not be the origin of anything at all. For the first time to be the first time, to be prior to all other moments, there must be a second time, a latecomer. (Incidentally, one should not forget to ask: If the first were *truly original*, how could it be recognized?) From this moment on, the first time is doubled, for it must necessarily keep this second time close to itself to exist; in fact, it can only exist in an unalterable and unadulterated proximity to a second time that reflects to it its firstness. Ironically enough, this second time now takes on a priority in the very constitution of the first time because it is this second time that makes the first time the first, and not the other way around. A remarkable consequence follows: because the first time depends essentially on its second time to appear as the origin, the first time, for all its claim to chronological priority or nonderivativeness, turns out to be *not* the first time but, rather, the third time; for it now exists in essential relation to both the second time and the supposedly pure first time that anchors the whole temporal sequence.

This tertiary constitution of the first time reveals that what is usually taken to be the origin of a sequence is in fact the effect of a proleptic cum analeptic fabulation. Signifying a beginning that has already begun, the firstness of the first time, that is, the apparent simplicity of origination of the first times, registers not the outset of a clean linear determination, but rather, the denouement of an obviated play of delay and anticipation, a play that stages an imaginary rupture as the phenomenon of beginning by repressing its own *fabulous* formation. It is this trackless "initial forgetting," captured by Freud's *Nachträglichkeit* and articulated more generally in Nietzsche's tropography of becoming, that instills a troubling murmur in the regular rhythm of numbering and, in doing so, actively disrupts the fast order that any act of counting must assume.

Reappearing as the trace of the third time, the first time never has its own proper place, for it does not and cannot take place when it is thought to take place; instead, it is constituted (and hence can only be recognized) as such *après coup*. This retroactive constitution ratifies the claim that any instance claiming to be the first, despite its nominal entitlement, can never be an absolute, unattached singular; rather, it insists as an effect and persists as its own trace in a series of the many—its topos stretches out through its own irrevocable othering as repetition, and its economy (*aikos-nomia*) ranges beyond its own home site. The first instance, if it were ever possible to locate it, can never be found as a *factum brutum* but only as always already historicized.

Retroactively constituted—that is, appearing as original provided that what constitutes it happens later—origin as such is essentially delayed: a delayed origin, plagued from start to finish by the specter of secondarity. Similarly, because the first time is in truth the progeny of the third time and can distinguish itself only to the extent that it does not make any radical break with its ancestral authorization, the act of counting cannot be but a belated act, and the voicing of "one," for the same reason, is essentially an echo of a silent "three." To begin the act of counting, to utter "one," is to repeat in that very verbalization a prior sounding of "one," "two," "three"; it is to reenact the opening scene of an untold history of numbering, to invoke, again and yet for the first time, the beginning episodes of a withdrawn or muted play that unfolds, imperceptibly and in advance of itself, the circulation of two plus one. Here Deleuze joins Derrida in Nietzsche's premises:

> Death is at the dawn because everything has begun with repetition. Once the center or the origin have begun by repeating themselves, by redoubling themselves, the double did not only add itself to the simple. It divided it and supplemented it. There was immediately a double origin plus its repetition. Three is the first number of repetition. (Derrida 1976, 299)

In the beginning was three. Before "one" can arrive, there must be this odd number "three," a number of asymmetry and hence of dynamism. Would repetition mean anything if there were not a surfeit of the same to fund its return? Would one continue to partake of the ritual of exchange, may I ask, if exchange were always *even*? Inasmuch as "one" characterizes identity, and "two" marks the emergence of difference, "three" signifies the anamnestic beginning of becoming, of the possibility that we can say "one" now and in the future, again, again, and again. It is this number, three, that grounds the act of counting by generating what *will have already begun* at the beginning, and it is the (un)voicing of "three" that, by having repeated itself in the first instance, fills the breath before speech and compresses the larynx to produce the phoneme. A certain patience, an exculpable miscalculation, and, one might say, a certain compromise of one's freedom is thus required before one begins the act of counting. One cannot begin all by oneself, and one does not really begin with "one." One must wait for the propitious moment in order to begin; in fact, as Derrida states, "We'd have to wait until there were more than two to begin." There must be more than two; there has always and already been three, a magic number that affords any first instance the possibility of infinite recurrence by carrying itself to the nth power.

In the beginning is another beginning; for every beginning, whenever it takes place, can only be the result of a quest for beginning and hence can only be a descendant of what has already begun. Herein lies the Kleinian/Mobian paradox of beginning as "eternal past"—an "always already" that, being exoteric to both memory and anticipation, breaks the indifference of One, the primordial stasis, thereby constituting the singular instant of the present as the durable foundation of history. "There would never be the *phenomenalization* of time itself," as Slavoj Zizek writes,

> without reference to a past which was never present—that is to say, temporality, in its original dimension, is not a single line of events that runs from the past through the present to the future, but involves the tension of relationship to an act which, precisely in so far as it was never present, in its very withdrawal, is always here as the (past) foundation of the present. (1996, 22)

The true beginning is not and cannot be at the beginning. And what stands at the beginning is not and cannot be present; for to begin is to have begun, and to have begun is to have actively forgotten the beginning's past, a past that, though forgotten, nonetheless never ceases to haunt the present—a present past as much as a past present that becomes the future *other*wise. When the past is taken into account, when the past is recognized as *effective*, all one can say is that every beginning is a *beginning over*, which is to say that no beginning, as such, ever existed. In the beginning was *was*. Beginning expresses itself, but only in the past tense. Beginning always withdraws itself into another beginning. In fact, it must withdraw itself if it wishes to express itself. Seen in this light, beginning is always and already doubled: a beginning *breaching* and *broaching* at the same time from the very beginning. One must begin, but one can begin only *in the middle*, before one or after three.

THE TIME OF PAINTING

Painting brings its lighting with it wherever it goes.

—LEONARDO DA VINCI

It is well known that Monet often lined up "as many as five or six" easels in his garden as he tried to commit to canvas what only "the innocence of the eye" could see (quoted in Smith 99). The day is good, the flora looks glorious, and the scenery, as always on a good day, fills the eye. A perfect day for painting. Carpe diem. Monet is ready; he is always ready. But why does he need so many canvases? Nothing in the garden seems capable of causing any damage to the piece(s) he is working on. What is in the scene that calls for this kind of multiple copying? Monet seems in a hurry, spending "only a few minutes" at each canvas, as his friend Maupassant reported (Smith 26). Why? What is the urgency that causes him to run from one canvas to another, applying paint to each in speedy touches of his brush? A curious scene indeed. If it is any indication of his method of capturing "primitive sensations," what does this method say about Monet, about "having an impression"? Specifically, what does it tell us about "impressionism," about Deleuze's statement that Monet's first water lily "repeats all the others," that is, about the relation between representation and singularity?

In retrospect, the twofold message behind *Impression: Sunrise* (1872), exhibited as part of a show by the group Societé Anonyme des Artistes-Peintres in April 1874, is clear. Two texts, slightly phased, are presented in the painting. On the one hand, the painting could be read as a gesture of defiance against the classicism-based hegemony affirmed annually by the Salon competition. On the other hand, and more significantly, the painting also posts a manifesto of a new photologic that, enfolded in the "glance" as an aesthetic stance, legitimated casual looking as a serious profession, the profession of the flaneur. The flaneur is bent on capturing the Other through trackless ambulation and diversionary voyeurism, the Other to which "modern" art ought to bear witness being the quotidian world (and the experience of constant movements in it), and the proper method of capturing it being the flickering brush stroke. What the group and, in particular, Monet introduced to the public in 1874 was nothing short of a moral vision that affirmed the self-sufficiency of subjective perception in its modern mode: a new cosmopolitan consciousness of which the rejection of what Paul Cézanne later referred to as "retinal paintings"—be they by Nicolas Poussin or by a certain Adolphe-William Bouguereau—was but a local symptom.

In *Impression: Sunrise*, the meaning and method of Impressionism are already clear. For Monet, to paint is to paint *according to necessity*. This means, first and foremost, submitting to the summons of the *manifest*, the absolute visible, the singular present one cannot not see. To paint, in other words, is to capture the *present* in the present, to re-present the present as present. For Monet, then, painting is essentially *photo-graphic* (writing with light); it remains from start to finish a matter of, to use Maupassant's word again, "printing"—making a copy of the other as color, as light. "A painter," as Jean-Luc Nancy remarks, "does not paint things in light, but the light of things, their luminous presence" (1995, 351).

In attempting to paint the light of things, however, the painter immediately encounters the second necessity of the act of painting: the struggle against time. This necessity is born the moment "the fixed, animally ecstatic eye" is greeted by what *passes* in front of it, and it is most acutely felt when the eye is trained on the light of things, when, that is, "subjective" vision confronts what seems to escape vision's appropriation, namely, the freedom, the *auto-nomos*, of time as it shows itself as the light of things. Light comes from the sun, the ultimate source of illumination, whose rays give things their luminous presence. The sun rises, it shines, and it shines in its coming. The coming of the sun brings things into broad daylight, giving them their proper place in light, defining their contours, their identities. No sooner does the sun rise, however, than it begins an arc that eventually leads downward. In fact, the sun's coming is at the same time its departing, and its rising is the same as its setting— depending on where one stands. As the sun departs, shadows elongate. As shadows grow, darkness descends; as darkness devours the field of vision, things withdraw into invisibility. The ultimate source of things' appearance, therefore, is also the ultimate source of their disappearance in that the periodic withdrawal of the sun's radiance means the regular loss of the illumination of things.

The sun's coming and going—rather, its coming by going and its going as immanent return—thus injects time into the act of painting. Inasmuch as the sun shines on everything under itself, time times everything passing through its flow. This flow of time times not only things of light but also the light of things. The sun rises and the sun sets; time passes; light changes. As a result, to paint things in their luminous presence becomes a struggle against time, a struggle against light-sensitive timing as the condition of things' time-sensitive illumination. As Paul Virilio says, any *take* (mental or instrumental) is simultaneously and inescapably a *time take*, a conquering of things' exposure against the limited *depth of time* (91). By *taking in* light, by *taking in* the luminosity of things in light, the painter—knowingly or not—graphs time. The painter is as much a photographer as a chrono-grapher.

"Painting brings its lighting with it wherever it goes." By the same token, light carries the painter with it wherever it illuminates things as the measure of time. The painter follows the light, as a child follows the mother. Light is thus captured by the paint; it is *within* the paint. However, there can be no "within it" without the experience of loss, just as there can be no "within the self" without the departure or absence of loved ones.[2] This is so without exception. Because the act of painting collapses time and light into one, the painter, as a writer of light, is characteristically nostalgic to the same degree that painting, being photo-graphic, is always after the light. Consequently, not only must painting be beholden to time's absolute passing, it must also surrender itself to the edict of optical othering, turning itself—immediately and imperceptibly—into an Icarian dream of parousia, a fatal pursuit of the runaway sun as the only response to a heliocentric imperative.

Because the present awaits light to be visible, the painter can never be punctual; his or her proper moment belongs solely to the past, perpetually timed, as it were, by what has passed absolutely. A belated chronographer, the painter sees the present but can record only the past. For this reason, painting, being photo-graphic, can never be more than recollection; it is always about a scene once seen. Painting, being photo-graphic, and the painter, as writer of light, both come to pass only in the past tense. To paint is to attempt to seize, against all odds, the passing of light, to overcome the gap separating the hand and the eye. The image of Monet dashing from canvas to canvas in the garden in Giverny is tragi-comic, but it is inevitable. Painting's truth dictates that Monet's acts be repeated.

PAINTING THE SERIES: *SINGULI, SERERE*

Each time, this, this drawing, this stroke, this splash, this color. Each time unique,
irrepeatable, irreplaceable: what the signs of discourse cannot be.

—JEAN-LUC NANCY

Nancy describes the painter as "the stealer of time, of each instant of
time, of his present . . . of the present given to him each day, the present
of the present day" and asks: "How can one steal what is given? It's a
painter's secret" (1995, 344). But what is the painter's secret? Where does
the secret lie? One steals what one knows or believes is already there: the
present. And one steals what one lacks but wishes to have: the present. To
say that the painter steals time is to say that he or she seeks to appropriate
it by making multiple copies of the present, and to say that the painter
steals the present is to recognize that the multiple copies he or she makes
of the present merely recollect the light that has already passed. The
painter's secret, if there is any, is precisely his or her inability to stop the
passing of time as light and of light as time:

> With discretion, the painting would say: painting is already past, with
> the passing of time. . . . But to say: painting has passed by, there
> where you're looking, and there nothing left to see, nothing but this
> passage, this passing, mobile-immobile, coming and going, barely
> existence, birth . . . and so perfectly real ("there is a point of perfec-
> tion . . . "). You see, you'd have to know how to do nothing but realize
> this. (Ibid., 362)

Herein lies the secret anguish accompanying the painter as his or her eye
and hand track the movement of photo-chrono-logical ousia. Now perhaps we understand better Monet's hurry in the garden, the heroic effort
behind his "dissolution of the evenly colored surface into spots and dabs
of color, the decomposition of local colors into *valeurs* . . . the play of
reflected light and illuminated shadows, the quivering, trembling dots
and the hasty, loose and abrupt strokes of the brush, the whole impro-
vised technique with its rapid and meshing sketching" (Hauser 169).

Although one cannot re-present the present without essential loss,
one must nevertheless paint things in their luminous presence. Two
mutually annulling theses thus characterize the anguishing fate of painting as photo-chrono-graphy: one cannot, and yet one must. The "must"

196 BRIANKLE G. CHANG

signifies an imperative to paint things in their luminous presence, and in response, the painter freezes a present, *graphing* a moment into eternity. On the other hand, there is a "cannot," a preordained message to the painter that foretells the failure of his action. This predestinal sending defines the act of painting as one of martyrdom, for all the painter can do is bear witness to things' passing luminosity without offering any real proof, testifying through passion rather than reason to an instance of light—each time, as a "this" that is always becoming "that." "Each time, this, this drawing, this stroke, this splash, this color. Each time unique, irrepeatable, irreplaceable" (Nancy 1995, 345). Each time, painting's telos is eclipsed; each time, its congenital nonsuccess is borne out, a fatality confirmed by the absolute singularity of a mummified "this," an entombed "past present" beyond knowledge and beyond mimicry. Each stroke, each color treads each time on the tail of a fleeting instance of light, a fleeing thisness that denies the possibility of generation and generality, of accumulation and growth.

As a photo-grapher, Monet began by printing a "this": the luminous presence of things, "each time singularly" (ibid., 346). Each time, this stroke, this color, this splash, again and again. "Colors, once and for all . . . Gone with the sun." Bear in mind, though, that "color is always the color of 'each time': each time, in each place, *local* color, literally" (ibid., 352). This green is not that green, although the two may look alike. This yellow is not that yellow, this blue, this pink, this ocher not that blue, that pink, that ocher, each being the monument to a unique, instantaneous stroke, one after another. Monet tried to fix on canvas the luminous surface of things, for this surface comes closest to his ideal of *instantaneity*; that is, this surface is coextensive with the painter's photographic attention, marking the singular other of which painting must take care, if only because this surface, the luminous face of things one cannot not see, is, as Nancy writes, "what constitutes the *discretion* of painting . . . in the mathematical sense of the word: the discontinuity of stroke-by-stroke" (ibid., 345). *Discrete, discretion, discretus*; separated, this set against that, as if in crisis (*krisis*: decision; *krinein*: to separate, to decide), almost catastrophic. Each stroke is unique, absolutely different, heterogeneous, and yet each stroke repeats itself by following the one preceding it, thus forming a sequence, a series, a *discourse*. *Discourse, discours, discursus, discurrere, discurrere*: running in different directions or running back and forth. A good painter must run; he or she must always be alert and swift, all the while observing the changing light of things. Monet was a master photo-graph-er. In exercising his discretion, he was at the same time *at* the discretion of an *other* urgency. He ran; he surrendered himself to running after the sun—not only in the garden but also on canvas—for time is running out.

One should thus restore painting to a discrete act, an *in*-directed act that places on painters the burden of controlling the frisson of pitting themselves against the transient experience of seeing. This stroke, this stroke again; one stroke after another, one canvas after another, one series after another. To paint is to paint again; in other words, to paint the reality of painting in and through painting. A painter's task is to pro-duce a series of discrete presences, a continuum of discrete thisnesses as testimony to the luminous presence of things. Painting is as much a dis-course on time as it is a discourse on thisness. Painting is a discourse on time because, whatever else it may be, it is always a discourse on thisness.

One could also speak of a growth of discrete colors into a painting, of their being thrown into space as patches of color on canvas. As color patches fill the coarse cloth, pigments start to blend. As a result, the paint-ed scene/seen gradually transforms itself until it settles into a picture, a figured flatness, that records the volume of passing impressions. The sun rises; amber meets lilies in the pond. A good day for painting. This sun-rise, this scene, this painting, again and again, quickly forming a series, a sequence of discrete thisnesses that bear witness to the luminous presence of sunlit things.

Singuli, one by one. *Serere*, one plus one. Water lilies then and there; water lilies again here and now. Haystacks, this one plus that one. Morning and afternoon; summer and fall. Paintings grow as organic pho-tographs, blooming in time, one after another, into a series. A series tracks the movement from one to many. It is an organized multiplicity, a composite whole whose unity synthesizes the modal expressions of its many parts. As an expressive multiplicity tracing the changing light of things, Monet's series realizes its virtue by spatializing time, namely, by *graphing* what in reality cannot be visualized as such. By keeping a particu-lar present in focus, a series, as time-lapse photography demonstrates, renders time's absolute passing into discrete monuments that in their proper sequence recall transient thisnesses accessible to the painter/pho-tographer as (pre)subjective impressions. This capacity of a series for dis-cretion is what catches the Impressionist's fancy, making the series a method favored by the writer of light.

PAINTING *THIS, THIS* PAINTING: *REPETITIO*

Leave it aligned, nothing more. *Nullus dies sine lines.*

—JEAN-LUC NANCY

Did Monet not align the visible? Did he not approximate—mimetically, or, more to the point, anecdotally—the *singuli* of light?[3] Through his paintings, he invites us to see the visible as he realigned it. "See the visible in this way"; this is the ordinary command of painting (Nancy 1996, 59). Before realizing itself, certainly before settling into a specific image, painting issues an invitation to the visible, luring it by promising to embody the visible in lighted scenes of color and shape. Come and see *this*: this scene, this image, this painting, this scene in this painting.

Bertrand Russell claims that "'this' is the only truly proper name" (Genova 39). He believes that "this" is the only word that, being equally attachable to and detachable from any particular referent irrespective of contextual variations, at once owns and is owned by the other that it indexes; it thus uniquely names that other by merging with it without residue. For him, "this" is the most deictic of all deictics: it indicates what it does as it does it. Is Russell justified? How could "this" be a *truly* proper name if, in naming others, it sinks flatly into them? If the other that "this" names completely absorbs it, how can "this" maintain its own identity, which is the basis of naming, its own naming included? To what is "this" a proper name? To the thing it names or to itself? How could "this" be *proper to* a thing simply because its utterance can be attached to it? Doesn't naming, and indexing too, presuppose distance and thus difference between words and things?

If, as Geoffrey Bennington remarks, the reality designated by deictics exists only in and through their own performance, shouldn't we consider deictics practically impotent signs, impotent because of their parasitic nature, their woeful reliance on an extrasemiotic other? (274–95). After all, how does "this" index anything if, in indexing, it does not at the same time index the fact that it is indexing? Would Russell ever take issue with the fact that indexes do not index themselves? It seems that before "this" can perform its indexing successfully, an act of indexing must have already taken place, a recursive, self-doubling act that no signifier, deictic or not, is able to achieve *on its own*. Indeed, if "this" were truly *proper*, if it belonged essentially to itself, it would not be capable of naming anything; conversely, to the extent that it names (or points to) something other than itself in the unique way it does, it does not seem to be truly *proper*.[4]

Painting as the becoming-sign of time; "this" as an improper index; obvious differences between painting and indexing notwithstanding, Monet's discursus can be interpreted as an acting out of Russell's belief, a light-sensitive enactment of indexes' peculiar "constitutive imperfection," an imperfection that "this" uniquely exemplifies. Although Russell never dreams of becoming a photographer, Monet philosophizes—photo-graphically—in the garden, painting a "this" with each painting in the series. However, in the same way that one cannot begin to utter "this" felicitously without having already committed to its use in the future, one cannot hope to paint a "this" without acknowledging that the "this" one paints can make itself present only as a "that." In this, there is not much mystery. *This* is here, and *here* is now here. But, however true that was a moment ago, now *this* has become that, and *here* is already there, at the beginning, for "something else was—and now, again, no longer is—here" (Frey 23). "This" and "here" are words with which one can only lie. Painting and writing thus share a similar fate, disappointing and disap-pointed in equal fashion by aiming at what always flees the scene of pres-ence.[5] One can conclude, for the moment at least, that just as Russell's belief regarding "this" is constitutively problematic, Monet's strokes exe-cuted against the glare decline into failure.

Painting as an event (*evenir*: to come out) of failure? Painting as failed event? Painting is failure insofar as it falls short of accomplishing what it intends to and is thus incomplete in some way, insofar as some-thing fails to come out in it. At the same time, the painter sooner or later stops painting: the work is finished, and the painting is complete, unalter-able, gallery-ready. For this one ought to grant the painter his or her accomplishment and the painting its completion. In light of these two opposing observations, one must immediately ask about Monet: What is it that, by refusing to come out and hence escaping his discrete acts, never-theless turns his water lilies series into a success? To phrase it in another way: What is necessarily lost in Monet's painting, and how does this neces-sary loss structure his serial discretion and so constitute itself as the cause of the photo-graphic fulfillment that the water lilies series is? Above all, how does this wheeling mutation of failure into success and success into failure in the event of painting relate to Deleuze's remark that Monet's "first water lily . . . repeats all the others"?

Instead of addressing these questions directly, let me begin with a simple thought experiment. Imagine a series of similar pictures, S. To economize my discussion, let us limit S to only three members, S^1, S^2, and S^3. Now suppose someone (call him P) is shown S^1, S^2, and S^3 and is told that one was copied off a lost original (call it S^0), a second copy was made of the first, and a third copy was made of the second, all on a discontinued copy machine that, unbeknownst to P, with each copying generates a subliminal distortion (call it SD). Moreover, the secretary who made S^1, S^2, and S^3 died years ago, and no one knows the order in which she completed her job. P's task is to place S^1, S^2, and S^3 in the exact order in which they were copied by the deceased secretary. How does P do it?

Because to P, S^1, S^2, and S^3 all look the same because the distortion is subliminal, P is justified in thinking that S^1, S^2, and S^3 are equally faithful reproductions of the original. To the extent that S^1, S^2, and S^3 are equal reproductions of S^0, P faces the considerable challenge of making a choice among six possible sequences:

1. $S^1 \rightarrow S^2 \rightarrow S^3$
2. $S^1 \rightarrow S^3 \rightarrow S^2$
3. $S^2 \rightarrow S^1 \rightarrow S^3$
4. $S^2 \rightarrow S^3 \rightarrow S^1$
5. $S^3 \rightarrow S^1 \rightarrow S^2$
6. $S^3 \rightarrow S^2 \rightarrow S^1$

How does P determine which of the sequences above corresponds to the secretary's copying procedure? Given the limitations of P's situation, barring pure luck there is no way for him to complete the task successfully. To determine the right sequence, P needs, above all else, to have access to S^0 and to know what S^0 looks like, but this is exactly what he lacks. The cause of his failure, in other words, is that because S^0 is unknown, P has no "effective reference" against which to contrast and compare S^1, S^2, and S^3, respectively. Without these contrasts and comparisons, P will not have at his disposal the kind of information—what can be called "discriminating differences"—necessary to determine how S^1, S^2, and S^3 stand in relation to S^0. Although a close inspection may reveal to P that S^1, S^2, and S^3 are indeed slightly different (assuming that P miraculously improves his vision so that he can perceive SD), the difference(s) so perceived, even if cumulative, are *internal to* the series itself. (It should be noted that although it is possible for P to seriate S^1, S^2, and S^3 on the basis of the perceived differences among them, the sequence so reconstructed reflects the distorting character of the copy machine, *not* the original sequence in which the copies of S^0 were fed into the machine by the secretary.) Because these differences remain internal to S, that is, because they cannot be used to relate various amounts of SD back to S^0, P's knowledge of them is of no use in helping him to determine the specific distortion that S^1, S^2, and S^3 each displays relative to S^0. The result is that S^1, S^2, and S^3, despite the perceived differences among them, will continue to appear to be equidistant from S^0. And this puts P exactly where he was at the beginning. However much his vision may improve, however closely he examines S^1, S^2, and S^3, he is in principle blocked from arriving at the "discriminating difference(s)" indispensable to reconstructing what by now can only be called the lost art of copying of a certain dead secretary.

We can redescribe P's predicament more generally as follows: As long as S^0 is unknown, no one will be able to identify the correct sequence successfully; for as long as S^0 is unknown, no one has the criterion by which to discriminate any one of the six possible sequences from the rest, and hence no one can decide which one corresponds to the secretary's modus operandi. (Even if someone chances upon the correct choice, we still have to say that he did not know what he is doing, for he cannot tell why or how he did it and could not guarantee to successfully repeat his feat.) To the extent that S^0 is *lost* and the dead do not talk, we are caught, just as P is, in the worst of all double binds: every choice we make is a blind choice, and every blind choice we make returns us to face the same challenge. In fact, every choice we make repeats the same failure for the same reason, if only because every selection we make renews a condition characterized by the same degree of uncertainty as that facing any subsequent selection. Although gazing intently at a set of pictures, we are nonetheless blind, (re)initiating with each move a predicament determined from the very beginning by probability, random distribution, or pure chance. This resembles the hopeless task designed by the gods to punish Sisyphus for disrespect. It is this Sisyphean loop, a fatal circle whose initial programming defines each act as futile repetition, that ensnares P and throws us blindly into the tragicomic drama staged by a certain lost original.

This tragicomedy of "eternal recurrences" says much about repetition and furthers our understanding of what Deleuze says about Monet. Whenever we try to repeat what *was already done*, don't we all find ourselves in P's quandary? Whenever we seek to re-present what *has already made* its presence, aren't we all trapped in the same predicament that

forces P to become a Nietzschean hero? Just as Monet studies the changing light, P examines the interchangeable copies. But Monet is in a different—though ultimately no better—situation than is P. P, confounded by
six possibilities, can only by chance beat the overwhelming, though calcu-
lable, odds, whereas Monet is well prepared methodologically and looks
directly at the origin of his challenge. Out in the sun, at the discretion of
the source of light, he photo-graphs the luminous presence of things/
scenes, turning what he sees, his impressions, into a series by using the
series as the proper method of photo-graphy. The first break of the sun,
causing/initiating the first brush stroke; the first water lily, leading to
another, then a third . . . seriatim and discretely.

Monet repeats, painting discretely. As a result, water lilies are repeated, forming a series through steady reflections. Of water lilies on canvas,
from the garden to the wall, one after another *in repetitio.* Are they different? How are they different? How do we know that they are different?
How do we know that they form *a* series? How do we know which painting
is the "first one" when they all repeat one another? Art historians may tell
us that this work here was painted after that one over there; the curator
may seriate the paintings in this or that order; the museum guide may
point to this water lily as the first and that one as the second, and so on.
Why should we believe them? How do we know that the descriptions in
the exhibition catalogs are not inaccurate? What if we enter the museum
through the back door, enter the exhibition room in reverse direction,
and observe what is on display (Are the paintings apocryphal? Does it
matter?) at random? How could we rely on historians when their evidence
includes hearsay? Monet, like the secretary, is long dead. When the so-
called experts say—on the basis of *historical* data and according to good
sense (good according to whom?)—that this one is the first one or that
one repeats this one, they are speaking from *their* point of view, and they
are repeating what *they* see.[6] But they are not Monet. Monet's view cannot
be their view; nor can theirs be his. The differences here are irreducible;
for whereas their view is set *against* a surface recorded by Monet, Monet's
view is not against theirs but is turned toward the sunlit scene. Between
these two views, there is no reciprocity. Monet was not looking at anyone;
he was looking at his brush and the changing light upon the scene, focusing on and managing the traffic between them. Each time, he was looking
at "this piece" and "this piece" only—a singular instance of light upon
things that, although written *momentarily*, was for all that *final.* From
Monet's point of view, each piece in the series is the *same* as the others,

for each piece is the (same) repetition of the (same) runaway sun that lights the (same) luminous presence of things. From where he stands in the garden, all attempts to seriate what he paints simply reflect an *other* point of view. It is *against* this *other* point of view, or conversely, from Monet's *own* point of view, a view that only he had or knew but that is now lost, that Deleuze says: "Monet's first water lily . . . repeats all the rest." Monet's first is his own first; from *his* point of view, his first is *the* first. It is this first that Deleuze returns to Monet and through him to the event of painting.

That the same repetition may be repeated differently, depending on the point of view taken, is the crux of both the similarity and the difference between P and Monet. Although P may eventually come to realize that his futile travail results from that fact that S^0 is lost and lost forever, Monet's series attests to his wise recognition that the first light is for his eyes only. To the art historian, the light is out. To our tragic hero P, the original is lost. To them, as to us, there is only the lost origin, and this lost origin comes to us as an original loss. This originless origin cannot be discovered, and, as we see in what happens by the pond and in the copy-machine room, this failure of discovery causes and compels repetitions to proliferate ad infinitum. There are only repetitions, compelling repetitions that, in spite of themselves, *initiate*. This is the truth of repetition; this is the principle of photo-graphy: what is lost cannot be retrieved; we can only discover its loss. But every act of discovery repeats the discovery of loss. What is lost cannot be repeated, but the discovery of loss causes/compels one to repeat. Deleuze speaks again through Monet, through the famed water lily series, on behalf of the lost origin: "Repetition repeats the unrepeatable."

ZERO RETURNS: REPETITION AND THE ABSENT CAUSE

> Of cause, so. And in effect, as?
>
> —JAMES JOYCE

To repeat, repetition repeats itself; it affirms itself by itself, by its own acts. Yet, in repeating itself, it also confirms its own failure by not being able to stop, by repeating itself endlessly. This failure of repetition to terminate thus doubles back upon itself as a windfall, an indirect success that trades on its own incompletion by improvising its provisional act repetitively. That being the case, "repetition as a conduct and as a point of view" would not come to pass if there were not already in it a genetic defect (e.g., S^0), an "irreplaceable" instance that, working as a cause in absentia, constitutes the very form of what it brings forth as its effects.[7]

In fact, as can be easily observed from the preceding discussion, what justifies the conclusion that S^1 repeats S^2 and S^3 is the (absent) existence of an original S^0, a *dis-stanced* "this" that exists prior to—and outside of—its own serial representations. As that which is repeated by its own reproductions, this lost original anchors the whole series by giving its elements an underlying, re-markable motif, namely, their perceived sameness across discrete registers in time. At the same time, however, because it will have to repeat itself *as* itself throughout the series, this S^0 must somehow keep itself *outside* the series, standing from start to finish *apart from* the scene of its own repetitions; that is to say, to the extent that it will have to (re)appear as the same, this S^0 must *except* (take out) itself from ever coming on the scene, *ex-sisting* as an excluded other that, precisely by being excluded, makes possible inclusion by creating a division between inside and outside. E pluribus unum: one *out of* many. It is this self-subtraction of one out of many—Deleuze's formula of structural unification: n - 1—that opens the space in which the many can be aligned and realigned. In contrast to the positions taken, respectively, by S^1, S^2, and S^3 in the series, the position of S^0, if it can still be called a position, is necessarily an *ex*-position, a position *ex*-posed to those of S^1, S^2, and S^3, each of which can stand in for S^0 and for one another despite the discrete locations of S^1, S^2, and S^3 in the series. In other words, as the absent cause of S^1, S^2, and S^3, S^0 is (presup)posed, its status as a lost cause being that of the necessary element of *inconsistency*, a structural *brisure*, indispensable to maintaining the phenomenal *consistency* of the series S.[8]

Using a more digestible analogy from simple mathematics, we can say that S^0 occupies the place of the number 0, a (non)number constituted ex post facto as taking the *place* before 1, before the actual beginning of the natural numbers. Rephrasing the idea in the language of formal semiotics, we can say that 0 designates the *necessary utopia* of the natural number universe, functioning as a metasign "whose meaning as a name lies in the way it indicates the absence of the names, 1, 2, . . . 9," without which one would not be able to, for instance, distinguish 96 from 906 or 12 from 120 (Rotman 12). In fact, it is this *ex*-positionality of S^0, an "intimate exteriority" of S^0 to its own others, that "engenders a secondary formation of itself" and, in so doing, makes possible S^1, S^2, and S^3 as multiple returns of the selfsame S^0 (ibid., 280). And it is S^0's expropriating character of "having already taken place" in relation to S^1, S^2, and S^3 that opens the possibility of the return of S^0's very own doubles as repetitive occurrence(s) of itself. Apropos of Jacques Lacan, one can say, "there's One (y'a de l'Un)": consistent rational order or structure must be anchored in an "irrational" (i.e., "unjustifiable" and "unobjectifiable" within the order) exception of One that, in its very capacity as exception, guarantees the structure's consistency, its seriality as such (Zizek 1996, 77). Following the same principle, and keeping in mind the all-powerful function that Lacan attributes to the empty set {0}, which transforms nothing into something by *marking* or *representing* it, one can go so far as to say that any system of meaning begins with the naming of the *void* that it (pre)supposes and to which all signifiers ultimately refer. In a parallel fashion, apropos of Deleuze, one can state that it is the pseudopoint of non-sense within the field of sense that distributes and regulates the series of sense atop the surface of sense-event. After all, repetition can become a predicate (i.e., S^0 is being repeated) only if what is being repeated, S^0, is already (self-) split, a self-becoming-other whose truth is a deliverance-to-come: it will become what it always already was.

This *dis-placed* S^0, or, more exactly, the very nonplace (*non-lieu*) that the virtual S^0 occupies (Roman Jakobson's zero phoneme, Filippo Brunelleschi's vanishing point, Marcel Mauss's *mana*, Claude Lévi-Strauss's floating signifier, Sigmund Freud's primal father, Jacques Lacan's fantasy object *a*, the *xeno*money in financial capitalism, etc.), thus functions as a curious negativity within a structure, a productive void that organizes and regulates the whole from a center that, being displaced, can only be located beyond the limit.[9] In marked contrast to a normal body, which can act only where it is, S^0 acts where it is not, performing effectively only in disappearance, absence, or self-exile. "This," to use Kojin Karatani's illustrative example,

> is exactly like the empty space in a puzzle of shifting numbers or letters that allows the pieces to be shifted around into some kind of order. What drives the movement of the game is not the differential system of signifiers, the 1, 2, 3, but the empty lot itself. While a player may think that she or he is relocating numbers, from another point of view it is the empty lot that is floating around and that enables this movement. (43)

206 BRIANKLE G. CHANG

On this game board, what is repeated by the players' moves is the movement of the empty lot itself, for each move made by the players depends on the lot's movability. In other words, with each move, the movement of the empty lot is repeated, and with each repetition of the empty lot's movement, the game as such is being played. Moreover, because one cannot remove the empty lot without destroying the game, the empty lot designates the only (irre)movable position—a constant "place value" that *belongs without belonging to* the game and that thus enables the game precisely because of its mobility. In this game, only the movement of the empty lot is truly repeatable.

The ex-posed S^0 is thus what S^1, S^2, and S^3 appear to have in common but do not possess. Operating like a missing link in a chain, it embodies a point of radical eccentricity that, by failing to come out and hence having no place, gives birth to a community as a multiplicity-in-unity. In other words, what is repeated by S^1, S^2, and S^3 is the absolutely lonely S^0, an "indivisible remainder," the Lacanian out-standing, ex-timate One, that, although authoring multiple representatives, nevertheless maintains its unrepeat*ability* by remaining unyieldingly hetero- or a-topic. To the extent that S^0 is *not* any of its fungible representatives but is nevertheless responsible for their coming out as they appear to be, this S^0, as a lost cause sui generis, designates the source of a difference that makes all the difference in the serial representation. It signifies "pure articulation" in the protostructuralist sense, a silent copula as an effective but self-effacing hinge or joint (*brisure*) that relates the different (e.g., S^1) to the different (e.g., S^2) without any mediation by the identical or the similar, the analogue, or the opposite.

Relating the different to the different, "pure difference" conceals its immediacy in mediacy, withdrawing itself behind the contrasts it sustains: "Difference is *behind* everything," Deleuze puts it emphatically, "but behind difference there is nothing" (1995, 80). What must not be overlooked here is that this simple statement carries a force that is easily refracted by its compound syntax. In fact, the first part of the sentence, "Difference is *behind* everything," in light of the second can be seen to mean something almost antithetical to what it suggested at first; for, if there is *nothing* behind difference, difference cannot be said to assume a dimension of its own—there is nothing to constitute a *background* for it. If difference occupies no *site* of its own, it can only exist parasitically—existing, that is, as a *para-site* on the same plane as do things whose distinction or identity it marks. Instead of being *behind* anything, difference is purely syncategorematic or connective, pulsating not so much *behind* things as *between* or *in* them.

Because it exists only *in* and *between* things, that is, because it comes to the fore only under the guise of what it is not, difference as such cannot be properly reflected except *en abîme*. For this reason, it eludes objectification and totalization, hiding itself as a "mark" (*marque*) along a chain that simultaneously erases and preserves itself in a process of "re-marking." At the same time, however, to be what it is, to keep itself "differently different," the difference of a series must make a difference in the series in which it exists. This necessity of making a difference, of keeping itself operative in the series, makes it impossible for the difference to remain indifferent. "One trope too many is thus added to the series," writes Rodolphe Gasché in reference to the concept of "re-mark":

> In the form of a proxy . . . it represents what does not really belong to the series . . . the nonmeaning against which the full marks stand out. If that trope is substracted from the series to be totalized by the concept (of the mark), however, this totalization leaves at least one mark unaccounted for. Thus re-marked by the space of inscription that demarcates all marks, no concept or theme of the mark could hope to coincide with what it aims to embrace. The re-mark is an essential limit to all coinciding reflection or mirroring, a doubling of the mark that makes all self-reflective adequation impossible. For structural reasons, there is always more than totality; the extra valence added by the delegate of the asemic space of diacritical differentiation of the totality of semes always—infinitely—remains to be accounted. (221)

Gasché's point is straightforward: the totality of a chain of marks is always re-marked by an additional, nontotalizable mark that, by marking what demarcates the marks, namely, the empty space between them, constitutes their ground by holding together their place of inscription—that is, their very differentiality, the difference between marks as such. "In any series of marks," as Zizek puts it, "there is always at least one which functions as 'empty' . . . which re-marks the differential space of the inscription of marks. It is only through the gesture of re-marking that a mark becomes mark, since it is only the re-mark which opens and sustains the place of its inscription" (1992, 75). That being the case, and as already betrayed by our use of the words *in* or *between* to characterize it, difference must be understood as "excessive lack," designating a blank- or surplus-element within a whole, thanks to which the whole becomes structured and can be accounted for.

As an empty space of other-inscriptions, difference as such remains void, its content being void itself and hence contentless, its form being difference itself and hence formless. It is this self-withdrawing character of difference as "re-mark," of difference as "excessive lack" serializing itself incognito, that repetition continuously affirms: "In its essence, difference is the *object* of affirmation, affirmation itself" (Deleuze 1995, 74). Re-marking itself through repetition, or rather, "lying between two repetitions," difference invites affirmation—an affirmation of a transeventual disjunction or discord, expressible as either not-all (*pas-tout*) or as more *and* less, and only discernible through the angle of a "fourth person singular" (Deleuze 1990, 102–3). Understood in this way, repetition cannot but stand in opposition to "exchange":

> For exchange implies only resemblance, even if the resemblance is extreme. Exactness is its criterion, along with the equivalence of exchanged products. This is the false repetition and causes our illness. True repetition, on the other hand, appears as a singular behavior that we display in relation to that which cannot be exchanged, replaced, or substituted—like a poem that is repeated on the condition that no word may be changed. It is no longer a matter of an equivalence between similar things, it is not even a matter of identity of the Same. True repetition addresses something singular, unchangeable, and different, without "identity." Instead of exchanging the similar and identifying the Same, *it authenticates the different.* (Ibid., 287–88)10

Authenticating the different—that is, authoring the different *as* different—true repetition works *unconsciously*, speaking only *as* and *through* an other. Inassimilable by any host, unequal to any gift, it "surges forth as the highest power of the unexchangeable," surging forth, in effect, as a "division" that "reunites" (ibid., 288). "It functions," writes Deleuze, "as the differenciation of difference, an in-itself which is like a *differentiator*, a *Sich-unterscheidende*, by virtue of which the different is gathered all at once rather than represented on condition of a prior resemblance, identity, analogy or opposition" (Deleuze 1995, 117). Simply put, it is "the in-itself of difference [that] hides itself in giving rise to what covers it" (154).[11]

The ex-posed S^0 never appears as such, and what does appear is nothing but the envoi of what never fails to disappear. Seen in this way, Monet's failure takes on a new light: It does not simply mean that even the most faithful recording of the full lumination of things inevitably falls short of the things illuminated. Nor does it mean that representation, serial or not, loses the represented along the way, or that between representation and presentation there lingers the irreducible phenomenological inadequation. Instead, Monet's failure should be seen as the very manner in which serial painting proceeds, revealing a mode of expression unique to painting as photo-graphy, a mode of expression that, through its unavoidable double exposure, does not and cannot silence the productive fiction of painting as verisimilar.

Much like the uttering of "this," a verbal act that becomes effective only in the moment of its illocutionary resolution, the painting of "this"— in fact, the light-sensitive inscription of subjective impressions in general—remains beneath the threshold of photo-graphic veracity until it actively forgets the ephemerality of lighted beings that breaks Being's promise of full exposure. Similarly, the claim that "Monet's first water lily . . . repeats all the others" also takes on a more precise meaning: it no longer suggests the eristic, counterintuitive proposition that an earlier act repeats later ones; far more radically, it states an architectural rule of timing: the so-called first impression, the first scene seen, the first stroke, in short, the very constitution of firstness as such, is already a repeated occurrence. As the Lacanian-Deleuzian refrains suggest, an event always take place twice before it really happens, or, as I dare to rephrase it, an event must take place *virtually* before it occurs *effectively*. It is this *twice-over* of an event that consolidates the event's phenomenal integrity, and it is its *virtual occurrence before the fact* that restores to the event its truth as retroactive happening, the aftermath of a "sombre precursor," that delivers what comes henceforth always in the form of *déjà pas encore*.

"To repeat is to behave," as Deleuze states time and again, "but in relation to something unique and singular that has no likeness or equivalent" (1995, 7). It is not that there is no universality of repetition; rather, the universal aspect of repetition is the universal of a structure, not of events; of a type, not of tokens; of a form, not of content; and finally, of a lost cause-in-remembrance, not of a marked antecedent. Instead of announcing anything positive, repetition exemplifies an exceptional falling: To repeat is to fall under the burden of retroactive secondarity, to fall by succumbing to the untimely othering of beings—or, as Emmanuel

Levinas has it, to have fallen "into that of which seeing, already assuming a plastic form, is but forgetfulness and re-presentation" (115).

THE COMING/SUFFERING OF BEING

In every now, being begins.

—FRIEDRICH NIETZSCHE

The inaugural is (the) absent. The true initial does not show up. And initiation is a game of failure that nevertheless manages to go on and on. These are the reasons why nothing should be accorded the status of *archē* simply because of its inaugural value. To repeat it in another way, the *archē* does not really deserve the values attributed to it insofar as it is attributed with the inaugural value. Because the inaugural appears to inaugurate but does not really initiate, it can only be a repeated event, an event that affirms itself through repetition. Such self-repetition compromises what the inaugural seeks to affirm, complicating its effects from the very beginning; for, through each repeated event, repetition comes back to its own emptiness in excess; it abandons itself by gathering others, infinitizing itself *in* others and, in so doing, returning to its own abandonment in full measure. Abandoning itself at birth, repetition adds nothing to what is repeated; conversely, what is repeated, to the extent that it stands in for the abandoned and hence is left with nothing to keep hold of, adds nothing and does nothing to the repetition that constitutes the immanent genesis of the phenomenality of things. In either case, repetition, as Nancy sagaciously observes, "obstructs or forsakes the very *position*, the initial position, of being, that empty position whose truth of nothingness, immediately turned back on and against being, mediates the becoming, the inexhaustible advent of being, its resurrection and the parousia of its absolute unity, truth, and goodness, arousing and pouring back into it the foam of its own infinity" (1995, 37).

Drowning itself in "the foam of its own infinity," repetition-in-(self)-abandonment prevents itself from ever becoming anything *substantial*; instead, it signifies the very *tension* (Deleuze's preferred word is *intensity*) of events and between events, a pure differential that *itself is not being* (*nicht selbst seende*) but that mediates between two aggregates of being, a having-been (past) and the yet-to-come (future), aggregates that are themselves differentially marked by the respective tensions that link and delink their own adjoining aggregates. It is here that one finds the true empirical (not empiricist) support for Nietzsche's "eternal return" in Deleuze, the "real genesis" of becoming: a no-nonsense view that does not treat beings as creations by a transcendental "ground" or any other self-aggrandizing instance but, instead, approaches them by way of the dif-ference (*Unter-Schied*), a "traumatic cut" as pain (*Schmerz*), that explicates recurrences as pure semblances effected by the internal contraction and expansion between unity and difference, between the one and the many, between the finite and the infinite, between the transcendental and the empirical.[12]

Repetition abandons itself in that it repeats itself; repetition repeats itself because it abandons itself. And because repetition abandons itself, repetition repeats the unrepeatable that it itself is on account of self-abandonment. To be abandoned is to be left with nothing to take hold of; to abandon oneself means to let go of oneself, completely and without calculation. But in neither case does "abandonment" mean "disappearance" or "death." Properly understood, "to abandon" means "to suffer." To suffer (*sub-ferre*), however, does not simply mean "to undergo." It means *to go under.* Suffering (*le subissement,* not *la souffrance*), says Maurice Blanchot, means "not so much what we undergo, as that which goes under" (3).[13] In the strict sense, to suffer is to surrender to what drags one down, to be affected passively and immeasurably by the weighty reality of an Other. Thus suffering is always associated with images of heaviness or falling, with the difficulty of standing up or of moving in any direction. In this light, to say that repetition abandons itself is to say that it sinks under its own weight.

Sinking under its own weight, repetition necessarily keeps itself and keeps to itself; it keeps (to) itself by perpetually (re)appropriating itself through self-suffering. In this sense, repetition properly characterizes the postal eco-nomy of presence as becoming-present, an Odyssean voyage in which going away is the same as coming back, in which the point of departure is the same as that of return, and in which sending is indistinguishable from receiving. Inasmuch as it is governed by the structure of return, repetition necessarily becomes itself because it always returns to itself; and by returning to itself, it remains itself. As a result, repetition is what remains; it remains in becoming qua becoming. Repetition *is becoming* proper.

What goes under is what remains, but "what *remains* is also what *resists* the most" (Nancy 1996, 81). This remaining resistance, a kind of

resistance that keeps itself by going under, causes and is capable of causing what goes under to return.[14] In fact, repetition as what remains will
not come to pass without its own resistance, which it then overcomes. This
is how repetition maintains its own "infinite identity," by traversing what
goes under as self-overcoming. And it is in this that we must awake to the
singular message of *becoming*-present as "the *inexhaustible* advent of
Being"—a barely audible message that speaks of Being as "inexhaustible"
by speaking for resistance as such. What this inexhaustible resistance
means, before it means anything else, is simply this: Being is not station-
ary; rather, it is constantly going under. Being *is* because it goes under,
because it suffers for its own sake. In so doing, it remains what it always is,
its self-overcoming immediately overcome by itself as repetition of the
same, by its own undividedness. For this reason, Being is as inexhaustible
as it is singular. Returning to itself, Being remains; "it remains without
remains," that is, by overcoming its own resistance *repetitively* (Blanchot
33). Thus, instead of saying that Being is abstract, unknowable, or anything else, one should say that Being is weighty, too weighty to be apprehended by thought, too heavy to be measured by any means. By going
under, it ex-sists as what it *already* is; at the same time, by going under
again, it also ex-sists as what it *not yet* is. Already but not yet, Being's
moment is always untimely, already out of joint. Already but not yet,
Being's destiny is to return to itself via its resistant Other, traversing/
repeating its own traces that bear witness to its radical becoming. When
all is said and done, what remains is only the becoming. There is only
becoming; there is *already but not yet* becoming—a becoming that comes
up by going under, that goes forward by circling back. A carrier of such
an unbearable weight, Being *is* already-but-not-yet, a No-thing into which
we are thrown, a suffering to which we are subjected all along, in the
future tense of a past and/or in the past tense of a future.

    If, as Nietzsche says, with every now Being begins, then Being's
beginning ends with every now, with its ever-renewed and ever-renewable
beginnings. And this can only mean that Being as such never comes, simply because perennial coming guarantees no arrival or delivery but only
affirms the repetition of a coming. Understood in this way, Being's presence can be taken to mean *prohibition* as such, provided that one under-
stands prohibition in the precise sense that the supposed object of prohibition is the *prohibition* itself, that the prohibited object *coincides with* the
principle or force that prevents its very attainment. Phrased a little differently, it is not that Being's presence is *withdrawn* by some unknown cause,

but rather, that presence *is* withdrawal itself, its own retraction.

Being comes forth by going under; Being unveils itself but only as "Nothing," as Heidegger says. To continue with Heidegger's language, one can say that "ontological difference" blocks the communication between Being and beings, staking out a region of "clearing" that remains nevertheless opaque to mortal vision; that is to say, the message of Being collapses completely and immediately into the passage of its sending, thus becoming silent: no message. In this silent sending, only the promise remains. And the promise, as one now realizes, is quite disappointing: Being comes, but *it comes only in the repetition of its coming.* Being returns, but it returns always blank or half-empty, for what actually comes back in this return is *either* the promise of returning, rather than Being as such, *or* the hedging avowal that it *will have come.* Consequently, one can only speak of a becoming that misses, coming either too early or too late, and thus excluding itself, its presence, its possibility of identity. There is only Being in its coming, a radical coming of Being that never arrives. Becoming becomes; Being does not come; Being *is not.*

The unbearable heaviness of Being causes everything to go down, to repeat, to suffer; suffering is *in* everything, and it never ceases to repeat. Look at the white spot on the canvas. Read the blank space between morphemes. Listen to the silence between words. Hiccups; stammerings; elisions; a stain . . . Where does one begin and where does another end? Where is the closure, the opening, or the space in between? When terminus subrogates telos, how does one "save the text from its book misfortune?" (Blanchot 101). One simply stops speaking, painting, writing . . . in order to begin.[15]

NOTES

1. Many almost identical expressions can be found in Deleuze's texts. For example: "True repetition . . . appears as a singular behavior that we display in relation to that which cannot be exchanged, replaced, or substituted—like a poem that is repeated on the condition that no word may be changed" (1990, 287).

2. For a discussion on the themes of loss, memory, and absence, see Derrida, *Mémoires for Paul de Man.*

3. By "anecdotal" I mean to suggest the referential sense emphasized by Meaghan Morris: "I take anecdotes, or yarns, to be primarily referential. They are oriented futuristically toward the construction of a precise, local, and *social* discur-

sive context, of which the anecdote then functions as a *mise en [abîme]*. That is to say, anecdotes for me are not expressions of personal experience but allegorical expressions of a model of the way the world can be said to be working" (14–15).

4. Bennington makes the same point succintly when, speaking of Derrida's "trace," he writes: "It is not simply that proper names and diectics do not manage properly to name or indicate something that escapes language while anchoring it somewhere, but that 'reality' thus improperly designated is present nowhere else" (1994, 114).

5. As Nancy writes: "One cannot dip one's pen in last night's water. Ink is always fresh. [Strokes] leave no trace or deposit in it. Everything must be started over; one can never begin to get it over with, unless it be by getting it over with before starting. And for that, as you see, it's already too late" (1995, 342).

6. The problem of "point of view" is crucial in this connection. And this explains why Deleuze emphasized it in the beginning passage of *Difference and Repetition* quoted earlier: "Repetition as a conduct and as a *point of view* concerns non-exchangeable and non-substitutable singularities" (emphasis added).

7. Clearly, the conclusion that S^1 repeats S^2 and S^3 appears paradoxical. Common sense and proper use of the word *repeat* tell us that what takes place earlier, S^1, cannot possibly repeat what occurs later, S^2 and S^3. Although the argument certainly does not refute common sense and sensible English, it nevertheless demonstrates one point crucial to the critical grasp of "repetition" as the structuring principle of a series: "repeated events (*événements*/tokens) are not necessarily instances that reproduce the universal rule" (Frank 376); that is to say, there is simply no guarantee that a reiterated word or a repeated gesture manifests one and the same universal. To rephrase the point positively: rather than submitting themselves to a governing principle of universal equivalence, a principle that rewrites similar phenomena as mere reflections of a "type" anchored in an untouchable instance of "essence," repeated events as *events* are irreclaimable singularities that, in the act of application, simultaneously transgress and incalculably alter the universal category under which they come forward; for, to continue with our example, although an observer, having looked at S^1, S^2, and S^3, may decide that they form a repetitive sequence, he is not justified in concluding that they share any underlying transphenomenal characteristics if only because the impression he forms of S^1, S^2, and S^3 as members of a repetitive sequence may result from their "family resemblances" and not from some essential S-ness that defines the identity of the series as a unifying and unified whole—a fact known to post-Scholastic nominalists long before it was rearticulated by Wittgenstein. Moreover, it must be recognized that S^1 and S^2, or any pair of entities, can be judged to have a common feature only if one first has available some objective criterion, a "third term," that functions as what philosophers call the "ground of relation" and singly determines whether S^1 and S^2 are either identical or different. Such a criterion, to the extent that it is summoned forth ex hypothesi to serve as a disinterested differentiator, is, strictly speaking, a *postulation*. And, as a postulated term, this first criterion would require the postulation of yet another criterion, another "third term," invoked by necessity as a second differentiator to mark its own identity. This act of postulating a differentiator in the very making of identity and differ-

ence would go on, leading straightaway to an infinite regress that undermines the possibility of any final discovery of an "essence" capable of assembling disparate individuals under the ruling of a general type or concept.

8. For a discussion of the absent cause as a structural principle, see Zizek 1994, 29–53.

9. For a helpful discussion on the development of formalism and the homology between "number," "money," and "pictorial representation," see Rotman. It should be noted that the existence of a "productive void" within a system results from a simple logical requirement: an element of a system is logically preceded by the place it occupies within that system. Thus, the number 0, for example, does not denote a boundless, contextless emptiness; instead, it should be seen as having been invented to designate the absence resulting from the removal of previously existing items, that is, for example, to designate the answer to the question, How many apples are left on the table after one has taken them all away?

10. Following this line of reasoning, one can also understand why Deleuze claims that "being neither the identity of the same nor the equivalence of the similar, repetition is found in the intensity of the Different" (1990, 288–89). Gilles Deleuze is Gilles Deleuze himself; there is only one Gilles, defined by a singular soul that he himself is. There are no two men who can both be taken to be Gilles. Yet the Gilles thirty years ago is not the same Gilles two years from now. But one cannot say that there are two beings in Gilles, two creatures inside the same individual. Thus, he is both the same as himself and different from himself. It is in this sense that Deleuze designates an "intensity" in himself: he composes a difference *in* himself, an internal inequality, which returns or repeats to make him the same individual across time. It is in this sense, too, that "repetition does not presuppose the Same or the Similar—these are not its prerequisites. It is repetition, on the contrary, which produces the only 'same' of that which differs, and the only resemblance of the different" (289).

11. According to Deleuze's conception, "difference" is best understood in topological terms, as a curvature that works as a "relative point of indifference" between adjacent curvatures. This explains why he insists on the distinction between difference and diversity. "Diversity" refers to the phenomenal distinction between individuals or between individuals belonging to two distinct species. "Diversity is given, but difference is that by which the given is given, that by which the given is given as diverse. Difference is not phenomenon, but the noumenon closest to the phenomenon" (1995, 222). The expression "closest to" is important, for, unlike the Kantian noumenon, which is distinguished by its postulated character as a final support for the Transcendental Object, *X*, the difference as noumenon in Deleuze, being closest to phenomenon, is not heterotopic to phenomenon.

12. Here one also finds the reason why in Deleuze Being's "condition of possibility" is at the same time its "condition of impossibility," why "the transcendental" is undecidably the same as "the empirical," why the "infinite" necessarily collapses into the "finite," and vice versa—conclusions that Deleuze shares with Derrida, though through different routes. This also explains how Deleuze reads Spinoza and Leibniz as reflecting the two facades of the Baroque decentered uni-

verse, Spinoza's constructed through the logic of explosion and Leibniz's through that of implosion.

13. In this connection, Freud's word *unterdrückt*, which Lacan translates as *chû en dessous*, comes to mind.

14. It might be interjected here that the usual interpretations of the claim that "individuals become (or rather, are constituted as) subjects" amount to no more than worn-out, quasi-sociological platitudes, in that they miss the radical meaning of becoming-in-repetition. Individuals do not become subjects, or anything else for that matter, because of influences exerted by forces "not of their own making" (such as ideology, race, gender, history, culture). According to Deleuze's materialism, individuals recognize themselves as subjects by returning to or becoming again what they always already are. Here the meaning of radical becoming, of the temporal structuration of "already but not yet," must be confronted honestly. Individuals are always already subjects, and their histories, seen from the present point of view, reflect the temporal expressions by which they will become again what they always already were. This also explains why Lacan emphasizes the "future anterior" dimension of the *sujet en procès*. Without this emphasis, one will not be able to answer the many difficult questions that arise in association with Lacan's notion that ego formation takes place during the stage of "the imaginary": for example, the simple question of how a child can recognize that the image he or she sees in the mirror is his or her own image if he or she does not know that it is his or her own image to begin with. This simple question shows, inter alia, how limited the "reflection model" is when it is used to explain the emergence of self-consciousness.

15. Like many ideas developed by postmodernist thinkers, Deleuze's singular reworking of the concept of repetition has far-reaching implications for cultural analysis. Readers interested in pursuing the questions of how Deleuze might be situated within the broader discussions of French poststructuralist thought can see Hardt, Patton.

WORKS CITED

Bennington, Geoffrey. *Legislations: The Politics of Deconstruction*. London: Verso, 1994.

Blanchot, Maurice. *The Writing of the Disaster*. Trans. Ann Smock. Lincoln: University of Nebraska Press, 1995.

Deleuze, Gilles. *The Logic of Sense*. Trans. Mark Lester. New York: Columbia University Press, 1990.

———. *Difference and Repetition*. Trans. Paul Patton. New York: Columbia University Press, 1995.

Derrida, Jacques. *Writing and Difference*. Trans. Alan Bass. Chicago: University of Chicago Press, 1976.

———. *Mémoires for Paul de Man*. Ed. Avital Ronell and Eduardo Cadava. Trans. Cecile Lindsay, Jonathan Culler, and Eduardo Cadava. New York: Columbia

University Press, 1986.

Frank, Manfred. *What Is Neostructuralism?* Trans. Sabine Wilke and Richard T. Gray. Minneapolis: University of Minnesota Press, 1989.

Frey, Hans-Jost. *Interruptions.* Trans. Georgia Albert. Albany: State University of New York Press, 1996.

Gasché, Rodolphe. *The Tain of the Mirror.* Cambridge: Harvard University Press, 1987.

Genova, Judith. *Wittgenstein: A Way of Seeing.* New York: Routledge, 1995.

Hardt, Michael. *Gilles Deleuze: An Apprenticeship in Philosophy.* Minneapolis: University of Minnesota Press, 1993.

Hauser, Arnold. *The Social History of Art,* vol. 4, *Naturalism, Impressionism, the Final Age.* New York: Vintage Books, 1951.

Karatani, Kojin. *Architecture as Metaphor.* Cambridge: MIT Press, 1995.

Levinas, Emmanuel. *Outside the Subject.* Trans. Michael B. Smith. Stanford, Calif.: Stanford University Press, 1994.

Morris, Meaghan. "The Banality of Cultural Studies." In *Logics of Television,* ed. Patricia Mellencamp. Bloomington: Indiana University Press, 1990. 14–43.

Nancy, Jean-Luc. *The Birth to Presence.* Trans. Brian Holmes et al. Stanford, Calif.: Stanford University Press, 1995.

———. *Muses.* Trans. Peggy Kamuf. Stanford, Calif.: Stanford University Press, 1996.

Patton, Paul. *Deleuze: A Critical Reader.* Oxford: Basil Blackwell, 1996.

Peirce, Charles Sanders. *Collected Papers.* Vol. 6. Ed. Charles Hartstone and Paul Weiss. Cambridge: Harvard University Press, 1935.

Rotman, Brian. *Signifying Nothing: The Semiotics of Zero.* Stanford, Calif.: Stanford University Press, 1993.

Schelling, F. W. J. von. *The Abyss of Freedom/Ages of the World.* Ann Arbor: University of Michigan Press, 1997.

Smith, Paul. *Impressionism.* New York: Abrams, 1995.

Virilio, Paul. *The Vision Machine.* Trans. Julie Rose. Bloomington: Indiana University Press, 1994.

Zizek, Slavoj. *For They Know Not What They Do.* London: Verso, 1992.

———. *The Metastasis of Enjoyment.* London: Verso, 1994.

———. *The Indivisible Remainder.* London: Verso, 1996.

Books Received

BATTEN, GUINN. *The Orphaned Imagination: Melancholy and Commodity Culture in English Romanticism.* Durham, N.C.: Duke University Press, 1998.

BLOCH, ERNST. *Literary Essays.* Trans. Andrew Joron and Others. Stanford, Calif.: Stanford University Press, 1998.

DI LEONARDO, MICAELA. *Exotics at Home: Anthropologies, Others, American Modernity.* Chicago: University of Chicago Press, 1998.

DOUGLAS, MARY, AND STEVEN NEY. *Missing Persons: A Critique of Personhood in the Social Sciences.* Berkeley: University of California Press, 1998.

ERICKSON, JOHN. *Islam: Postcolonial Narrative.* Cambridge: Cambridge University Press, 1998.

ESCOFFIER, JEFFREY. *American Homo: Community and Perversity.* Berkeley: University of California Press, 1998.

FOSTER, DAVID WILLIAM. *Buenos Aires: Perspectives on the City and Cultural Production.* Gainesville: University Press of Florida, 1998.

FROMENT-MEURICE, MARC. *That Is to Say: Heidegger's Poetics.* Trans. Jan Plug. Stanford, Calif.: Stanford University Press, 1998.

GILMAN, SANDER L. *Love + Marriage = Death, and Other Essays on Representing Difference.* Stanford, Calif.: Stanford University Press, 1998.

GUNDAKER, GREY. *Signs of Diaspora, Diaspora of Signs: Literacies, Creolization, and Vernacular Practice in African America.* New York: Oxford University Press, 1998.

HALBERSTAM, JUDITH. *Female Masculinity.* Durham, N.C.: Duke University Press, 1998.

HASS, KRISTIN ANN. *Carried to the Wall: American Memory and the Vietnam*

218

Veterans Memorial. Berkeley: University of California Press, 1998.

HIRSCH, SUSAN F. *Pronouncing and Persevering: Gender the Discourses of Disputing in an African Islamic Court.* Chicago: University of Chicago Press, 1998.

IAMPOLSKI, MIKHAIL. *The Memories of Tiresias: Intertextuality and Film.* Trans. Harsha Ram. Berkeley: University of California Press, 1998.

KAUFFMAN, LINDA. *Bad Girls and Sick Boys: Fantasies in Contemporary Art and Culture.* Berkeley: University of California Press, 1998.

KIRSHENBLATT-GIMBLETT, BARBARA. *Destination Culture: Tourism, Museums, and Heritage.* Berkeley: University of California Press, 1998.

KNOWLTON, ELOISE. *Joyce, Joyceans, and the Rhetoric of Citation.* Gainesville: University Press of Florida, 1998.

MORRIS, DAVID B. *Illness and Culture in the Postmodern Age.* Berkeley: University of California Press, 1998.

NAREMORE, JAMES. *More Than Night: Film Noir in Its Contexts.* Berkeley: University of California Press, 1998.

PEYSER, THOMAS. *Utopia and Cosmopolis: Globalization in the Era of American Literary Realism.* Durham, N.C.: Duke University Press, 1998.

POOVEY, MARY. *A History of the Modern Fact: Problems of Knowledge in the Sciences of Wealth and Society.* Chicago: University of Chicago Press, 1998.

RHODES, CHIP. *Structures of the Jazz Age: Mass Culture, Progressive Education, and Racial Discourse in American Modernism.* London and New York: Verso, 1998.

ROY, PARAMA. *Indian Traffic: Identities in Question in Colonial and Postcolonial India.* Berkeley: University of California Press, 1998.

SANDBORN, GEOFFREY. *The Sign of the Cannibal: Melville and the Making of a Postcolonial Reader.* Durham, N.C.: Duke University Press, 1998.

SCHORK, R. J. *Greek and Hellenic Culture in Joyce.* Gainesville: University Press of Florida, 1998.

SIMPSON, MICHAEL. *Closet Performances: Political Exhibition and Prohibition in the Dramas of Byron and Shelley.* Stanford, Calif.: Stanford University Press, 1998.

SMITH, PHILLIP, ED. *The New American Cultural Sociology.* Cambridge: Cambridge University Press, 1998.

WACHTEL, ANDREW BARUCH. *Making a Nation, Breaking a Nation: Literature and Cultural Politics in Yugoslavia.* Stanford, Calif.: Stanford University Press, 1998.

Contributors

MAIA BOSWELL teaches social theory and cultural studies, nineteenth-century British literature, and modernism at the University of North Carolina at Chapel Hill. She is currently completing a book manuscript, "Crossing and Transgression: Sites of Impasse in Blake, Barrett Browning, and D. H. Lawrence."

LESLIE BOW is assistant professor of English at the University of Miami, where she specializes in Asian American literature, ethnic autobiography, writing by women of color, feminist theory, and theories of race and ethnicity. She is currently completing a manuscript titled "Betrayal and Other Acts of Subversion: Feminism, Sexual Politics, Asian American Women's Literature."

BRIANKLE G. CHANG teaches cultural studies in the Department of Communication, University of Massachusetts, Amherst, where he also serves as the director of the Center for the Study of Communication. He is the author of *Deconstructing Communication: Subject, Representation, and Economies of Exchange* (University of Minnesota Press, 1996).

EVA CHERNIAVSKY is associate professor of English at Indiana University. She is the author of *That Pale Mother Rising: Sentimental Discourses and the Imitation of Motherhood in Nineteenth-Century America*. Her current projects include a book on race and commodity culture, *Hot Voodoo: The Body Politics of Global Capital in Classic Hollywood Film.*

PENELOPE INGRAM has just completed her doctoral dissertation in English at the University of New South Wales, Sydney, Australia. Her dissertation, "Becoming-Woman: 'Difference Feminism' and the Race for the Other," examines the problematic relationship between sexual and racial difference in the work of Luce Irigaray, Trinh Minh-ha, Rosi Braidotti, and others.

DONALD M. NONINI is associate professor of anthropology at the University of North Carolina at Chapel Hill. His most recent book, coedited with Aihwa Ong, is *Ungrounded Empires: The Cultural Politics of Modern Chinese Transnationalism.* His articles have appeared in *positions: east asia cultures critique* and *American Ethnologist.*

JOHN W. ROBERTS is chair of the Department of African American and African Studies and professor of English at the Ohio State University. He is author of *From Trickster to Badman: The Black Folk Hero in Slavery and Freedom* and *From Hucklebuck to Hip Hop: Social Dance in Philadelphia's African American Community,* as well as numerous articles on African American folklore. He is president of the American Folklore Society.

hypatia

BORDER CROSSINGS:

Multicultural and Postcolonial
Feminist Challenges to Philosophy 1
Edited by **Sandra Harding** and **Uma Narayan**

CONTENTS

"Globalizing Feminist Ethics" **Allison Jaggar**

"Feminism, Women's Human Rights, and Cultural Differences" **Susan Moller Okin**

"Chandra Mohanty and the Re-Valuing of Experience" **Shari Stone-Mediatore**

"Essence of Culture and a Sense of History" **Uma Narayan**

"Cultural Alterity: Cross-Cultural Communication and Feminist Thought
in North-South Contexts" **Ofelia Schutte**

"How to Think Globally" **Lorraine Code**

"*Un Sitio y una Lengua*: Chicanas Theorize Feminism" **Aida Hurtado**

and more

hypatia 13.2 Price: **$16.95**

BORDER CROSSINGS:

Multicultural and Postcolonial Feminist Challenges to Philosophy 2
Edited by **Sandra Harding** and **Uma Narayan**

CONTENTS

"Locating Traitorous Identities: Toward a View of Privilege-Cognizant
White Character" **Alison Bailey**

"Burnt Offerings to Rationality: A Feminist Reading of the Construction of Indigenous
Peoples in Enrique Dussel's *Theory of Modernity*" **Linda Lange**

"Dualisms, Discourse, and Development" **Drucilla K. Barker**

"Maquiladora Mestizas and a Feminist Border Politics:
Revisiting Anzaldua" **Melissa W. Wright**

"It's All in the Family: Intersections of Gender, Race, Class, and Nation"
Patricia Hill Collins

"Resisting the Veil of Privilege: Building Bridge Identities as an Ethico-Politics
of Global Feminisms" **Ann Ferguson**

"Multiculturalism as a Cognitive Virtue of Scientific Practice" **Ann E. Cudd**

"What Should White People Do?" **Linda Martin Alcoff**

"Gender, Development, and Post-Enlightenment Philosophies of Science"
Sandra Harding

and more

hypatia 13.3 Price: **$16.95**

Shipping and handling: Add $3.00 for one issue and $1.00 for each additional

Indiana University Press
601 North Morton Street
Bloomington, IN 47404
Phone: 1-800-842-6797
Fax: 1-812-855-8507
E-mail: Journals@Indiana.Edu
URL: www.indiana.edu/~iupress/journals

hypatia:
journal of feminist philosophy
Edited by Laurie J. Shrage and Nancy Tuana

New from MINNESOTA

MARK FENSTER
Conspiracy Theories
Secrecy and Power in American Culture

"Mark Fenster has provided a solid and illuminating study of the public's fascination with conspiracy theories and sets forth a stimulating correlation between the popularity of such theories and the social and political values of our society. This is a comprehensive and intriguing analysis of our often obsessive interest in conspiracy theories."–Gerald Posner

$24.95 cloth (3242-1) • 272 pages • 1999

TROY MESSENGER
Holy Leisure
Recreation and Religion in God's Square Mile

"Felicitously titled *Holy Leisure*, this evocative study of a summer community at Ocean Grove, New Jersey, is a major contribution to the study of religious life in the United States. . . . This lucid and insightful book speaks not only to the cultural history of religion, but also suggests new directions for the study of tourism and leisure."–Barbara Kirshenblatt-Gimblett

$29.95 cloth (3253-7) • 176 pages • 1999

DAVID LENSON
On Drugs

A critical exploration of the user's perspective on drug consciousness—now in paperback!
"Lenson's magnificent book is a perceptive mapping of the rippling waves of undiscovered solar systems within our brain. It will comfort the fearful and guide the unprepared. A classic."–Timothy Leary

$16.95 paper (2711-8) • $29.95 cloth (2710-X)
256 pages • 1999

JEFF LAND
Active Radio
Pacifica's Brash Experiment

"To commemorate the 50th anniversary of the independent Pacifica Radio Network, Land, a media critic and activist, recounts the network's history in a tight, accessible narrative. . . . For Land, Pacifica embodies the power of the First Amendment, exemplifying the salutary effects of the 'disruption of convention encouraged by vigorous dissent.'"
—*Publishers Weekly*

$16.95 paper (3157-3) • $42.95 cloth (3156-5) • 184 pages• 1999
Commerce and Mass Culture Series, Volume 1